SAP Interface Programming

 **PRESS**

SAP PRESS and SAP Technical Support Guides are issued by
Bernhard Hochlehnert, SAP AG

SAP PRESS is a joint initiative of SAP and Galileo Press. The know-how offered by SAP specialists combined with the expertise of the publishing house
Galileo Press offers the reader expert books in the field. SAP PRESS features
first-hand information and expert advice, and provides useful skills for professional decision-making.

SAP PRESS offers a variety of books on technical and business related topics
for the SAP user. For further information, please visit our website:
www.sap-press.com.

Liane Will
SAP APO System Administration
Principles for effective APO System Management
2003, 240 pp., ISBN 1-59229-012-4

A. Rickayzen, J. Dart, C. Brennecke, M. Schneider
Practical Workflow for SAP
2002, 504 pp., ISBN 1-59229-006-X

Frédéric Heinemann, Christian Rau
Web Programming with the SAP Web Application Server
The complete guide for ABAP and web developers
2003, 528 pp., ISBN 1-59229-013-2

Horst Keller, Joachim Jacobitz
ABAP Objects. The Official Reference
2003, 1094 pp., 2 Volumes and CD Set
ISBN 1-59229-011-6

Helmut Stefani
Archiving Your SAP Data
A comprehensive guide to plan and execute archiving projects
2003, 360 pp., ISBN 1-59229-008-6

Johannes Meiners, Wilhelm Nüßer

SAP Interface Programming

A comprehensive reference for RFC,
BAPI, and JCo programming

 PRESS

Contents

8 Calling BAPIs from Clients 283

Introduction

This book deals with the most important ways to develop interfaces for R/3 systems and external software. The primary focus is on the RFC Library. Newer technical approaches used by SAP are also addressed, which include the recent Business Application Programming Interface (BAPI) technology and Java Connector (JCo).

So this is a book about SAP interface programming with the RFC Library as the main attraction, with C programs, certainly, but without a word about Web services, SAP XI, and .Net? Because it's sometimes necessary to "talk" to the SAP system, it's understood that interfaces are important, but is Remote Function Call (RFC) technology—which has its roots in the days of R/2—still relevant today in the age of J2EE, .Net, and Web services? Even SAP puts considerable marketing effort into promoting these technologies and approaches, and no longer wants to be known as a vendor of purely proprietary solutions and protocols.

The question (Is RFC technology still relevant?) is rhetorical because if we were to answer "no," this book would not exist. On the contrary, there are good reasons to write about this subject:

1. The RFC interface is a central component of the SAP Application Server, which is an integral part of the SAP Web Application Server. It is still used internally by SAP and by many customers to implement very complex solutions.

2. Many SAP customers still use SAP software releases that don't support, or only partly support, the new technologies we mentioned. These customers will continue to rely exclusively on the RFC Library.

3. Even if new technologies can be used, however, either they're based on the RFC interface or they offer only some of the functions available with this established interface. We'll illustrate this issue in the last chapter of this book, using JCo as an example.

4. Lastly, the programming models that play a role in RFC programming can be transferred to many client-server environments. There are educational reasons why a developer should take a closer look at the RFC Library—even if there are simpler APIs than the RFC interface.

For this last reason, in particular, we ease into the subject of RFC programming so as not to overwhelm the reader. Experienced SAP developers will encounter familiar concepts and can jump ahead, while those new to the world of SAP will need background information to enable them to proceed independently after reading this book.

This book is divided into nine chapters:

- ▶ **Chapter 1** offers a brief introduction to the basic concepts of the R/3 System. We present important elements such as the SAP Application Server, work processes, and the Gateway.

- ▶ **Chapter 2** presents the most important tools in the ABAP Workbench. Experienced SAP developers can skip these first two chapters.

- ▶ In **Chapter 3**, we start the actual programming with SAP RFCs. We begin with the programming language C because it is the original language of the RFC interface. Here, you'll learn about simple client-server applications.

- ▶ **Chapter 4** develops the approaches mentioned in Chapter 3. We highlight an important subject here—the data types in the RFC Library and in the R/3 system. Both this chapter and Chapter 3 constitute the core of the book.

- ▶ Since you will certainly be in a position to develop and implement complex programs after reading the earlier chapters, it would seem appropriate that in **Chapter 5** we present tools for error diagnosis and troubleshooting. An SAP expert can also skip this chapter, as he or she will already be familiar with most tools.

- ▶ **Chapter 6** focuses on some less well known and what could be characterized as "advanced programming" aspects of the RFC interface. Here, we deal with subjects such as tRFCs, qRFCs, and parallel processing.

- ▶ **Chapter 7** discusses a conceptually very important form of interfaces for the SAP system—BAPIs. Defined by SAP, BAPIs are an object-oriented method for stable interfaces that are ultimately addressed using the RFC interface.

- ▶ One of the most important uses of BAPIs is with ActiveX Controls, which is the subject of **Chapter 8**. From here, we leave behind what has been a mostly platform-independent context and focus on the world of Microsoft.

- ▶ However, **Chapter 9** focuses on the Java Connector, which requires only the common Java Virtual Machine (JVM) as its runtime environment, so it can run on all platforms. It's also the cross-over to the aforementioned modern technologies. For example, it forms part of the SAP Connector and therefore is instrumental in connecting SAP to J2EE servers.

The C/C++ programming examples in Chapters 3 to 6 have been developed on Windows 2000 operating systems so you must make the appropriate adjustments if you're developing programs for other platforms.

We could have included many other subjects in this book. Today's frequently mentioned Web services pose a real technological alternative to RFC. Therefore, it was appropriate for us to focus on subjects that could be called "classic"—

they're relevant for a large number of current systems. Web services are an option for the future but currently the standards and software have not been conclusively consolidated, so they're not yet suitable for inclusion in this book.

The book is primarily intended for developers, that is, those who try to create a "clean" program based on a consultant's vision of what this program should be and do. We'll show you the ways to create interfaces for the R/3 System and external systems. We'll also discuss the role that consultants play in this process of developing interfaces. Although consultants don't have to implement their own interface designs, it's often helpful in the planning phase if they're aware of the options available for creating interfaces.

To spare you the exasperating task of having to type numerous long examples, you'll find the source code for the complete programs on the catalog page for this book at *www.sap-press.com*.

There are always many people who are directly and indirectly involved in the publication of a book. Johannes Meiners would particularly like to thank Prof. Nowack from the Münster Fachhochschule (a technical college), who gave him access to the college's SAP lab. He would also like to thank the departments of development and technical consulting at itelligence AG, Bielefeld, for their help and support in answering technical questions. Wilhelm Nüßer would particularly like to thank the Heinz Nixdorf Foundation, without whose generous support he would not have been able to contribute to this book, and the Fachhochschule der Wirtschaft (University of Applied Sciences) in Paderborn. We would both like to thank the employees at SAP—and in particular Thomas Becker—who have been there for us with moral and practical support, which contributed greatly to the completion of this book. Lastly, we would like to thank Florian Zimniak at Galileo Press for his helpful and friendly assistance.

1 The Basics of R/3 System Architecture

To develop external clients and servers, you need to understand the basics of R/3 system architecture and the ABAP programming language, which are introduced in this chapter and Chapter 2, respectively.

The R/3 System is divided into three levels:

▶ The data level

▶ The application level

▶ The presentation level

Each level performs different tasks. On the data level, persistent data is managed and provided for the application level. The application level processes incoming queries using this data. The presentation level accepts queries from the end user and presents the answers provided by the application level.

Each of these conceptual levels is generated with special software, sometimes referred to as the *server*. The server provides the *services* offered at a certain level. A server consists of one or more programs required to implement the functions (see Figure 1.1).

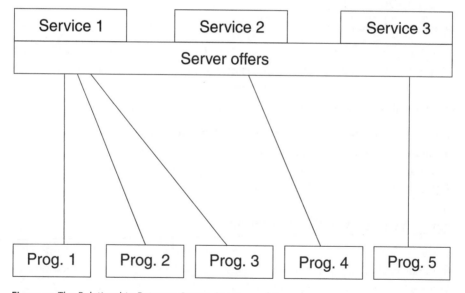

Figure 1.1 The Relationship Between Server, Service, and Program

In keeping with this three-tier architecture, the following servers exist in an R/3 System:

▶ Presentation server

▶ Application server

▶ Database server

The user communicates with the R/3 System via the presentation server. He or she is provided with input templates on the presentation level to facilitate communication. The user enters data and selects menus for processing it. The SAP GUI, the interface used by the end user, makes up part of the presentation server.

The primary tasks of the presentation server are:

▶ Creation of the user interface, for example, presentation of the input templates

▶ Transport of data from and to the application level of the R/3 System

The R/3 System communicates with the database via the database service. To facilitate this communication, SAP currently uses relational databases. Access to and modification of data is done using SQL commands. The SAP R/3 System provides two SQL dialects for communication with the database:

▶ Open SQL standard

▶ Native SQL standard

The Open SQL standard guarantees a SQL language environment that is supported by all databases—after conversion by the SAP application level if necessary. ABAP programs (see Section 1.2) that comply with this standard can be used on all databases supported by SAP.

The Native SQL standard enables access to the complete SQL environment of the database in question. Native SQL commands are included in an ABAP program with the statements EXEC SQL and ENDEXEC. Programs that use database-specific SQL commands cannot, of course, run on all databases.

1.1   The Application Server

The application level is the hub of the R/3 System. Its primary task is to process the end user's data. The application server provides the programs necessary to process the data. Because it is integral to each R/3 System, it makes sense to take a closer look at its services and its structure.

The application server in an R/3 System can provide:

▶ Dialog service

▶ Update service

▶ Enqueue service

▶ Batch service

▶ Spool service

There are also two other services for communication inside an R/3 System, between different R/3 Systems, and between R/3 and external systems:

▶ Message service

▶ Gateway service

As we already mentioned, the services are provided by one or several programs. Depending on the service that the programs carry out, in the R/3 System we can differentiate among the following:

▶ Dialog process

▶ Update process

▶ Enqueue process

▶ Batch process

▶ Spool process

▶ Message process

▶ Gateway process

In SAP nomenclature, the processes that provide the first five services are referred to as *work processes*.

Figure 1.2 shows the structure of an application server. You can see that each application server has a dispatcher. The dispatcher monitors the coordination of processes and services. It takes in all requests and distributes them to the appropriate services. The message server is not shown here because it does not run under the control of a single application server; rather it coordinates communication between application servers.

Of the processes named, we'll examine the dialog process, the update process, the enqueue process, the gateway server, and the message server.

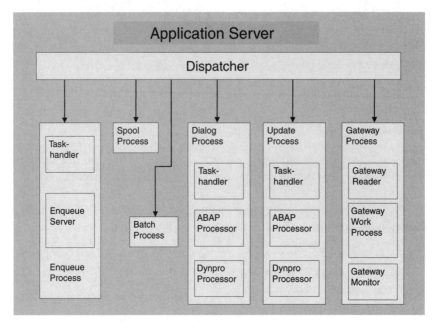

Figure 1.2 Structure of the Application Server

1.2   The Dialog Process

The dialog process provides all the programs necessary to process requests from the presentation level and from external programs. Each application server usually has several dialog processes.

The dialog process is divided into three basic components:

▶ ABAP processor or ABAP interpreter

▶ Dynpro processor

▶ Taskhandler

The *ABAP processor* executes the statements in an ABAP program. The ABAP programming language was developed for the R/3 System. Most SAP business applications have been and continue to be written in ABAP. The task of the ABAP program is to process the incoming data. It checks for data consistency, generates results, and so on.

When a user works with the SAP system, sequences of screen templates are usually run on the GUI. Between two consecutive screens, ABAP code is executed to process the input (called *Process After Input*, PAI) and to generate the following screen (called *Process Before Output*, PBO). The *Dynpro processor* controls the implementation of these screen templates and the associated PAI and PBO program code. In SAP terminology, this grouping of screen and code is referred to as a *screen or dynamic program* (*Dynpro*) and the flow from one screen to another is called a *dialog step*. The Dynpro processor manages the interaction of the user with the SAP system. The control of these steps is also referred to as *dialog step control*.

Finally, the *Taskhandler* coordinates the screen processor and the ABAP processor; that is, it generates an executable working environment for these two components. This includes, in particular, forwarding data to the screen processor and the ABAP processor. This may be, for example, data from an SAP GUI or from another client. Part of this book will address the programming of specific clients—*RFC clients*.

A dialog process is not a fixed assignment to a client; rather the dispatcher assigns an incoming request from a client to a dialog process that is currently available. This process carries out one dialog step at a time and is then available again to process other requests. A dialog step includes the following individual steps (see Figure 1.3):

1. A user or an external client sends a data package to the dispatcher in the application server.

2. The dispatcher determines which dialog process is currently free and assigns processing to it. First, an attempt is made to select the process that processed the user's previous request. If this work process is occupied, the request is sent to the next available process.

3. If the work process that is to process the current request was previously used by another end user, the data of the current user will be provided for the work process from the *user memory*. This procedure is also known as a *roll-in*. The user memory is a memory area in which user data is temporarily stored. It contains, among other things, the *roll area*. The current work process receives all user-specific information from the roll-in.

4. If the program that is necessary to process the data has not yet been loaded in the ABAP program buffer (*Program eXecution Area*, PXA), this is done now so that the work process can begin processing the data.

5. Processing of the request begins now. This includes checking the data, reading new data, and so on. In some cases, the database server still participates in the processing of a request, particularly if additional data needs to be read from the database.

6. Once the user's request has been processed, an answer can be sent.

7. Concurrently, the user-specific data is saved again to the roll area so that another dialog process can continue working with the information. This procedure is also known as a *roll-out*.

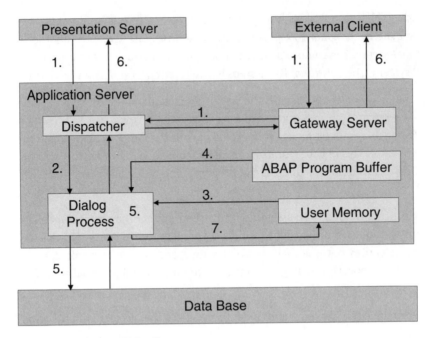

Figure 1.3 Executing a Dialog Step

1.3 The Update Task

The *update task* starts working the moment data is written to the database. The R/3 System does not necessarily write every change to the database immediately; rather it may collect changes first in a log structure. These temporarily stored change requests are sent to the database only after final confirmation, for example, using the ABAP command COMMIT WORK. The update work process controls the actual storage.

SAP selected this method of temporarily storing the data and delaying the writing for several reasons. One reason was to reduce the communication effort necessary between the database server and the application server, which considerably improves the response time performance of programs.

Another, conceptually more important reason was the need to bring together actions that sometimes execute different (dialog) work processes for a user into a logical unit. The transaction concept of the underlying databases is, of course, no longer sufficient because in the database, different clients (work processes) were involved. The temporary storage described above constitutes one solution to this problem. The update process can bring the data collected to the database in an *atomic* action (i.e., all or nothing) and thus also maintain the logical unit of the ABAP program on the database.

The temporary storage of data can be done in different ways. The usual form is temporary storage in special database tables (update tables).

The concepts *synchronous* and *asynchronous updates* are also frequently mentioned in this context:

▶ With synchronous updates, the execution of the work process is delayed until the data has been stored on the database. The caller waits during this time.

▶ With asynchronous updates, the work process doesn't wait for the data to be written to the database. The data is written by a separate process—usually the update task—at a later time.

Many SAP programs use asynchronous updates because users can continue to process their data without waiting for the update. One typical example of this is the creation of sales orders.

1.4   The Enqueue Process

The enqueue process controls locks on data records. When creating a lock mechanism that would take into account the change of work process, SAP had to develop the concept of a logical lock. The basic idea behind the SAP lock concept can be found in the administration of a single lock table for the entire R/3 System: It's located in the main memory of the application server, the enqueue process runs on it, and it is administered by the enqueue server. All programs that want to lock a data record should read and check the entries in the lock table to determine whether the object is locked or free.

When a data record is locked, the following steps occur between processes, for example, a dialog process and the enqueue process:

1. One process (for example, a dialog process) sends a request to the enqueue work process containing all the necessary information on the object to be locked. This information is also known as the *object key*. An object may be a sales order or a bid, for example. The dialog process will send a request only if it has no information on whether the user currently has the object. The process obtains this and other information from the user memory (see Figure 1.4).

2. The enqueue process uses the entries in the lock table to verify whether the data record is already locked. If it isn't, the enqueue process locks the object for the user. If the object is currently locked by another user, the enqueue process sends a message to the requesting process. Among other things, the message contains information on the owner of the current lock on the object.

3. At the end of the dialog step, the dialog process saves all information on objects currently locked by the user in the user memory

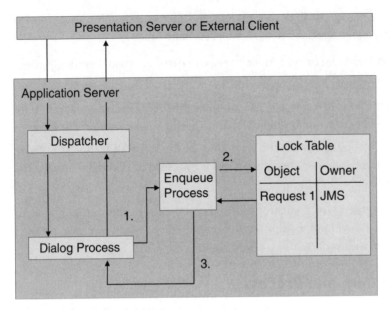

Figure 1.4 Communication Paths of the Enqueue Process

SAP supported the concept of a logical lock table, which is contrary to the lock mechanism in the database, for two reasons:

1. Database locks lock only one table. The data on an object is frequently contained in several tables. Therefore, in a sales order, for example, the data for the order header and the order items is saved in separate tables. Only the application knows which tables need to be locked if an object is to be changed. It is therefore useful to shift the job of locking to the application.

2. R/3 applications usually involve many dialog steps that can be processed and edited by different dialog processes. From the point of view of the database, however, each dialog process is a database client that would like to lock data. If the database lock concept were used, dialog processes that process the same application could obstruct each other, because from the perspective of the database, two processes want to process a single data record. As databases usually hold locks per client, it is difficult to reproduce cross-work-process processing in the SAP system on the database. These two problems can be avoided by shifting the lock logic to the application server.

The disadvantage of this concept is that it requires a high degree of discipline when developing programs. Nobody compels a developer to read the lock table when developing a program. It is very important that external programs also adhere to the concept. You can achieve this (as for ABAP programs) by calling particular function modules—the so-called *enqueue* and *dequeue function modules*—and observing their results.

1.5   The Gateway Server

The central service in the SAP system for communication between application servers and external programs is the *Gateway Server*.

Generally, to facilitate communication between two programs on different servers, from a software perspective, the following two elements are necessary:

▶ Protocol

▶ Programming interface

The protocol defines the rules—the syntax of communication. This includes, for example, the format of the data to be transferred. It defines how the data packages to be exchanged between two programs should be structured. One well known protocol is TCP/IP, which is the standard on the Internet. Another recognizable protocol is LU 6.2 from IBM, which is important in the world of IBM Mainframe.

The programming interface makes a batch of functions available. The functions support:

▶ Configuration of the connection

▶ Conversion of data into the protocol data format

The functions of the programming interface are used by programs that want to communicate with another program.

Familiar programming interfaces designed for communication between programs in the SAP world are the CPI-C interface (*Common Programming Interface Communication*) or SAP's own RFC interface (*Remote Function Call*). Other well known interfaces include, for example, BSD Sockets, RPC by Sun, Java RMI, and CORBA. There is no fixed link between programming interface and protocol. Which protocols are supported depends on the actual implementation of the interface functions.

Figure 1.5 illustrates the relationship between the programming interface and protocol: A Java program can use the RMI API to communicate with, for example, a program written in C++ using CORBA. The important thing here is that the protocol between the two programs is understood by both (in this case, for example, IIOP).

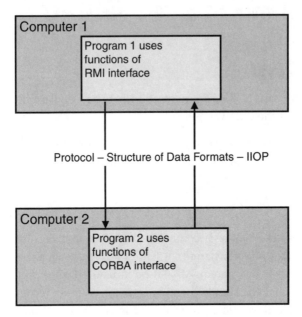

Figure 1.5 Relationship Between Interface and Protocol

Let's go back to the Gateway Server. The programs on the Gateway Server were developed with the functions of the CPI-C interface. Consequently, the gateway server is frequently referred to as the *CPI-C-Server*. Since the R/3 System is used in heterogeneous system landscapes, the gateway server must also support different protocols. A rule of thumb here is:

▶ The TCP/IP protocol is used for communication between R/3 Systems or between R/3 systems and external systems.

▶ The LU 6.2 protocol is used for communication between R/3 and R/2 Systems and for communication between R/3 Systems and programs on an IBM mainframe.

The Gateway Server contains three programs:

1. Gateway Reader

2. Gateway Work Process

3. Gateway Monitor

The Gateway Reader is responsible for communication based on the TCP/IP protocol. It's started by the dispatcher on the application server. The program that executes the Gateway Reader is called gwrd.

The Gateway Work Process is responsible for communication based on the LU 6.2 protocol. It's implemented by the program gwwp.

The Gateway Monitor is used to administer all connections with external programs. Figure 1.6 illustrates the structure of the Gateway Server.

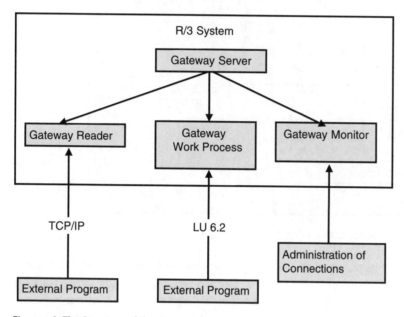

Figure 1.6 The Structure of the Gateway Server

Communication between an external program and the R/3 System proceeds in the following steps (see Figure 1.7):

1. An external client sends a request to the SAP system. In order for the SAP system to process the request, the client must log on to the Gateway Service on the application server.

2. The gateway informs the dispatcher on the application server that there is a request from an external program.

3. The dispatcher dispatches the request to a dialog process, for example.

4. The dialog process processes the request from the external client.

5. After processing the request, the process sends the result to the dispatcher.

6. The dispatcher sends the result of the request to the Gateway Service.

7. Finally, the Gateway Service sends the result back to the external program.

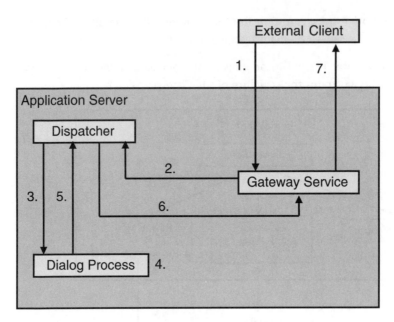

Figure 1.7 External Applications Communicate with the SAP R/3 System

On the other hand, a dialog process can also use the Gateway Service to request the services of an external server. The communication path is the same. The only difference between this scenario and the one outlined above is that now the ABAP program is the controlling unit.

Finally, here we determine the usefulness of the gateway, which is what we questioned initially. Like the update task and SAP lock management, the gateway resolves a problem that occurs due to using several work processes to process a user request. An external program cannot and should not be able to verify which work process is currently processing its request. Therefore, communication cannot be directly via the work process; instead, it must be via an end point that will not change, unlike the work processes. This end point is the gateway. This procedure could be described as *virtualizing* the communication partner.

1.6 Distributed Load Systems and the Message Server

Until now we've acted as if there were only one application server at application level. In reality, this is not the case. Rather, there are several application servers at this level to process requests from the presentation level or from external applications. Here, each application server normally offers only a fraction of the services available. Thus, for example, there are application servers that offer only dialog services—they are known as *dialog servers*. The advantage of this type of distributed system is that all requests from the presentation level or from external clients can be distributed evenly over the existing application servers. This distribution of requests, for example, to spread load evenly over the application servers, is referred to as *load balancing*. It's important to note here, however, that once a user is logged on to an application server, he or she will not be moved to a different server during that session. Logon/load balancing is therefore done only at the moment of logging on to the SAP system.

In a distributed system, application servers are frequently grouped according to the applications that run on them. A group of application servers is also referred to as a *logon group*. With this grouping, it is hoped that similar requests, for example from Financial Accounting (FI), can be located in a single group.

The conceptual advantage of this type of approach is obvious: Similar requests generate similar and clear demands on resources. The application servers can work with these requests more efficiently. This is relevant for SAP buffers in particular. These are areas in the main memory in which, among other things, database data is stored for faster access. In a logon group—for FI, for example—it's conceivable that eventually hardly any requests will be passed on from the buffers to the database, because the buffers will be able to get almost all of the data required from the main memory. Overall, this may also help to improve response time behavior.

In a distributed system, there is often a service that knows all the application servers that exist in the system and the services they offer. In an R/3 System, this is known as the *message service*. There is only one message service in any SAP system. The dispatchers of all application servers log on to the message server and inform it of the services they offer. Thanks to the message server, it is possible to offer certain services centrally in a distributed system, which includes, for example, shared lock management. The message service also contains precise statistics on the load on the participating application servers and can therefore be used by clients to determine which application server has the best performance.

Figure 1.8 shows the logon process for an external client using load balancing:

1. All dispatchers in the application servers log on to the message server.
2. An external client receives a list from the message server showing the systems that currently present the best response times.
3. The external client logs on to the gateway of the appropriate application server.

The SAP GUI follows similar steps. In the third step, however, it logs on directly to the dispatcher.

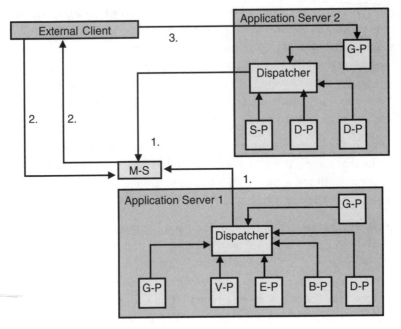

Figure 1.8 Logon Procedure in a Distributed R/3 System

Incidentally, grouping application servers together in logon groups is not mandatory for load balancing. The existence of several application servers and a message server is sufficient.

1.7 The RFC Interface Within the R/3 System

There's a long tradition of connecting the SAP system to other systems. It began with the predecessors of the R/3 System, in particular, the R/2 System. This system, which is still used by some customers today, stood within a mainframe-based environment. These mainframes housed applications that frequently needed to exchange data with the SAP system.

Several techniques can be used for this type of data exchange. On the one hand, data from the source system can be saved in a neutral format on a file system or on drives and then imported into the target system. In many cases, this asynchronous procedure is too slow and laborious.

An alternative is to transfer data directly between programs. The medium for this can be a network. During the 1980s, IBM developed the CPI-C interface, which supports a message-oriented model. The CPI-C interface allows for connections between partners to be established and then broken, and for data to be transferred. Right from the start, the R/3 System has supported this CPI-C interface.

In many cases, however, the direct transfer of data—whether by data files or by CPI-C—is not enough for complex applications. In many cases, the option to execute entire functions on other servers or in other programs is also needed. This represents a step from the data-oriented to the modular or procedural view of programs.

Outside the world of SAP, this transfer was even performed in the 1980s. We can cite the example of the change from TCP sockets to the RPC interface[1].

Within the SAP world, this procedural approach was provided with the RFC interface. Remote Function Calls—like RPCs—allow for procedures to be called in other systems. Inside the SAP system, these procedures are expedited by special ABAP function modules. Thanks to the RFC Library, you can also call procedures and functions in other programming languages in external programs.

Today, the RFC interface is a central component of the SAP Application Server. It forms the basis for communication with the vast majority of external partners. The RFC interface also supports all important aspects that can arise regarding function calls. Important examples are the conversion into different data formats and Unicode capacity.

All intensive work on the programming of interfaces for the SAP system will eventually have to resort to the RFC Library. This dominant role may change over the next few years if Web service technology takes hold in the SAP environment, too.

Programming the SAP RFC interface requires some basic knowledge of the ABAP programming language. In the next chapter, we'll give a brief description of working in the ABAP environment, so that in subsequent chapters we can examine and work with the RFC interfaces in detail.

---

1 TCP sockets provide for a byte stream-oriented communication whereas RPC is based on the ability to call functions on remote servers in a way that is almost identical to a local function call.

2 The Basics of the ABAP Programming Language

To work more intensively with SAP interface programming, it's important to understand the basics of the SAP programming language ABAP. This language is used to implement a large number of internal program flows that can be triggered using RFC interfaces. To a certain extent, you should think of the SAP system as an interpreter or virtual machine for ABAP. In subsequent chapters, elements of this language will be used time and again, and the nature of the examples will assume that you're familiar with the ABAP basics presented here.

The ABAP programming language was developed for the R/3 System. It differentiates between the program types:

▶ Reports

▶ Dialog applications

▶ Function groups/function modules

Reports are programs that are predominantly used to present data records in the form of lists. In the simplest variant, reports select data from database tables, summarize the data, and output it. This form of report is static, but reports can also have interactive characteristics. Thus users can display additional information on data records, for example. Complex interactive reports are similar to dialog applications in the options they provide. In this book, however, we'll focus on the development of simple reports, because we'll use reports solely to test external servers.

Dialog applications are complex programs that facilitate interactive data processing. They provide the user with menus from which he or she can select a processing type. Internally, dialog applications consist of two important elements:

▶ Screen programs (often called DYNamic PROgrams or Dynpros)

▶ ABAP statements

The screen program determines the layout of a data-entry screen and the flow control. Flow control determines which ABAP statement will be executed when. Dialog applications can be started only with transactions. Most of the well known SAP applications are implemented as dialog applications. We won't go into further detail on dialog applications in this chapter. In client-server programming, however, dialog applications can be instrumental. For example, they can be used to execute the various services of a server. Or, the user can control other processes in real time, such as stock removal.

Function modules are an element for cross-program modularization. They encapsulate logical units—for example, all the steps for updating data records on a database table—and can be used by different programs. Each function module has an interface that defines the way it exchanges data with the calling program. Function modules cannot be executed on their own. Each function module can also be addressed by external programs, provided that the process type is set to **Remote-enabled module** in its attributes. Function modules are therefore a key element if an R/3 System is to offer services to external programs.

Function groups bring together several function modules in a logical unit. The function group provides shared administration functions for the modules it contains. A function group can therefore be considered the ABAP counterpart of a *normal* library in C/C++ or a package in Java.

2.1 The ABAP Development Environment

To develop programs in the R/3 System, you need to master the ABAP development environment. Therefore, we have included it here only in the detail necessary to understand this book and execute its examples.

The ABAP development environment includes the following tools:

▶ ABAP Editor
▶ Object Navigator
▶ Data Dictionary
▶ Function Builder
▶ Screen Painter
▶ Menu Painter
▶ Class Builder

The tools in the ABAP development environment are started using *transactions*. In the R/3 System, transactions are the smallest program units that can be executed by users. Every ABAP program can be linked with a transaction. When you enter the name of the transaction, the program linked to the transaction is executed. The transaction code for a program can be entered directly or can be called from a menu.

The *ABAP Editor* is the tool used to develop code for ABAP programs. It provides all the menus for developing programs. It is presented in greater detail in the context of developing reports and function modules.

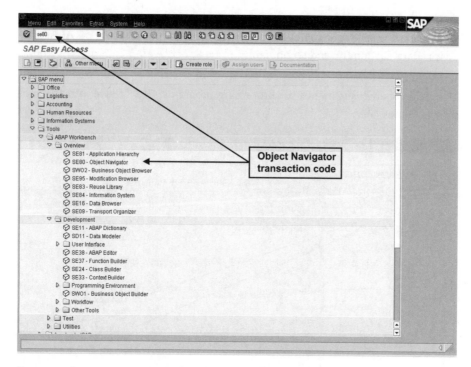

Figure 2.1 Alternative Possibilities for Executing a Program Using the Transaction Code

The ABAP Editor doesn't provide information on the contents of a program—you won't learn about a program's subroutines, data declarations, and other elements. This void is filled by the *Object Navigator*, which is the tool you use to get an overview of all elements in a program and to navigate easily among the program's elements. When you select a particular program element in the Object Navigator, it's automatically displayed, along with the appropriate tools for processing it. You can also call the Object Navigator from the ABAP Editor. Most developers use the Object Navigator as a starting point for program development.

The Object Navigator comprises the following elements:

▶ **Navigation area**
Contains a list box for selecting the program type (program, function group, and so on) and a list box for entering the program name.

▶ **The Program object list**
Displays all the elements used in a program in a tree structure. It's used to navigate among the different program elements. To display an element in the source code editor, for example, double-click on it in the program object list.

▶ **Display window**

Displays the selected element and the tool necessary to process it—ABAP Editor, Data Dictionary, and so on.

▶ **Menu bar**

Provides numerous menus for processing programs. We'll delve into the specific menus later.

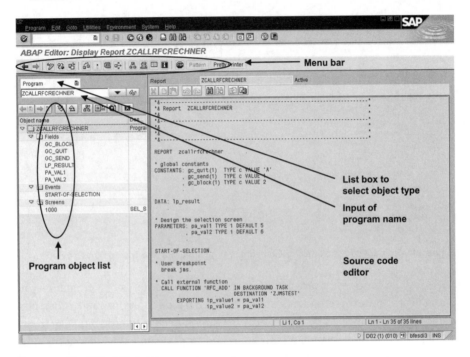

Figure 2.2 The Object Navigator

The *Data Dictionary* (also *ABAP Dictionary*) is the tool used to create descriptions of tables, data elements, domains, etc. Knowledge of the Data Dictionary is critical for client-server programming because the Data Dictionary can be used to quickly determine information about the data model of an application or the technical properties of a table. We'll explain the Data Dictionary in greater detail in the next section.

The *Function Builder* is the tool used to create and administer function groups and function modules. The Function Builder is the most important tool when working with RFC programming.

The *Screen Painter* and *Menu Painter* are tools used to develop data-entry screens. Typically, they're used in the development of dialog applications. Because the development of dialog applications does not fall within the scope of this book, these tools will not be discussed in greater detail here.

The *Class Builder* is a tool used in the development of global classes. It is started using Transaction SE24. Because the development of classes is not discussed, we won't go into further detail on the Class Builder.

Typically, when creating new elements with these development tools, you're asked which *development class* and *transport request* the new elements should be assigned to. Development class and transport request are integral to the administration of every type of element within the R/3 System. For a more detailed description, refer to the literature on software logistics of SAP systems. In this book, we'll outline only the main features.

Every program or database object must be assigned to a development class. The development class determines which target system the object of the transport request should be delivered to. Customer developments are usually assigned to a customer development class, the names of which begin with Y or Z. If you don't want to transport the object to another system, it can also be assigned to the local development class $TMP.

If, however, an object is assigned to a transport-enabled development class, it must be recorded in a transport request. All objects belonging to a development can be in one such transport request. In this way, you can transport all objects of a development to the target system together; however, transport to the target system will take place only when the transport request has been released. If necessary, you can delete each transport request manually.

When developing test programs and tables, you should administer them in a transport request, as this gives you a good overview of your developments at all times.

There is an important naming convention that must usually be observed when creating your own objects in the R/3 System. Customer developments usually begin with Y or Z. The prefix allows the SAP system to identify programs or tables as customer developments and they will not be overwritten in the event of a release change or similar event. The namespace is valid for all objects of any type. In larger projects, it may be advisable to sidestep the aforementioned restrictions by using your own namespaces. For more information, see books on ABAP development that deal with this topic.

In Table 2.1, you'll see the transaction codes for the main development tools of the ABAP development environment.

Development Tool	Transaction Code
ABAP Editor	SE38
Object Navigator	SE80
Data Dictionary	SE11
Function Builder	SE37

Table 2.1 Important Transaction Codes in the ABAP Development Environment

2.2 Creating Database Tables

The data exchanged between R/3 Systems and external programs is often extracted from tables that come with the SAP R/3 System. However, when working in the area of client-server programming, we don't recommend that you work with these tables. First, it is not advisable to write data directly to SAP tables because the data has not previously been checked. Furthermore, you cannot change the semantic and technical properties of table fields when conducting tests. Consequently, here we'll create our own database tables, data elements, and domains in the R/3 System that can be modified as needed.

2.2.1 The Data Dictionary

The Data Dictionary in the development environment provides information about:

▶ The database model, which defines the structure of the database tables, and contains all information about the data and table definitions used and the relationships between the tables; this information is also referred to as *metadata*

▶ The use of the tables and structures in a program package

The Data Dictionary of the R/3 System has the following properties:

▶ Integrated

▶ Active

Integrated means that all information about the elements in the database model is recorded only once in the Data Dictionary and is managed centrally there. When developing programs, this information can be accessed at any time. Thus, for example, during the development you can check whether tables exist in the database. Similarly, for variables that have a data element as a data type, you can determine the properties of the data element from the Data Dictionary.

Active means that all programs are immediately notified of changes to an element in the Data Dictionary. This is because ABAP programs are checked at runtime to determine whether the description of the tables they access has changed in the Data Dictionary. If, for example, a column is deleted from a table, all programs that access that column will no longer be executable because they will know that the table no longer contains this column.

2.2.2 Relationships Between Domains, Data Elements, and Tables

For the purposes of this book, only transparent tables are required. Therefore, only that table type will be discussed. Transparent tables are characterized by the fact that the physical database table corresponds exactly with its description in the Data Dictionary.

A *table* is a two-dimensional array made up of columns and rows. The point of intersection of a row and a column is called a *field*. All fields in a column have the same properties. The properties of a field are described in the R/3 System by a two-tiered domain concept. We can differentiate between:

▶ Technical domains

▶ Semantic domains, which are also referred to as *data elements* (this name is also used in this book)

The technical domain determines the formal properties of a field. This includes, among other things, the data type, byte size, or possible fixed values. The data element specifies the meaning of the field. Note that fields with the same technical properties may be very different from one another. For example, two fields may have a domain of the type Character with a length of 10 characters, but the first field may be a customer number and the second field might be the number of a sales order. Both fields, therefore, have the same formal properties, but they have inherently different meanings.

The link between the semantic and the formal properties is achieved by assigning a domain to a data element. The data element is assigned to the field in a table so that the table field is given formal and semantic properties.

When creating a transparent table, a maximum of three steps is necessary:

1. Create a domain.
2. Create a data element.
3. Create a table.

2.2.3 Create a Domain

A domain is created in the Data Dictionary, which is started using transaction SE11. In the initial screen, you must define the dictionary element type and name it. Once you have entered this information, click on **Create** (see Figure 2.3).

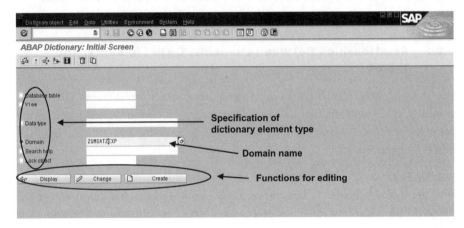

Figure 2.3 Initial Screen for Creating a Domain

The program branches to a dialog screen in which the properties of the domain are maintained (see Figure 2.4). These include:

▶ **Short description**

▶ **Data type**

▶ **Number of characters**

▶ **Number of decimal places** (only for packed numbers)

▶ **Output length**
This is determined and entered by the SAP system itself.

▶ **Conversion routine**
This controls the conversion of values into an internal and an external format. It is optional. One example is the Alpha conversion routine to display customer numbers. It ensures that customer numbers are displayed without leading zeros in dialog boxes, whereas they're saved in the database table with leading zeros.

▶ **+/– sign indicator**
This controls whether number data types have a place for the +/– sign.

▶ **Lowercase indicator**
This controls whether lowercase letters are allowed in character strings. If the indicator is not set, lowercase letters are converted to uppercase.

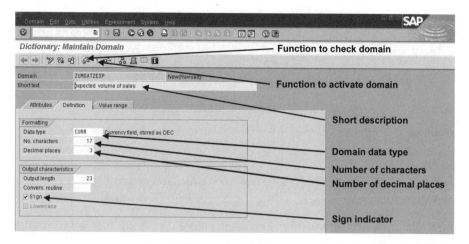

Figure 2.4 Dialog for Entering the Properties of the Domain

You can also create fixed values for domains. To do this, click on the **Value range** tab.

Lastly, the domain must be activated. Only then is it created on the database. Figure 2.4 shows the location of the **Activate** function. Once you have selected the **Activate** function, the dialog boxes for entering the development class (see Figure 2.5) and the transport request (see Figure 2.6) will appear. However, note that the dialog box for entering the transport request will appear only if the domain has already been assigned to a transportable development class.

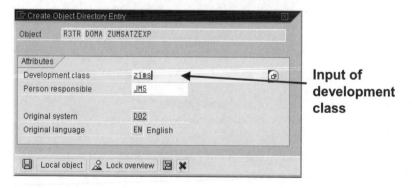

Figure 2.5 Dialog Box for Defining the Development Class

Input of transport request

Figure 2.6 Dialog Box for Defining the Transport Request

The dialog boxes displayed in Figures 2.5 and 2.6 will always appear once a new object is created in an R/3 System. Here, the term *object* means not only database objects, but program objects, such as reports and function groups.

After all necessary information has been entered into the dialog boxes, the domain is created on the database and can be used.

2.2.4 Create a Data Element

The data element assigns a logical meaning to the domain. Several data elements can use the same domain. The data element is also created in the Data Dictionary.

In the initial screen (see Figure 2.7), you must activate **Data type** as the object type and then click on **Create**. Select the appropriate data type in the dialog box that opens. Because we want to create a data element, we select the **Data element** type.

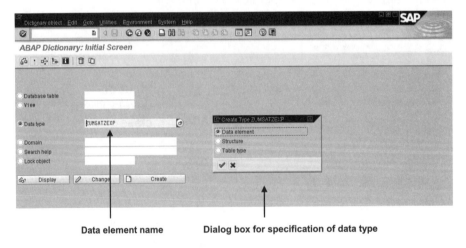

Data element name   **Dialog box for specification of data type**

Figure 2.7 Initial Screen for Creating a Data Element

On confirmation of the entries, the system branches to the maintenance dialog for data elements. For a data element:

▶ The technical properties must be maintained.

This is done either by linking the data element to a domain or by entering a database data type directly. In the R/3 systems, the first of these options is more commonly used.

▶ The alternative field labels for the data element must be maintained.

The text maintained here is used in reports as column headers, for example.

Figure 2.8 shows the maintenance screen used to define the technical properties of a data element. You can use the tabs to branch to different maintenance dialogs. And finally, the data element must also be activated.

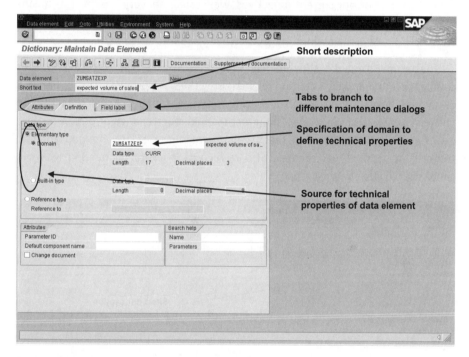

Figure 2.8 Maintenance Dialog for a Data Element

2.2.5 Create a Transparent Table

A database table is also created using the Data Dictionary. To do so, in the initial screen of the Data Dictionary (e.g., Figure 2.3), select the object type **Database table** and enter the name of the table. Once you have filled in the required fields and clicked on **Create**, you must go to the maintenance screen for database tables.

First, enter a short description of the table. This should make it easier to search for tables based on their content at a later stage.

To create a transparent database table, you must fill out the following three types of fields:

1. Properties of the database table

2. Fields of the database table

3. Technical properties of the database table

The properties of the database table define, among other things, the table type. In the standard delivery, transparent table is the default value. The delivery class controls how the data records are to be handled by the different tools in SAP software logistics. For our current objectives, we'll select delivery class A. This means that the table is an application table, in which master and transaction data is stored. The data is maintained by a customer program.

The **Table maintenance allowed** flag should also be set (see Figure 2.9). This enables you to manually edit data records using the Data Browser. This option will always be flagged for our tables because it means that specific data can be changed very quickly for tests. The direct manual maintenance of data records is very beneficial, particularly in the development phase of user-defined applications. If the manual maintenance of data records is no longer needed, you can simply deactivate the property.

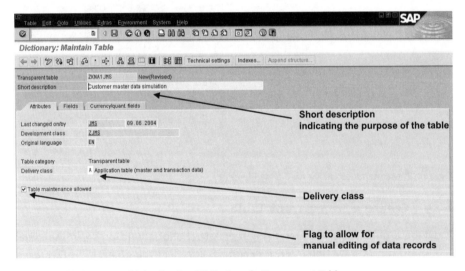

Figure 2.9 Maintenance Dialog for the Attributes of a Transparent Table

You can use the **Fields** tab to access the screen for creating the table fields. The names of the table fields are stored in the column on the left. The name of the data element with which the field should be linked is specified in the **Data element** column. Here you can enter either data elements delivered by SAP or customer-developed data elements. If the R/3 System does not have an appropriate data element and if you don't want to enter your own data element for tests, you can also enter a database type directly. To do so, simply click on the **Data element/Direct type** function key and the fields for the direct input of the data type will be activated. Figure 2.10 shows the screen for maintaining the fields in a database table.

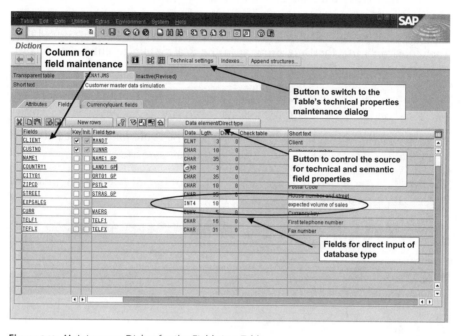

Figure 2.10 Maintenance Dialog for the Fields in a Table

After you have defined the structure of the table, you must maintain its technical properties. These include:

▶ Buffering

▶ Buffering type

▶ Data class

▶ Size category

The **buffering** flag is used to define whether data records read should be held in the main memory. We recommend that you keep your data records in the main memory if they're accessed frequently; however, this does reduce the memory space available for other applications. Typically, this flag is not set. In the buffering type you set how the data records read are to be stored in the main memory. The data type and the size category control how much memory space should be reserved on the database for the table when it is created and by how many bits the memory area needs to be extended. After the table has been created, it must be saved and activated.

2.2.6 Maintaining Data Records Using the Data Browser

We have now created a table on the database. But there are still no data records in the table. Normally, data records are written to a database table or changed by programs, however, for our current needs, this procedure is too time-consuming. Therefore, we'll use the Data Browser in the SAP system to enter data records manually. You can use the Data Browser for the following:

▶ To display the contents of database tables, provided that the table has been created on the database using the Data Dictionary

▶ To change the content of a database table, if the **Table maintenance allowed** attribute is activated in the properties of the database table

The Data Browser is started using Transaction SE16. The most important functions of the Data Browser are displayed in Figure 2.11.

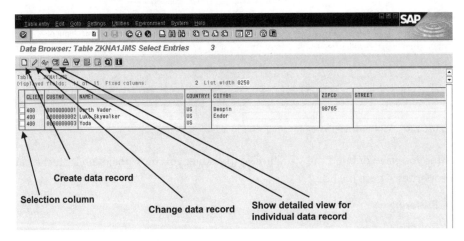

Figure 2.11 Overview of the Functions of the Data Brower

2.3   A Simple Program

The easiest way to learn a new programming language is to develop a short test program. We'll also use this method to learn the basic features of the ABAP programming language. Our first program—following in a long programming tradition—is a report to output the text "Hello World."

To create the program, we start the Object Navigator. Then, we click on **Edit Object**. The following dialog boxes appear:

▶ The dialog box for selecting the object type (see Figure 2.12)
Here, we select the **Program** tab and, in the dialog box that then appears, we select the **Program** object type. We also enter the name of the program and then click on **Create**.

▶ The dialog box to determine whether the program should have a TOP include (see Figure 2.13)
Global data is declared in a TOP include. In the ABAP development environment, however, this indicator is also used to control the program type—report or dialog application. If the indicator is set, a dialog application is created and not a report. Therefore, for our program, we will not set this indicator. The entries must be confirmed.

▶ The dialog box for recording the program attributes (see Figure 2.14)
Here, you need to enter only a short description of the program. All other values will remain unchanged.

▶ The dialog box for entering the development class

▶ The dialog box for entering the transport request

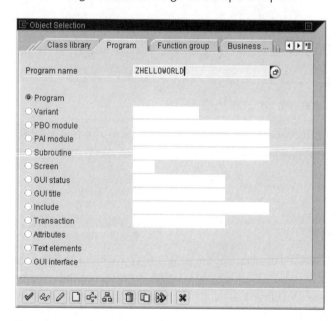

Figure 2.12 Initial Dialog Box for Creating a Report

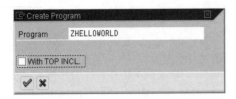

Figure 2.13 Dialog Box for Adding the TOP Include

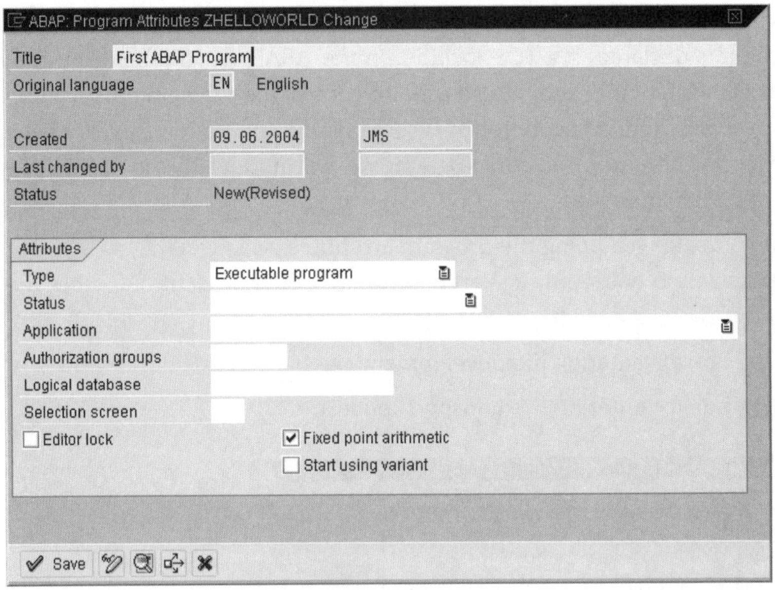

Figure 2.14 Dialog Box for Maintaining the Program Attributes

After you've made the appropriate entries in the dialog boxes, we go to the ABAP Editor. This is where the actual program is written. Our first program has three lines.

```
REPORT ZHELLOWORLD.
START-OF-SELECTION.
WRITE: / 'Hello World'.
```

The REPORT statement is already available in the program, so we need to add only the START-OF-SELECTION and WRITE statements. The meaning of these commands is succinctly defined in Table 2.2. Note the importance of ending ABAP statements with a period (.).

The REPORT statement triggers a program of type Report. A number of optional additions exist for this statement, but these options aren't relevant to the development of simple test programs. The REPORT statement is automatically set by the ABAP development environment and should not be deleted or replaced by other statements.

Because the ABAP programming language is event-driven, a report is divided into several logical areas. Statements can be assigned to each event and they are executed as soon as the event occurs. The link between the event and the corresponding statements is provided by event statements. If a particular event occurs, the control logic in the program looks for the corresponding event statement and executes all following statements. This involves the statements that come after the event statement right up until the event for the next event statement. There are no statements to mark the end of an event statement. The following events exist, among others:

Event	Event statement	Meaning
Initialization	INITIALIZATION	Event that is sent once, as soon as the report is started
Start of data selection	START-OF-SELECTION	Initiates the main part of a report, which includes the actual data selection
End of data selection	END-OF-SELECTION	Event that is sent when the data selection has been executed; it is usually omitted.

Table 2.2 Events in a Report

The START-OF-SELECTION event statement should be used in every report, especially if other events are to be used after it.

The contents of a variable are output with the WRITE statement. The output destination is usually the monitor. The presentation of the value can be influenced by numerous options. The syntax of the WRITE statement is:

```
WRITE: </> Variable1 <Editing options>
     , Variable2 <Editing options>
     .
```

The colon (:) initiates a list and is necessary only if several variables are to be output. The optional control character (/) initiates a line feed, which is followed by variables to be output in the current row. The editing options can come after the variables. We won't go into further detail on the editing options that are available.

After the programming lines have been added, you must activate the program. Then, you can execute the program by pressing the function key **F8** (see Figure 2.15).

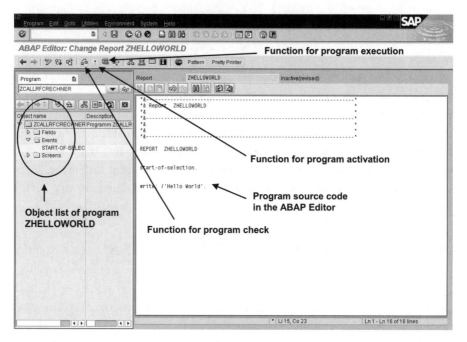

Figure 2.15 View of the First Program in the ABAP Editor

2.4   ABAP Data Types and Variable Declaration

A variable identifies—with a name—a location to which values can be saved. The size of the memory location and the format of the values saved depends on the variable data type. In the ABAP programming language, we differentiate among the following data types:

▶ Predefined data types

▶ Structures

▶ Table types

Structures and table types are also referred to as *data aggregates* because they comprise several predefined data types.

The predefined data types in the ABAP programming language include:

Data Type	Predefined Size	Possible Size	Initial Value	Description
C	1	1–65.535	Blank character	Character string
N	1	1–65.535	'0'	Numeric character string
T	6	6	'000000'	Time in internal time format HHMMSS
D	8	8	'00000000'	Date in internal date format YYYYMMDD
F	8	8	0.0	Float
I	4	4	0	Integer
P	8	1–16	0	Packed number
X	1	1–65.535	X'00'	Hexadecimal value
STRING	0	Any	Zero string	Character field of variable length
XSTRING	0	Any	Zero	Byte field of variable length

Table 2.3 Predefined Data Types

A variable is declared in an ABAP program using the DATA statement:

```
DATA: <Name of variable> TYPE <Data type>
```

The declaration of an integer variable would look like this:

```
DATA: iValue TYPE I.
```

If you are declaring several variables with a DATA statement, the individual variables are separated from each other with commas. The syntax would be:

```
DATA: iValue1 TYPE I
    , iValue2 TYPE I
    .
```

When you are declaring variables of data types C and N, you must enter the length of the variable in the declaration. If, for example, you wanted to create a string and a numeric string of length 10, the declaration would be as follows:

```
DATA: String(10) TYPE c
    , Numc(10) TYPE n
    .
```

If the length is not specified, the fields will have the length 1. Apart from the predefined data types, variables can also be of the type of an element in the Data

Dictionary. If there is a data element in the Data Dictionary with the name String10, then with the statement

```
DATA: String TYPE String10.
```

there could be a variable in an ABAP program of the data element type.

The data type Character of length 1 is the default for all variables. If a variable is declared in a program without any further details, it will automatically have this data type.

Structures group together several fields in a logical unit. In ABAP, we differentiate between local and global structure definitions. Local structure definitions are known and can be used only inside a program. Global structures, on the other hand, are known and usable across programs. Global structure definitions are frequently stored in the Data Dictionary.

The syntax for defining a local structure in a program is:

```
TYPES: BEGIN OF <Name of structure>
            , <Fields in structure, separated by commas>
       , END OF   <Name of structure>
```

A structure with customer information, for example, would be defined as follows:

```
TYPES: BEGIN OF st_CustomerInfo
            , custno   TYPE custno
            , name(40) TYPE c
       , END OF st_CustomerInfo.
```

A variable with a structure type as its data type would be declared in a program as follows:

```
DATA: ls_Customer TYPE st_CustomerInfo.
```

A variable that refers to a structure definition in the Data Dictionary would be declared in the same way as a variable that refers to a local structure definition:

```
DATA: ls_kna1 TYPE kna1.
```

In the preceding example, the variable LS_KNA1 refers to the structure definition of the database table KNA1 in the Data Dictionary.

The table type is the third very important data type. The table type defines the structure of a data record and reserves a memory area for saving numerous data records. A variable that has a table type as data type is also known as an *internal table* in ABAP. Internal tables can be compared to an array of structures in the C programming language. Internal tables are frequently used in ABAP to save the results of a database selection temporarily inside the program.

Several methods are allowed for declaring internal tables in ABAP. One way to create an internal table is to define a table type and then declare a variable that has the table type as its data type.

The syntax for defining a table type is as follows:

```
TYPES: <Name of table type> TYPE <Table type>
                            OF   <Row type>
       <optional additional attributes>
```

If you want to define a table type that has the structure type st_CustomerInfo as its row type, it would look like this:

```
* Definition of structure type
TYPES: BEGIN OF st_CustomerInfo
             , custno    TYPE custno
             , name(40) TYPE c
      , END OF st_CustomerInfo
* Definition of table type
       , tt_CustomerInfo TYPE standard table
                         OF   st_CustomerInfo
                         INITIAL SIZE 0

    .
* Declaration of the internal table
DATA: lt_CustomerInfo TYPE tt_CustomerInfo.
```

Listing 2.1 Creating an Internal Table

In this listing, we defined the table type tt_CustomerInfo. The table type has the structure st_CustomerInfo as row type. In this case, it is a standard table. A differentiation is made in ABAP among standard, sorted, and hashed tables. The forms are different in the way the data records are recorded in the internal tables and in how the data records can be accessed. In the standard type, the data records are saved and unsorted. The addition INITIAL SIZE in the definition of the table type tt_CustomerInfo is used to determine how much memory should be made available for the internal table in the main memory of the R/3 System. Overestimating the value for INITIAL SIZE will increase memory pressure on the system. This in turn reduces the processing speed. The null value means that the R/3 System itself must determine how much memory space should be reserved for the internal table. Specifying the null value is usually sufficient and will also be used for our example.

2.5 Elementary Programming Statements in ABAP

In this section, we'll present the most important elements for controlling the program flow. These include:

▶ Value assignments

▶ Branches

▶ Loops

▶ Access to data records in internal tables

▶ Database accesses

2.5.1 Value Assignments

The ABAP programming language offers many possibilities for assigning a value to a variable. The most frequently used form is the equal sign (=) operator. Thus, the statement

```
<Variable1> =  Value.
```

assigns the value Value to Variable1. If you want to assign the same value to several variables, this can be done as follows:

```
<Variable3> =  <Variable2> =  <Variable1> = Value.
```

Type conversion takes place implicitly in ABAP. If, for example, Variable2 has the data type C (Character) and Variable1 has data type N (Numeric string), in the assignment

```
<Variable2> =  <Variable1> .
```

the numeric string will automatically be converted into a string. Automatic type conversion in the ABAP programming language goes much further, however. If, in our example, Variable2 has the data type I (Integer) and Variable1 has data type C, then in the assignment

```
<Variable2> =  <Variable1> .
```

the value of Variable1 is automatically converted into an integer value, if the value of Variable1 is a valid number. Explicit type casting is not possible in the ABAP programming language, however.

When referring to strings, offset and length details also allow for the possibility of accessing certain substrings. The following example should help to explain this:

```
DATA: Variable1(4) TYPE c VALUE 'lift'
    , Variable2(4) TYPE c VALUE 'move'
```

```
Variable1+2 = Variable2+2(2).
```

According to the assignment, the value of `Variable1` is "live."

Structures are frequently used in the ABAP programming language. The fields of a structure can be accessed using

```
<Structure name>-<Field name>
```

Therefore, value assignment to a field in a structure would be

```
<Structure name>-<Field name> = Value.
```

If you want to exchange content between two structure variables that refer to the same structure type, you can do so with an assignment:

```
DATA: ls_customer1 TYPE kna1
    , ls_customer2 TYPE kna1
    .

ls_customer2 = ls_customer1.
```

There is another variant, however, for assigning values between structure variables. It also works with structure variables that refer to different structures. The statement is as follows:

```
MOVE-CORRESPONDING <Source> TO <Target>.
```

On assignment, the statement `MOVE-CORRESPONDING` checks whether the field names are the same. The fields of the target structure variables are assigned the values of fields of only those source structure variables that have the same names. The following example should help to clarify this:

```
TYPES: BEGIN OF st_customer
             , custno(10) TYPE c
             , name1(40)  TYPE c
        , END OF st_customer
      , BEGIN OF st_document
             , document(10) TYPE c
             , custno(10)   TYPE c
        , END OF st_document
      .

DATA: ls_customer TYPE st_customer
    , ls_document TYPE st_document
    .

MOVE-CORRESPONDING ls_document TO ls_customer.
```

The structures `st_customer` and `st_document` are defined in this section of the program. The two structures have only the `custno` field in common. The structure variables `ls_customer` and `ls_document`, which refer to the corresponding structures, are then declared. In the subsequent value assignment from `ls_document` to `ls_customer` only the value of the field `custno` is transferred, because the structures share only the field `custno`.

2.5.2 Branches

Branches can be realized in ABAP in two different ways:

▶ `IF` branches
▶ `CASE` branches

The syntax of the `IF` branch is:

```
IF <Condition>.
    <Processing block1>.
ELSEIF <Condition>.
    <Processing block2>.
ELSE.
    <Processing block3>.
ENDIF.
```

The `ELSEIF` and `ELSE` branches are optional and can be omitted. The relational operators in a condition can be represented through either an operator or a text symbol for the operator. The following operators exist:

Operator	Text Symbol for the Operator	Meaning
=	EQ	equals
<	LT	less than
>	GT	greater than
<=	LE	less than or equal to
>=	GE	greater than or equal to
<>	NE	not equal
	NOT	Negation linking operator
	AND	Logical operator And
	OR	Logical operator Or

Table 2.4 Relational Operators for the ABAP Programming Language

The term *processing block* represents a number of ABAP statements. All ABAP statements that come after a branch—until the next branch or until the IF statement is closed with an ENDIF—belong to the current branch.

Multiple case distinction is possible thanks to the CASE statement. The syntax of the CASE statement is:

```
CASE <Variable>.
      WHEN VALUE1.
            <Processing block1>.
      WHEN VALUE2
        OR VALUE3.
            <Processing block2>.
      WHEN OTHERS.
            <Processing block3>.
ENDCASE.
```

The CASE statement is used for extensive case distinctions. Each distinction has its own branch. The WHEN OTHERS branch is optional. Here you can enter what should happen if none of the preceding cases is applicable.

2.5.3 Loops

The ABAP programming language identifies, among others:

▶ Counting loops

▶ Loops with entry requirement

The simplest form of the syntax for counting loops is:

```
DO <counting variable> TIMES.
    <Processing block>.
ENDDO.
```

The counting variable is a positive whole number that determines how often the loop should be run through. The system field sy-index contains the value of the current loop run at runtime.

The syntax for loops with entry conditions is as follows:

```
WHILE <Condition>.
      <Processing block>.
ENDWHILE.
```

The condition is analyzed before the loop is run through. If the condition is met, the loop is run through; otherwise, it is exited.

Loops can also be abandoned explicitly using the statement

```
EXIT.
```

The EXIT statement thus ends the innermost enclosing loop:

```
WHILE <Condition>.
      DO <counting variable>.
          EXIT.
      ENDDO.
ENDWHILE.
```

In this example, the counting loop is ended with the EXIT statement and the program returns to the WHILE loop.

2.5.4 Access to Internal Tables

Internal tables record multiple data records. There are numerous statements that assign read and write access to data records in an internal table. Here, we'll take a closer look at the following statements:

▶ LOOP and ENDLOOP

▶ READ

▶ MODIFY

The LOOP statement allows for the sequential processing of all data records in an internal table. The syntax is as follows:

```
LOOP AT <Internal table> INTO <Structure variable>.
      <Processing block>.
ENDLOOP.
```

The argument for the LOOP loop is the internal table, the data records of which should be read sequentially. The INTO statement is used to specify the output area to which the currently read data record should be written. The variable here should have the same data structure as the internal table. The number of loop runs is determined by the number of data records in the internal table. If the internal table contains 10 data records, then the LOOP loop is run through 10 times. If the internal table contains no data records, then the LOOP is not run through. The current loop run can be determined by the sy-tabix system field.

The READ statement reads a single data record from an internal table and makes it available in an output area. It can use the data record index or a key for access.

If there are 10 data records in the internal table lt_CustomerInfo and the third of these records should be read, then the access using the index would be programmed as follows:

```
READ TABLE lt_CustomerInfo INTO ls_CustomerInfo
                     INDEX 3.
```

If the data record is to be accessed with the *Customer number* key, access should be programmed as follows:

```
READ TABLE lt_CustomerInfo INTO ls_CustomerInfo
                     WITH KEY custno = '0000000135'.
```

We should point out that the aforementioned form of access is a sequential access. A binary search is not carried out. This means that this form of access is time-consuming if the internal tables are very large.

The MODIFY statement is used, among other things, for write access to data records in an internal table. The syntax is:

```
MODIFY <ITAB> FROM <Structure variable>
              INDEX <Index>.
```

The ITAB variable refers to the internal table in which contents are to be modified. The Structure variable specifies the memory area from which the information for this modification should be read. The Index variable identifies the data record within the internal table for which the content is to be changed. In addition to this index-oriented access, you can also use conditions to identify which data records are to be modified:

```
MODIFY <ITAB> FROM <Structure variable>
              WHERE <Condition>.
```

2.5.5   Access to Database Tables

The ABAP programming language provides you with many options for accessing database tables. Within the context of this book, we'll present only the following statements:

- ▶ SELECT
  for reading data records
- ▶ INSERT
  for writing data records

The SELECT statement is very important. It is used for reading data records from database tables. Because the syntax of the SELECT statement is so extensive, we'll display it here only to the extent needed to understand the following section. In the simplest case, the syntax of the SELECT statement is as follows:

```
SELECT <Column data>
    FROM <Database table>
    INTO CORRESPONDING FIELDS OF TABLE <Internal table>
  WHERE <Column2> = <Condition1>
      AND <Column1> = <Condition2>.
```

With the column data, the SELECT statement defines which columns of the database table should be read. The FROM keyword specifies the database table. The INTO keyword determines the target area for the data record selected. In the above syntax, a high-performing form is used to execute a database selection. If you enter CORRESPONDING FIELDS OF TABLE after the keyword INTO, an internal table is designated as the target for saving the read data records. This has the effect that all data records that fulfill the selection conditions are read with one database access and written to the internal table. You can enter the conditions that the data records should fulfill after the WHERE keyword. The conditions can be linked to each other with AND or OR operators. If all columns in a table should be read, the asterisk (*) character can be used instead of listing all the column names.

The sy-subrc system field informs us whether the SELECT command has been successfully executed. The value zero indicates successful execution. A value higher than zero indicates that there has been an error. If the execution was successful, the sy-dbcnt system field contains the number of data records found.

If you want to search for a specific data record, you can do this by using the variant

```
SELECT SINGLE <Column data>
    FROM <Database table>
    INTO CORRESPONDING FIELDS OF  <Structure variable>
  WHERE <Column content> = <Condition1>
      AND <Column content> = <Condition2>.
```

The effect of the SINGLE keyword is that the first data record that satisfies the selection criteria will be read. The SELECT SINGLE variant should therefore be used only if the database table is read with the complete primary key.

The following relational operators can be used in the WHERE condition:

Operator	Text Symbol for the Operator	Meaning
=	EQ	equals
<	LT	less than
>	GT	greater than
<=	LE	less than or equal to
>=	GE	greater than or equal to
<>	NE	not equal
	BETWEEN <Upper limit> AND <Lower limit>	Selects all data records that lie in an interval between the upper and lower limits specified
	(NOT) IN (<Value1>, <Value2>)	Quantity of values that are, or are not in the data records sought
	(NOT) LIKE <Template>	Template that the data record sought should or should not comply with. To structure the search sample, the characters '_' = any individual character and '%' = any character string are used.

Table 2.5 Relational Operators for the SELECT Statement

Data records can be written to a database table with the INSERT command. There are numerous options for this. Here, we'll show you how a data record can be written to a database table from a structure. The syntax for this option is:

INSERT <Name of the database table> FROM <Structure variable>.

If the data record is successfully written to the database table, the value of the system field sy-subrc will be zero. Otherwise, it will have a value greater than zero—usually four. To definitively write the changes to the database table, you must execute the

COMMIT WORK.

statement. If an error occurs when writing the data records, you can undo the database changes with the

ROLLBACK WORK.

statement.

Writing the content of an internal table to a database table can be programmed as follows:

```
DATA: gt_customer TYPE STANDARD TABLE OF zknaljms
                  INITIAL SIZE 0
    , gs_customer TYPE zknaljms.
         .
LOOP AT gt_customer INTO gs_customer.
     INSERT zknaljms FROM gs_customer.
* Check if the data record was successfully
* written to the database table
* yes => Commit database changes
     IF sy-subrc = 0.
        COMMIT WORK.
     ELSE.
        ROLLBACK WORK.
     ENDIF.
ENDLOOP.
```

In this listing, the internal table `gt_customer` contains the customer master data that is to be inserted into the database table ZKNA1JMS. In a loop via the internal table `gt_customer`, the data records are first written to the structure variable `gs_customer`. An attempt is then made to write the current customer master data record to the database table ZKNA1JMS. If this has been completed successfully, the database changes are saved with the `COMMIT WORK` statement. In the event of an error, it can be undone with the `ROLLBACK WORK` statement.

2.5.6 Configuration of Selection Screens

We want to use reports to test external servers. It's commonplace to test external servers with different data. At this point, we'll introduce the `PARAMETERS` statement so that you don't have to change and activate the report for every data combination.

Variables that are declared using the `PARAMETERS` statement are presented on a selection screen at the start of the program so that the variable can be filled with values at runtime. The syntax of the `PARAMETERS` statement is:

`PARAMETERS: <Name> TYPE <Data type>.`

The type of the parameter is specified after the name. Multiple selection parameters are separated from each other with a comma. There are many optional entries for the `PARAMETERS` statement that will not be considered here.

The following program shows how selection variables are used:

```
REPORT  ZCALLRFCCALCULATOR LINE-SIZE 256.
DATA: lp_result TYPE i
          .
* Structure of the selection screen
PARAMETERS:  pa_value1 TYPE i DEFAULT 5
           , pa_value2 TYPE i DEFAULT 6
          .
START-OF-SELECTION.
lp_result = pa_value1 + pa_value2.
WRITE: / 'The result of the addition is: ', lp_result.
```

In this program, the selection variables `pa_value1` and `pa_value2` are declared using the `PARAMETERS` statement. The selection variables are then added and the result is output.

2.6   Creating Function Modules

Function modules are integral to client-server programming because they're the option most frequently used in the R/3 System for offering services to non-SAP software components.

We'll demonstrate the creation of function groups and modules using a function module that reads data records from the database table ZKNA1JMS. The name of the function group to be created is `Z_RFC_SERVICES`, which should indicate that the function modules in the function group can also be used by external programs. The name of the function module is `Z_RFC_GET_SINGLE_CUSTOMER`.

Function modules are developed in two steps. First, the function group for managing the function modules is created. Secondly, the function modules themselves are created. Customer-developed function groups and function modules also begin with Y or Z.

We use the Object Navigator as the starting point for developing function groups. After you have clicked on the **Edit Object** function, the dialog box for selecting the object to be edited is displayed again. Select the **Function group** index tab. In the dialog box that opens, you'll see all the objects that can be created for a function group. First, select the **Function group** object and enter the name of the function group to be created. Next, select the **Create** function, at which point the following dialog boxes will appear (see Figures 2.16 to 2.19):

▶ Maintaining a short text for the function group

▶ Determining the development class

▶ Entering the transport request, if the function group is assigned to a transportable development class

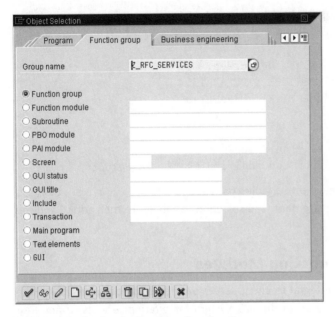

Figure 2.16 Dialog Box for Creating a Function Group

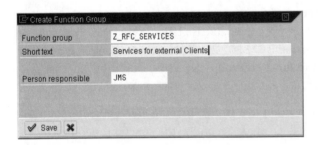

Figure 2.17 Maintaining a Short Text for the Function Group

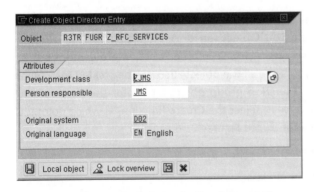

Figure 2.18 Dialog Box for Defining the Development Class

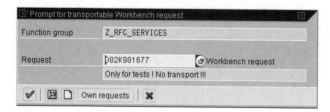

Figure 2.19 Dialog Box for Entering the Transport Request

After the appropriate entries have been made in the individual dialog boxes, the function group is created in the R/3 System and the function modules for our function group can be created.

A function module is created in the same way as the function group. The only difference is that in the **Select Object** dialog box, you now mark the **Function Module** object type. Note that in the **Group name** field you also enter the name of the function group to which the function module is to be assigned. After they have been created in the Object Navigator, the function group Z_RFC_SERVICES and the function module Z_RFC_GET_SINGLE_CUSTOMER are displayed as shown in Figure 2.20.

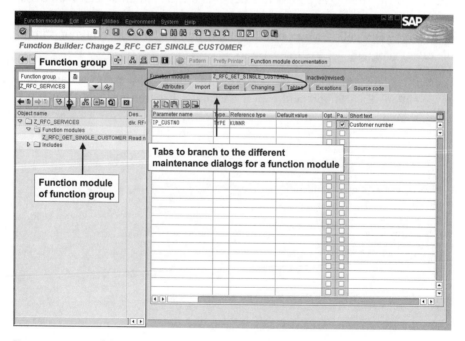

Figure 2.20 View of the Function Group in the Object Navigator

Although the function module Z_RFC_GET_SINGLE_CUSTOMER now exists in the R/3 System, it cannot be used in its current form. It still needs two important elements:

▶ The interface
▶ The processing logic

The interface of a function module defines which variables the function module can exchange with an external program. The interface of an SAP function module comprises the following elements:

▶ Import parameter
▶ Export parameter
▶ Changing parameter
▶ Tables
▶ Exceptions

The *import*, *export*, and *changing* parameters determine which variables are transferred to the function module, returned by it, or transferred to it, and then returned by it. The *tables* parameters determine which internal tables are transferred to the function module or are returned by the function module. The *exceptions* parameters define which errors the function module can communicate to the calling program.

For our first function module, we need only the import and export variables and an exception. Each import and export parameter has the following properties, which should be defined when the parameter is created:

Property	Import Parameter	Export Parameter
Name	X	X
Data type	X	X
Default value	X	
Optional parameter flag	X	
Pass by value flag	X	
Short text	X	X

Table 2.6 Properties of the Import and Export Parameters

When entering the data type, you should note that it must be known globally. Structure variables, therefore, always refer to a structure description in the Data

Dictionary. Also, for RFC-enabled function modules, no generic data types may be used for a variable in the interface. The reason for this is explained in Chapter 4. The **Optional Parameter** indicator controls whether a variable must be or can be transferred. For optional variables, we suggest that you define a value that will be used if the calling program does not provide a value. The value is saved in the **Default Value** attribute. The **Pass by value** property controls whether what is being transferred is a **Pass by value** or a **Pass by reference**. For RFC-enabled function modules, you should note that only the **Pass by value** is allowed with import parameters. The short text describes the meaning of the variables.

Our function module Z_RFC_GET_SINGLE_CUSTOMER needs the customer number as import parameter, and its export parameter is the structure variable ES_CUSTOMER_DATA, which contains the customer data record for the customer number. Figure 2.21 shows how the attributes for the structure variable ES_CUSTOMER_DATA are maintained.

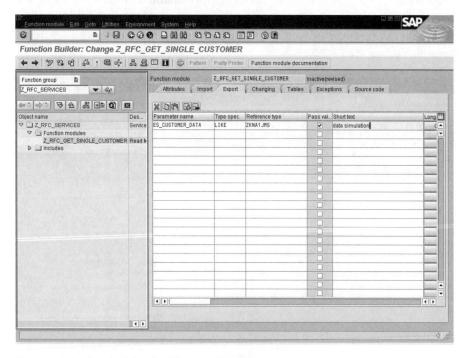

Figure 2.21 Attributes of the Variable ES_CUSTOMER_DATA

The exception ERROR_CUSTOMER_DOES_NOT_EXIST is created in the event that there are no data records for the customer number to be transferred.

After the interface for the function module has been implemented, you must implement the processing logic—you must program what the function module is to do. For this we select the **Source code** tab, which opens the source code editor. Our function module should import the data record in question from the database table ZKNA1JMS into a customer number. The following statements are suitable for this:

```
SELECT SINGLE *
  FROM zkna1jms
  INTO CORRESPONDING FIELDS OF es_customer_data
 WHERE CUSTNO = ip_custno.
* If no data record is found, trigger the exception
IF sy-subrc <> 0.
    RAISE error_customer_does_not_exist.
ENDIF.
```

To ensure that our function module can also be called by external programs, the **Processing type** attribute must be set to **Remote-enabled module**. To do so, we select the **Attributes** tab whereupon the maintenance dialog for the function module properties is displayed. Here the **Processing type** attribute is changed accordingly (see Figure 2.22).

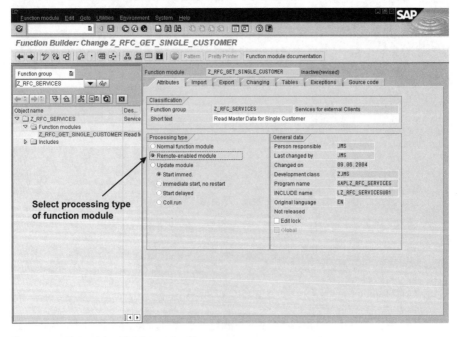

Figure 2.22 Maintaining the Processing Type

Finally, the function group and the function module must be activated. From the **Function module** menu, we select **Activate**. All of the program objects that have not yet been activated are displayed in a dialog box (see Figure 2.23). In this dialog box, we mark all the objects that belong to our function group and then confirm the entry.

Once the function module has been activated successfully, we can verify that it works correctly. We select the **Test** function—function key **F8**—and go to the test environment (see Figure 2.24). Here we can assign values to all the import parameters in our function module and then click on the **Execute** function. Provided that we've entered an acceptable customer number, the function module should return the corresponding data record.

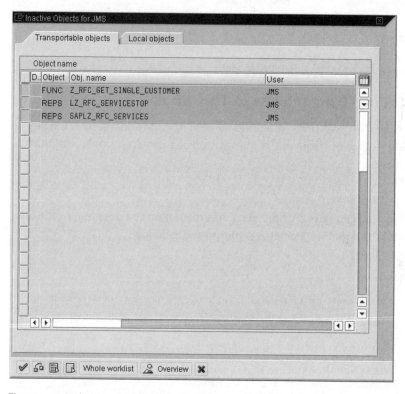

Figure 2.23 Dialog Box for Selecting the Objects to Be Activated

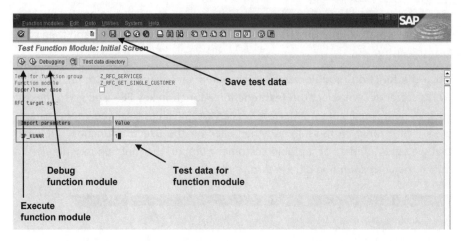

Figure 2.24 Test Environment for Function Modules

2.7 Coding Conventions in This Book

In this last section, we present additional naming conventions for variables as used by SAP. Variables frequently begin with a three-character prefix with the following structure:

XX_.

The first X is a placeholder that provides information on the direction or the area of validity of the variables. Values are interpreted as follows:

Value	Meaning
I	Import parameter = variable that is transferred to a function module or a subroutine
E	Export parameter = variable that the function module or subroutine returns
G	Global variable = variable that is known to all parts of a program
L	Local variable = variable that is known only in a specific part of the program, for example, in a function module or subroutine

The second X specifies the type of variable in question. Values are interpreted as follows:

Value	Meaning
P	Parameter = individual variable

Value	Meaning
S	Structure variable
T	Table = internal table

Therefore, in our function module, the ES_ prefix for our variable ES_CUSTOMER_ DATA means that this is a variable that the function module returns to the calling program. The S indicates that this is a structure variable. This naming convention should be observed during development because this will make the program easier to read.

In some listings, you'll find the colon (:) and the ellipsis (...) to indicate that some lines of the program have been omitted in those places.

These explanations bring us to the end of our explanation on the basics of ABAP programming. With the information provided here, you should be in a position to understand the ABAP programs in this book.

3   Introduction to Programming with the RFC API

The RFC Library forms the basis of RFC programming. It has been available since Release 3.0E and it provides a set of functions that can be used to develop external clients and external servers for communication with the R/3 System.

Figure 3.1 shows how the RFC Library fits into the overall picture with the rest of the SAP interface components.

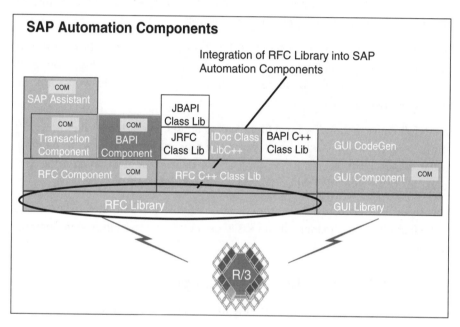

Figure 3.1 Integration of the RFC Library into the SAP Automation Components

The diagram shows that the RFC Library is the central software component on which all other communication technologies depend. These technologies envelop and enhance the RFC Library. The reason for packing or *wrapping* the library in various covers was and is to include new developments in the general interface technologies for software components within the SAP system. COM and ActiveX technologies in particular have become very common on Windows operating systems over the past few years. This has also prompted SAP to supply the RFC Library in the form of ActiveX components. A similar development is currently indicated for the area of Web services. Therefore, the capabilities of the RFC Library have a direct influence on the technologies that are connected to it. Furthermore, with the RFC Library wrapping, the new software components have not adopted all of the options available. Sometimes these higher layers can do less than the RFC Library itself. This is particularly true with regard to the development of external servers, for which the RFC Library is still the optimal solution. Thus, for example, the classic ActiveX components, which we describe in Chapter 8, cannot be used for server programming.

Another advantage of the RFC Library is that it adheres to the ANSI-C standard and can therefore be used trouble-free on all current operating systems. Consequently, it is possible to develop programs that can be used on Windows and Unix/Linux systems, provided that the rest of the program also adheres to the ANSI-C standard. This isn't possible with other technologies. ActiveX controls, for example, run on Windows operating systems only.

Therefore, if an SAP customer uses the C function library to connect external software components, it still gets a very up-to-date interface technology from SAP, which will remain current for some time. It is thus worthwhile to work with the RFC Library in every case.

In the following sections, we will first develop an RFC client that makes RFC calls to the SAP system. This will also illustrate the preparations that need to be done in the system itself. We will then look at the development of an external RFC server for processing RFC calls originating in the SAP system.

We use a Windows-based development environment here so that it will be of use to the majority of our readers. It can easily be transferred to a Linux environment, however.

3.1 The Task for the First Example

An external RFC client must consistently fulfill three important tasks:

1. Set up a connection to the R/3 System
2. Send data
3. Receive data

We'll show you a reliable way to implement these requirements via a simple example application, by which we wish to use the SAP system as a part of a "pocket calculator." The pocket calculator client will send two values to the SAP system, request that the system execute the calculation, receive the result of the calculation from the SAP system, and display it. Figure 3.2 shows the software components that will be involved in our first program.

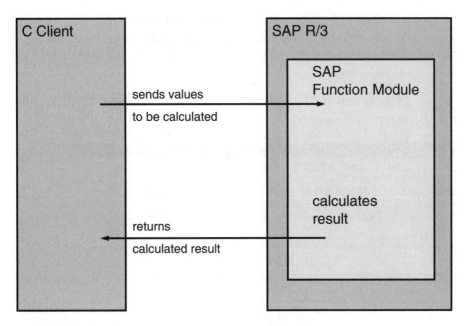

Figure 3.2 Software Components of the Pocket Calculator

The following software components must be developed:

▶ A function group in the SAP system that provides the function modules for executing the addition and subtraction

▶ A client that receives data from the SAP system and the user, and calls up the function modules in the system

3.2 Programming the SAP Function Modules

In Chapter 2, we showed you the basic procedure for developing function modules. There, we created the function group Z_RFC_SERVICES. Here, we will use it to develop the function modules.

The function modules Z_RFC_ADD and Z_RFC_SUB are added to the function group. The two modules have the same interface, so we'll only describe the interface of the function module Z_RFC_ADD.

The function module Z_RFC_ADD has two import parameters and one export parameter.

The import parameters are two integer variables called IP_VALUE1 and IP_VALUE2. In the declaration, it's important to note that the **Pass by value** indicator is set for the variables, because only one **Pass by value** is allowed with import variables in RFC function modules (see Figure 3.3). One transfer per reference is not possible because the client and the server don't share a common memory area. The result is that the server cannot directly access the client's memory area. The server therefore receives a copy of the parameter value and works with it in its own address space.

The export parameter is also an integer variable and it is called EP_RESULT. It returns the result of the calculation.

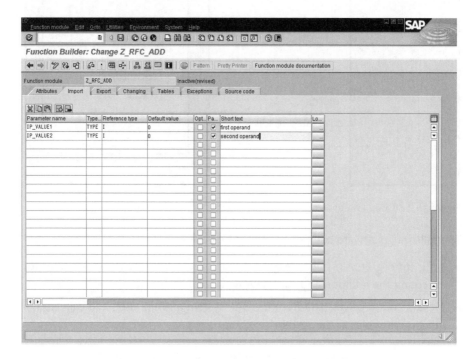

Figure 3.3 Interface for the Import Parameters

Also, in the properties of the function module, the processing type must be set to **Remote-enabled module** (see also Chapter 2).

Finally, the logic of the function modules must be implemented. This is rather trivial for our first example. For the function module Z_RFC_ADD, we need only the following program lines:

```
EP_RESULT = IP_VALUE1 + IP_VALUE2.
```

and for Z_RFC_SUB:

```
EP_RESULT = IP_VALUE1 - IP_VALUE2.
```

The function modules must then be activated. As a last step, they should be checked in the test environment of the R/3 System.

3.3   Programming the Client

For our current purposes, the client will be programmed as a console or shell application—this means that the user enters all data via a command prompt. We selected this method so as not to divert attention from the functionality to GUI techniques.

The client should accomplish the following:

▶ Check whether the user wants to execute a calculation

▶ Log on to the SAP system

▶ Receive the type of calculation and the values to be calculated

▶ Address the function modules Z_RFC_ADD or Z_RFC_SUB in the R/3 System

▶ Present the result

The program flowchart for the client looks like the diagram shown in Figure 3.4. You will find the full program on the Web site for this book at *www.sap-press.com*.

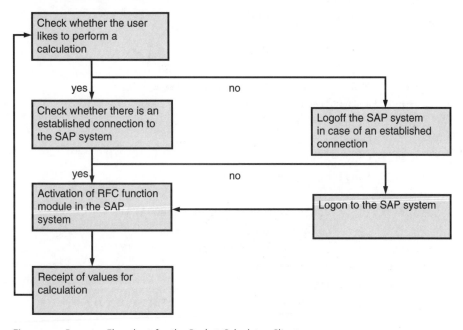

Figure 3.4 Program Flowchart for the Pocket Calculator Client

The components of the RFC software development kit (SDK) are required to develop the client. In the compile and linker options of the development environment in question, it is necessary to complete the references to the header file and the library of the RFC SDK.

The continuously required central header file is called *saprfc.h*. In Windows, this file is located in the following directory:

C:\Program files\SAP\FrontEnd\SAPgui\rfcsdk\include\saprfc.h

The nomenclature in the RFC Library itself depends to a certain extent on the operating-system platform. With Unix for example, the file name is often *librfc.so*. With Windows, the library *librfc32.lib* is located in the following directory:

C:\Program files\SAP\FrontEnd\SAPgui\rfcsdk\lib

3.3.1   The Configuration of the main() Function

Every RFC-enabled program must integrate the central header file *saprfc.h*. In our very simple case, we can then immediately start to program the `main()` function. For this, we will also use typical Windows Boolean and calling conventions, which may exist in different forms in some C/C++ environments:

```
#include <saprfc.h>
int main (int argc, char** argv)
{
    RFC_RC          rc = RFC_OK;
    RFC_ERROR_INFO_EX ErrorInfo;
    RFC_HANDLE      hConnection = RFC_HANDLE_NULL;
    int    iValue1  = 0,
           iValue2  = 0,
           iResult  = 0;
    char cInput = 'Y';
    static iBool bLogon = iFalse;

  printf("%s\n", "Would you like to do a new"\
                "calculation?");
  while((cInput = (char)toupper(getchar())) == 'Y'){
/* Execute logon to SAP system */
    if(bLogon == iFalse){
       if((rc = LogonToSAP(&hConnection, &ErrorInfo))
             != RFC_OK){
          printf("%s\n", ErrorInfo.message);
          exit(rc);
       }
       bLogon = iTrue;
    }
    _flushall();
```

```
/* Function for entering the operation and
   calling the SAP function module */
     if((rc = Compute(hConnection, &ErrorInfo,
                      &iValue1, &iValue2, &iResult))
        != RFC_OK){
/* If errors occurred with RFC call, output errors */
         printf("%s\n", ErrorInfo.message);
         exit(rc);
     }else{
/* If RFC function was called successfully, output result */
         printf("The result of the calculation is: "\
                "%i\n", iResult);
         printf("%s\n", "Would you like to do a new "\
                "calculation?");
     }
   } /* End of while-loop */
/* Close connection */
   RfcClose(hConnection);  return rc;
}
```

Listing 3.1 The main() Function of the Pocket Calculator

The main() function consists of three parts:

▶ Logging on to the SAP system, which is executed in the LogonToSAP function

▶ Executing the calculation, which is done in the Compute function. The function is cloaked in a loop that will be run through for as long as the user answers "Y" to the question *Would you like to do a new calculation?*

▶ Closing the connection

If we take a closer look at the main() function, we can see three new data types:

▶ RFC_RC

▶ RFC_ERROR_INFO_EX

▶ RFC_HANDLE

The data type RFC_RC is an enumeration type of the RFC Application Programming Interface (API). It is frequently used by the functions of the RFC API as a return type to inform the calling program as to whether the function call was successfully executed. The return value RFC_OK indicates a successful function call. The RFC_RC type has the following values, among others:

Value	Meaning
RFC_OK	Function was executed successfully.
RFC_FAILURE	Error occurred during the execution of the function.
RFC_EXCEPTION	Exception triggered by the SAP function module that was called.
RFC_CLOSED	Connection has been terminated.
RFC_RETRY	Sent to an external server if there is no request in the SAP system for the execution of a callback function (polling not successful).
RFC_NO_TID	Error in the area of the transactional server. No transaction ID was transferred.
RFC_MEMORY_INSUFFICIENT	If an RFC API function requires more space than is currently available, this value is triggered.
RFC_INVALID_HANDLE	Invalid connection handle
RFC_INVALID_PARAMETER	Invalid parameter

Table 3.1 Values of the Type RFC_RC

You can use the function RfcLastErrorEx to get more precise information on any error that occurs. This function receives a reference to a variable of the structure RFC_ERROR_INFO_EX. The structure has the following fields:

Field	Meaning
group	Error group
key[33]	Error code to identify the error
message[513]	Text that describes the error that has occurred

Table 3.2 Fields of Structure RFC_ERROR_INFO_EX

The message field is particularly important because it contains a precise description of the error that has occurred. Therefore, you should combine calls to RFC API functions with an error-check. The realization of an RFC call could be as follows:

```
if((rc = RfcFunction()) != RFC_OK){
    RfcLastErrorEx(&ErrorInfo);
}
```

The data type RFC_HANDLE is the last new data type. From a C perspective, it is an unsigned integer. It picks up the handle of the current R/3 connection. The connection handle is a unique identifier for an R/3 connection. If no connection is currently open to an R/3 System, the variable of this type will have the value RFC_HANDLE_NULL.

3.3.2 Open a Connection to the R/3 System

Before a client can exchange data with the R/3 System, it must first connect to the R/3 System. In our example program, the connection is made in the LogonToSAP function. Within this function, the function RfcOpenEx is called. The arguments for logging on to the R/3 System are transferred to the function RfcOpenEx in the form of a string.

The values are entered into the connection string in the form

Argument=Value

When entering the argument and the associated value, you should note that the value is case-sensitive, contrary to the name for the argument. Furthermore, if it contains blank spaces, the value for an argument is enclosed in quotation marks. If, for example, you're working with a configuration file (see also Chapter 4) and if the value for the argument Dest is "RFC SERVER," this value must be entered in the connection string as follows:

Dest="RFC SERVER"

The entry

Dest=RFC SERVER

would be wrong.

The connection arguments can be divided into three groups:

▶ User-specific data

▶ System-specific data

▶ Values with which the properties of the connection can be set

The user-specific data includes the following information:

Argument	Meaning
client	Client
user	User
passwd	The user's password
lang	Logon language

Table 3.3 User-Specific Connection Data

The following sub-groups can be created for the system-specific information:

▶ Data for logging on to an application server

▶ Data for load balancing

▶ Data for working with a configuration file (*SAPRFC.INI*)

Working with a configuration file and load balancing will be explained in Chapter 4. Here, we'll describe the arguments for logging on to a particular application server.

Argument	Meaning
ashost	IP address of the application server
sysnr	System number

Table 3.4 Data for Logging on to a Specific Application Server

When entering the IP address for the application server, we must specify whether the connection is being made via an SAP router. If the connection is made directly to the application server, it is specified as

ASHOST=10.10.34.131

If, on the other hand, an SAP router is involved in creating the connection to the application server, this is incorporated. The value for the ASHOST information would then look like this:

ASHOST=/H/sapgate1/S/3297/H/10.10.34.131.

We can see that the details of the SAP router have been included in front of the IP address. One possible way to determine the system data is to use the SAP Logon. If you select the target system in the SAP Logon and then execute the **Properties** function, the system data for the target server is displayed (see Figure 3.5).

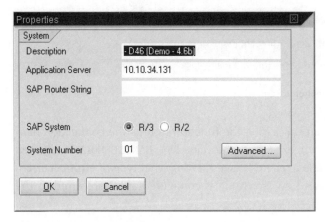

Figure 3.5 Determining the Server Data

In addition, the properties of an active connection can be influenced by the following attributes:

Value	Meaning
abap_debug	Activate the ABAP debugger 0 = off; 1 = on
lcheck	Activate the logon check. With the logon check, the user data is checked at logon. 0 = off; 1 = on
trace	Activate the trace—see also Chapter 5 0 = off; 1 = on
use_sapgui	Activate the SAP GUI 0 = off; 1 = on

Table 3.5 Attributes for the Properties of a Connection

If the use_sapgui option is activated, screens of the R/3 System can be displayed in the external client. The SAP GUI is automatically activated if the abap_debug option is active.

The string with the connection arguments is finally transferred to the RfcOpenEx function. The interface of this function is displayed in the following table:

Value	Meaning
connect_param	String with connection arguments
error_info	Reference to a structure of type RFC_ERROR_INFO_EX

Table 3.6 Interface of the Function RfcOpenEx

If the connection has been successful, the function returns the connection handle. If an error occurs during execution, the value RFC_HANDLE_NULL is returned and in the ErrorInfo variable a record is saved stating what type of error occurred. The following listing shows how the string is configured and transferred to the RfcOpenEx function:

```
char ConParam[] =
     "DEST=RFCRECHNER CLIENT=099 USER=<USER> "\
     "PASSWD=<Password> LANG=EN ABAP_DEBUG=0 "\
     "ASHOST=10.10.34.131 SYSNR=01";
RFC_ERROR_INFO_EX ErrorInfo;
memset(&ErrorInfo, NULL, sizeof(RFC_ERROR_INFO_EX));
if((hConnection = RfcOpenEx(ConParam, &ErrorInfo))
                == RFC_HANDLE_NULL){
   printf("%s\n", ErrorInfo.message)
   rc = RFC_FAILURE;
   return rc;
}
```

Listing 3.2 Logging on to the R/3 System

In this listing, in addition to logging on to the R/3 System, we can also see that the return value for the function LogonToSAP is manually set to RFC_FAILURE if the function returns an invalid connection handle. This is necessary because the function LogonToSAP has the data type RFC_RC as return type to return the status of the execution of functions to the RFC API directly. Because the function RfcOpenEx has another return type, however, it is necessary to manually adjust the value rc to ensure consistency.

Working with a string to manage connection data is not so clear, however. It is better to manage the values in structures and to build the connection string from the data in the structures. Incidentally, SAP used to manage connection data in structure variables itself (see also Chapter 4). In keeping with the SAP concept, we will create three structures. The structures are:

▶ RSSYSTEMDATA
for managing the system data

▶ RSUSERDATA
for storing user data

▶ RSSPECIALFLAGS
for setting specific data for the connection

A suggestion for the creation of the structures might look like this:

```
typedef struct
{
    rfc_char_t *ASHost,
               *SysNr;
} RSSYSTEMDATA;
typedef struct
{
    rfc_char_t *Client,
               *User,
               *Password,
               *Language;
} RSUSERDATA;
typedef struct
{
    unsigned int ABAP_Debug,
                 LCheck,
                 Trace,
                 Use_SAPGUI;
} RSSPECIALFLAGS;
```

Listing 3.3 Structures for Managing Logon Data

In this way, the structure RSSYSTEMDATA is currently limited to the information for logging on to a specific application server. It must be enhanced to allow the use of load balancing or configuration files.

The following steps are required to create the connection string from the structure variables:

1. Create templates for the connection argument groups.

2. Fill the template with the values of the structure variables.

3. Copy individual groups of connection arguments to the connection string.

The `BuildConnectString` function shows how the aforementioned steps can be implemented:

```c
char* BuildConnectString(RSSYSTEMDATA   SystemData,
                         RSUSERDATA     UserData,
                         RSSPECIALFLAGS Specialflags)


{
    char PatternUser[] =
            "Client=%s User=%s Passwd=%s Language=%s",
         PatternASHost[] =
            "ASHost=%s SysNr=%s",
         PatternSpecialFlags[] =
            "ABAP_Debug=%u LCheck=%u Trace=%u "\
            "Use_SAPGUI=%u",
       *ConnectionString = NULL;
    int iSize = 500;
    ConnectionString = (char*)malloc(iSize);
    memset(ConnectionString, NULL, iSize);
/* Set the user data */
    _snprintf(ConnectionString, iSize, PatternUser,
            UserData.Client, UserData.User,
            UserData.Password, UserData.Language);
/* Blank character to separate the new block */
    strcat(ConnectionString, " ");
/* Set the system data */
    _snprintf(ConnectionString+strlen(ConnectionString),
            iSize, PatternASHost,
            SystemData.ASHost, SystemData.SysNr);
    strcat(ConnectionString, " ");
/* Setting the control flags */
    _snprintf(ConnectionString+strlen(ConnectionString),
            iSize, PatternSpecialFlags,
            Specialflags.ABAP_Debug, Specialflags.LCheck,
            Specialflags.Trace, Specialflags.Use_SAPGUI);
    return ConnectionString;
}
```

Listing 3.4 Function for Configuring the Connection String

We can see that the function manages templates for individual groups of connection arguments internally and copies the templates, including the values assigned to them, to the `ConnectionString` variable. For additional information on the `RfcOpenEx` function and, in particular, on the possible values for the connection, see the detailed SAP documentation.

The function `RfcClose` closes an existing connection. The interface of the `RfcClose` function is displayed in the following table:

Variable	Meaning
handle	Handle of the connection to be closed

Table 3.7 Interface of the Function RfcClose

Please note that the function should not transfer the value `RFC_HANDLE_NULL`, because otherwise all existing connections will be closed.

3.3.3 Calling Up Function Modules in the R/3 System

Once our client has successfully made a connection to the R/3 System, we are in a position to call up RFC-enabled function modules in the R/3 System. We shall now look at what a client program has to do to control and exchange data.

A client program has to execute two steps:

1. It must reproduce the interface of the function module so that it will be possible to transfer the data.
2. It must call the function module in the SAP system.

The implementation of the interface in the client includes the following aspects:

▶ All variables that are to be exchanged with the R/3 function module must also be created as variables of the same data type and the same byte size in the client.

▶ A description must be created for every variable that will be transferred when the `RfcCallReceiveEx` function is called, for example.

▶ You should also note that the interface parameters are created as a reversed image in the client. By reversed image we mean that import parameters on the SAP side become export parameters on the client side and vice versa.

To create variables on the client side all that is required is a declaration of the corresponding variables. For our example, we'll need three integer variables:

```
int  iValue1 = 0,
     iValue2 = 0,
     iResult = 0;
```

The description of the technical properties of the data type of the variables to be exchanged is saved in an array of variables of type RFC_PARAMETER. A separate array must be created for the import and export parameters. An array of variables of type RFC_TABLE is used for exchanging tables. The exchange of tables is displayed in Chapter 4. The RFC_PARAMETER type is a structure with the following fields:

Field	Meaning
name	Name of the variables in the function module interface
nlen	Name length
type	Variable type
leng	Field byte size
addr	Reference to the corresponding variable in the client code

Table 3.8 Fields of the Type RFC_PARAMETER

The need to describe the interface parameters is an important difference from using ABAP function modules from an ABAP program. If you call a function module in an ABAP program, you transfer the values to the interface parameters directly. There is no need to transfer a description containing the technical properties of the data types to be exchanged.

In an ABAP program, the function module Z_RFC_ADD is called as follows:

```
CALL FUNCTION 'Z_RFC_ADD'
    EXPORTING
        ip_value1  = 5
        ip_value2  = 10
    IMPORTING
        ep_result  = lp_result.
```

In an external client, the circumstances are somewhat different. In this case, the function module is called indirectly, for example, with the function RfcCallReceiveEx. This function has the following interface:

Parameter	Meaning
handle	Connection handle
function	Name of the function module to be addressed
exporting	Array of type RFC_PARAMETER with a description of the technical properties of the export parameters
importing	Array of type RFC_PARAMETER with a description of the technical properties of the import parameters
changing	Array of type RFC_PARAMETER with a description of the technical properties of the changing parameters
tables	Array of type RFC_TABLE with a description of the tables to be exchanged
exception	Reference to a pointer of data type char to include the function module exception

Table 3.9 Parameters of the Function RfcCallReceiveEx

RfcCallReceiveEx is a function that refers not only to a certain function module, but to any RFC-enabled function module and can therefore call up any RFC-enabled function module in an R/3 System. In its declaration, it cannot be aligned to the specific interface of a function module. Consequently, the program that calls the RfcCallReceiveEx function must provide a description of all interface parameters itself, including their technical properties. This is the effect of the generic nature of the RfcCallReceiveEx function.

As we have seen, the structure RFC_PARAMETER has the fields type and leng, among others. In the type field, you must enter the data type of the variable to be exchanged and in the leng field, the byte size of the data type is transferred. The RFC API recognizes the following data types:

Data Types of the RFC API	Identifier	Meaning
RFC_BYTE	TYPX	1-byte field, which means that the field content is not interpreted
RFC_BCD	TYPP	Packed number in BCD format, corresponds to the ABAP data type P
RFC_CHAR	TYPC	Character string ending with a space
RFC_DATE	TYPDATE	Date type in internal representation YYYYMMDD
RFC_FLOAT	TYPFLOAT	Float with double precision

Table 3.10 RFC API Data Types

Data Types of the RFC API	Identifier	Meaning
RFC_INT	TYPINT	Integer, size 4 bytes
RFC_INT1	TYPINT1	Integer, size 1 byte—obsolete
RFC_INT2	TYPINT2	Integer, size 2 bytes—obsolete
RFC_NUM	TYPNUM	NUMC-numeric field with a fixed length
RFC_TIME	TYPTIME	Time type in internal representation HHMMSS

Table 3.10 RFC API Data Types (cont.)

The type to be entered in the `type` field depends, naturally, on the interface of the SAP function module that we want to address. You can determine the byte size of the data type using the `sizeof()` operator. You should note that the `sizeof()` operator as an argument implicitly contains the RFC data type and not the C data type.

To better understand this, let's look at the configuration of the technical description for the import parameter `IP_VALUE1` of the function module `Z_RFC_ADD`. The parameter `IP_VALUE1` is defined in the interface of the function module as an import parameter of type `I`. It must therefore be understood in the client coding as an export parameter. This results in the following configuration for the structure `RFC_PARAMETER`:

```
int  iValue1 = 0;
/* Array to describe the technical properties.
   A separate array is needed for the export and
   import parameters. In addition, export parameters
   in the client then become import parameters in
   the SAP function module and vice versa */
RFC_PARAMETER ExportParameters[3],
              ImportParameters[2];
:
/* Configuration of the structure RFC_PARAMETER
for the exchange of parameters IP_VALUE1; IP_VALUE2 analog */
:
ExportParameters[0].name = "IP_VALUE1";
ExportParameters[0].nlen = strlen("IP_VALUE1");
ExportParameters[0].type = TYPINT;
ExportParameters[0].leng = sizeof(RFC_INT);
ExportParameters[0].addr = &iValue1;
```

In the declaration of the ExportParameters array, you'll notice that it is one higher than the number of import parameters in the SAP function module. The reason for this is that the function RfcCallReceiveEx recognizes the end of an array only if there is a final zero in the Name field. Therefore, the size for each array can be determined as follows:

Array size = Number of import or export parameters + 1

It is clearer if you write an additional function for filling the fields in the structure RFC_PARAMETER. It could look like this:

```
RFC_PARAMETER BuildSimpleParam(char *pName,
                               int   iType,
                               int   iLength,
                               void* pCallbackVariable)
{
    RFC_PARAMETER NewParameter;
    NewParameter.name = pName;
    NewParameter.nlen = strlen(pName);
    NewParameter.type = iType;
    NewParameter.leng = iLength;
    NewParameter.addr = pCallbackVariable;
    return NewParameter;
};
```

Listing 3.5 Additional Function for Filling the Fields in the Structure RFC_PARAMETER

Calling the function for the parameter IP_VALUE1 of function module Z_RFC_ADD would be as follows:

```
ExportParameters[0] = BuildSimpleParam(
            "IP_VALUE1", TYPINT, sizeof(RFC_INT), &iValue1
            );
```

After the two arrays have been configured in the client with the description of the interface for the function module Z_RFC_ADD, the SAP function module can be addressed. There are basically two alternatives for communicating with the R/3 System:

▶ Asynchronous data processing

▶ Synchronous data processing

For asynchronous data processing, the functions RfcCallEx and RfcReceiveEx are required. The RfcCallEx function calls the function module and only transfers the values for the export parameters. It returns immediately after the data has been transferred. It does not wait for the result of the processing by the function module. The interface of the `RfcCallEx` function is:

Variable	Meaning
`handle`	The connection handle that was previously determined with the function `RfcOpen`
`function`	The name of the R/3 function module
`exporting`	Array with the technical description of the export parameters from the client's perspective, that is, import parameters from the viewpoint of the SAP function module
`changing`	Array with the technical description of the changing parameter
`tables`	Array with the description of the tables to be exported

Table 3.11 Interface of the Function RfcCallEx

The result of this processing by the function module is determined by calling the function `RfcReceiveEx`. The interface of the `RfcReceiveEx` function is:

Variable	Meaning
`handle`	The connection handle that was determined with the function `RfcOpen`
`importing`	Array with a description of the import parameters from the client's perspective, that is, export parameters from the viewpoint of the SAP function module
`changing`	Array with a description of the changing parameters
`tables`	Array with a description of the tables that should be imported
`exception`	Reference to a character array to include the function module exception

Table 3.12 Interface of the Function RfcReceiveEx

The more frequently used method, however, is that of synchronous data processing. With this method, the client sends the data and waits for the result of the processing by the function module. It is also used in our first example. The function `RfcCallReceiveEx` is used for synchronous data processing. Its interface has been described above.

If an SAP function module does not have an interface parameter type, the corresponding pointer in the function `RfcCallReceiveEx` is simply set at `NULL`. Our SAP function module `Z_RFC_ADD`, for example, has only import and export parameters, but no table parameters. Calling it would therefore be as follows:

```
RFC_PARAMETER ExportParameters[3],
              ImportParameters[2];
char *pException = NULL;

rc = RfcCallReceiveEx (hConnection, "Z_RFC_ADD",
                       ExportParameters, ImportParameters,
                       NULL, NULL, pException);
```

3.4 Frequent Errors on the Client Side

Once we have implemented the call for the function module Z_RFC_ADD using the function RfcCallReceiveEx, the pocket calculator client is ready. After compilation and linking, we should be in a position to log on to the R/3 System and execute the calculation (see Figure 3.6).

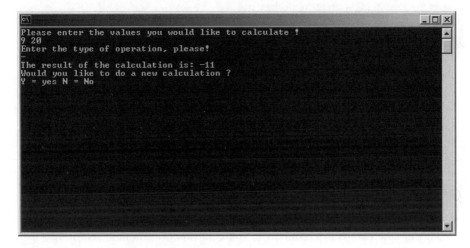

Figure 3.6 The Pocket Calculator in Action

If the pocket calculator doesn't work, there are two possible reasons. The first is incorrect logon data, which results in failure to log on to the SAP system. People often make mistakes here. If you cannot connect to the system, take a close look at the values.

One option for testing the connection data is to use the SAP program rfcping.exe. In Windows systems, it can be found in the directory

C:\Program files\SAP\FrontEnd\SAPgui\rfcsdk\bin

Here you will find a whole range of useful extra test programs. As standard values, the program expects the client, the user, the password, the logon language, the IP address of the server, and the system number (see Figure 3.7).

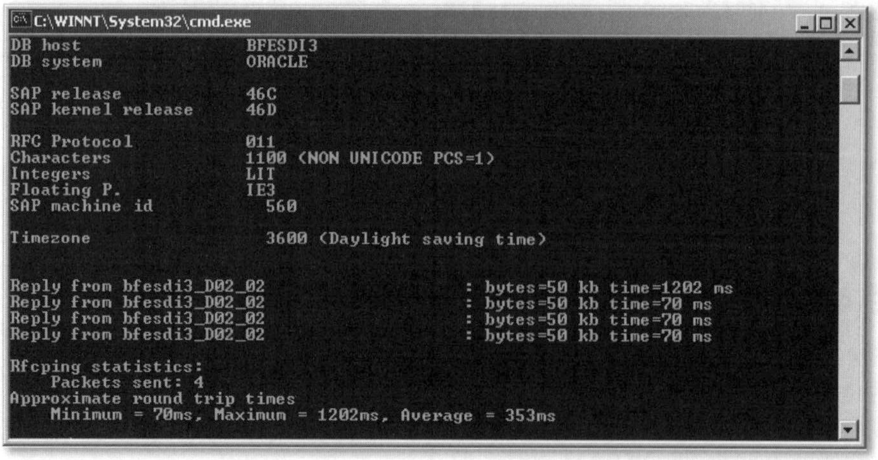

Figure 3.7 Results of the Program RfcPing

When you start the program, it first checks only whether the server can also be reached. It does not check the user and the password. If this data should also be checked, you have to set the optional argument use_sapgui to either value 1 or 2.

If your pocket calculator always returns the value zero, or if for other reasons the result is not comprehensible, we recommend that you check the names of the interface parameters in the ABAP function module and in your program—the value of the name field in the structure RFC_PARAMETER. Typing errors may also be at fault. Unfortunately the SAP system does not trigger an exception if the interface parameter is incorrect; it simply ignores it, which leads to incorrect results.

If this advice does not help you to achieve a satisfactory result, you can try remote debugging. Two steps are required to debug a function module remotely. First, you must set a breakpoint in the function module. The best thing here is to use a user-specific breakpoint so that other programs that also use the function module will not be interrupted in program flow. Second, you must transfer the option ABAP_DEBUG, with value 1, to the connection string. If we start our pocket calculator again, we should be able to pause at the breakpoint and debug the function module in the R/3 System. In Chapter 5, we'll describe how to work with the ABAP Debugger and other tools to eliminate errors.

3.5 Overview of the Functions and Structures Used

In our first example, we programmed a simple client that exchanges data with the SAP system, using the functions listed below:

Function	Meaning
RfcOpen	Open a connection to an R/3 System
RfcClose	Close existing connection
RfcLastErrorEx	Request information on the last error that occurred
RfcCallReceiveEx	Synchronous sending and receiving of data to or from an R/3 function module
RfcCallEx	Send the data to an R/3 function module
RfcReceiveEx	Receive the data from an R/3 function module

Table 3.13 Overview of the Functions Used

The following structures are also used:

Structure	Meaning
RFC_PARAMETER	Structure for describing the technical properties of import and export parameters

Table 3.14 Overview of the Structures Used

3.6 From an RFC Function Call to the Function Module

We have now used an external client to address a function module in the SAP system. In doing so we have accepted the fact that the function module is called somewhere in the SAP system. To conclude, let's look at how the call from a function module in the client reaches the function module in the SAP system.

The fact that the function module can be addressed by our client should not be underrated. SAP function modules are not standalone, executable program units. A function module can be executed only by using the ABAP program statement CALL FUNCTION. However, our client was written in the C programming language, which does not have power over ABAP language elements. Therefore, the client cannot execute the function module directly. An ABAP environment must exist in the SAP system that deals with the virtual function module call. This environment is the program SAPMSSY1.

The SAPMSSY1 program is an R/3 System program that runs permanently in the background. It has four tasks:

▶ Receive the RFC call from the external client

▶ Import the data sent by the client

▶ Call the function module in the SAP system

▶ Return the result from the function module to the client

This task is performed by the subroutine REMOTE_FUNCTION_CALL in the program SAPMSSY1. The subroutine is implemented as follows:

```
FORM REMOTE_FUNCTION_CALL USING VALUE(TYPE).
  DO.
    CALL 'RfcImport' ID 'Type' FIELD TYPE.
    PERFORM (SY-XFORM) IN PROGRAM (SY-XPROG).
    RSYN >SCONT SYSC 00011111 0.
  ENDDO.
ENDFORM.
```

Listing 3.6 The Subroutine REMOTE_FUNCTION_CALL in the Program SAPMSSY1

First, the program calls the C function `RfcImport` in the SAP kernel. The task of this function is to import data from the client. The function module is then addressed by the statement

```
PERFORM (SY-XFORM) IN PROGRAM (SY-XPROG).
```

Finally, the function module results are sent back to the client.

The observant reader will now argue that the subroutine REMOTE_FUNCTION_ CALL does not contain any CALL FUNCTION statement, only the dynamic calling of a subroutine. In fact, an RFC update include is automatically created for every RFC-enabled function module. The developer does not notice any of this procedure, because the SAP system doesn't provide any information about it. You can view the include via the menu path **Goto · More jump destinations · Generated RFC/Update include** in the Function Builder. The RFC/Update include consists of a single subroutine. The subroutine reproduces the import and export parameters of the function module, and it also calls the function module.

```
* * * * * * * * * * * * * * * * * * * * * * * * * * * * * * * * * * * * * * * * * * * * * *
* THIS FILE IS GENERATED BY THE FUNCTION LIBRARY   **
* NEVER CHANGE IT MANUALLY, PLEASE!                **
* * * * * * * * * * * * * * * * * * * * * * * * * * * * * * * * * * * * * * * * * * * * * *
FORM Z_RFC_ADD %_RFC.
* Parameter declaration
DATA IP_VALUE1 TYPE I
DATA IP_VALUE2 TYPE I
DATA EP_RESULT TYPE I
..
* Assign default values
  IP_VALUE1 = 0 .
  IP_VALUE2 = 0 .
* Call remote function
  CALL FUNCTION 'Z_RFC_ADD' %_RFC
    EXPORTING
      IP_VALUE1 = IP_VALUE1
      IP_VALUE2 = IP_VALUE2
    IMPORTING
      EP_RESULT = EP_RESULT

  .
ENDFORM.
```

Listing 3.7 RFC/Update Include for an RFC-Enabled Function Module

Why does SAP choose to make a detour via a subroutine, and not call the function module directly? Once more the reason is that it should be possible to address any RFC-enabled function module using the program SAPMSSY1. If a specific function module is called in the subroutine, then the call would no longer be universally applicable. We have also seen this generic quality in the function RfcCallReceiveEx in the RFC API. This is a continuation of the same.

Figure 3.8 shows the relationship between the RFC call and the function module.

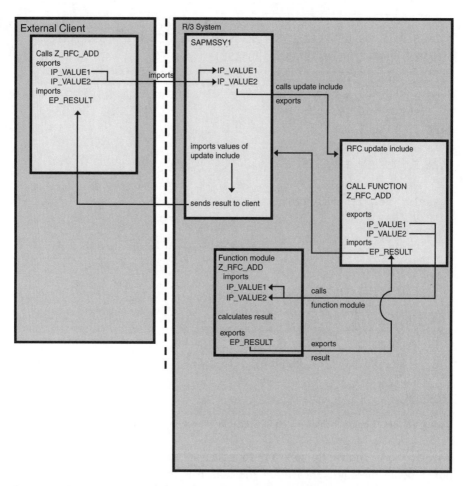

Figure 3.8 Communication Path from RFC Call to Function Module

3.7 Programming the External Server

After we have dealt with the programming of a simple external client, we now take up the reverse situation and look at programming a simple external server. In this case, the SAP system is the client. The external software component is the server. The R/3 System calls on the services offered by the third-party software.

We will again use the example of a pocket calculator to demonstrate developing an external server. This time, the R/3 System requests a third-party software component to execute the addition or subtraction of two values.

Figure 3.9 shows the relationship that exists between the software components.

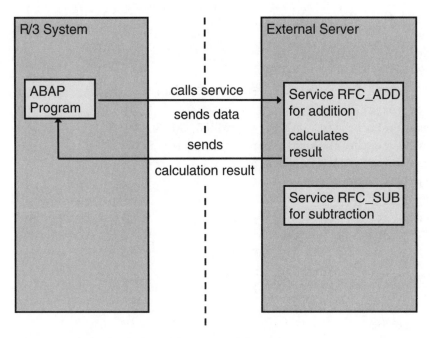

Figure 3.9 Relationship Between R/3 System and External Server

When developing a server for the R/3 System, you must perform the following steps:

▶ Conduct an independent logon of the server to the R/3 System (applies only to registered servers).

▶ Implement the services that the server offers the R/3 System.

▶ Determine which service the R/3 System has called and control the function that carries out this service.

3.7.1 Configuring the main() Function for an External Server

The main() function of the calculator does the following:

▶ It registers the server at the SAP gateway.

▶ It informs the R/3 System of the services offered by the server.

▶ It implements a message loop to determine which service the R/3 System has requested.

The main() function for the server could be programmed as follows:

```c
int main (int argc, char** argv)
{
    RFC_RC rc = RFC_OK;
    RFC_ERROR_INFO_EX ErrorInfo;
    RFC_HANDLE hConnection = RFC_HANDLE_NULL;
    char* argv1[3];
    memset(&ErrorInfo, NULL, sizeof(RFC_ERROR_INFO_EX));
/* Configure the arguments for using an INI-file */
    argv1[0] =  -DRFC_CALCULATOR";
    argv1[1] = "-t0";
    argv1[2] = NULL;
/* Accept connection */
    if((hConnection = RfcAccept(argv1))
                    ==  RFC_HANDLE_NULL){
        RfcLastErrorEx(&ErrorInfo);
        printf("%s\n", ErrorInfo.message);
        rc = RFC_FAILURE;
        return rc;
    };
    printf("%s\n", "Connection accepted!");
/* Register Callback Function */
    if((rc = RfcInstallFunction("RFC_ADD", RFC_ADD,
                                NULL)) != RFC_OK){
        RfcLastErrorEx(&ErrorInfo);
        printf("%s\n", ErrorInfo.message);
        return rc;
    }
    if((rc = RfcInstallFunction("RFC_SUB", RFC_SUB,
                                NULL)) != RFC_OK){
        RfcLastErrorEx(&ErrorInfo);
        printf("%s\n", ErrorInfo.message);
        return rc;
    }
/* Start message loop */
    do{
        if((rc = RfcDispatch(hConnection)) != RFC_OK){
            if(rc != RFC_CLOSED){
                RfcLastErrorEx(&ErrorInfo);
                printf("%s\n", ErrorInfo.message);
                break;
```

```
        }
    };
  }while(rc == RFC_OK);
  RfcClose(hConnection);
  return rc;
}
```

Listing 3.8 Configuring the main() Function for an External Server

The individual aspects of this listing are presented in greater detail in the next section.

3.7.2 Open a Connection with the R/3 System

For a server to receive data from an SAP client, the server must be known to the R/3 System. This means that the system must know where the server is located. There are two procedures by which the R/3 System can learn the location of the server. The procedures depend on the type of server. We differentiate between:

▶ Started servers, and

▶ Registered servers

Started servers are started by the SAP system itself. The server program is activated only at the moment when the SAP system calls a service from the program. Once the program has been executed, it is ended. In the case of a started server, all information on the location of the server is maintained with Transaction SM59.

The more common type of external servers are *registered servers*, however. They can be identified by the following characteristics:

▶ They are started autonomously, not by the SAP system

▶ They log on to the SAP gateway independently

▶ They run permanently in the background

The advantage of a registered server, in comparison to a started server, is that it uses fewer resources. If two SAP clients want to call a service on the same server with a started server, the program would be started twice. Consequently, system resources are required for two instances of the program. With a registered server, the program is started only once and the requests from the SAP clients are processed one after the other. In addition, the processing speed of a registered server is usually faster because there is no need for a restart when the R/3 System wants to execute a function on the server.

To log on to the SAP gateway, the registered server needs the following:

▶ ID with which the server identifies itself to the SAP system

▶ IP address of the server on which the SAP gateway is located

▶ ID of the SAP Gateway Service (and with it the Gateway Port)

▶ Information on whether the trace has to be activated

The information is administered in a field of data type "pointer to char." What information appears in the field depends on how the information is made available via the SAP gateway. There are two possible alternatives:

▶ Setting fixed values in the server

▶ Working with a configuration file (*SAPRFC.INI*) that prepares the values for logging on to the SAP Gateway

The size of the array, independent of the variant selected, is always the same as the number of connection arguments plus one, for a final zero. This zero enables the corresponding function of the RFC API to identify the end of the field.

If working with fixed values, the information listed above is provided in an array as constant. The values for the connection contain a prefix that allows the SAP system to identify what sort of information is specified by the value transferred. The following table shows which information is transferred with which prefix when working with fixed values.

Prefix	Meaning
-a	Server ID
-g	IP address of the Gateway Host
-x	ID of the Gateway Service
-t	Trace

Table 3.15 Connection Arguments for Working with Fixed Values

The following listing shows how the array for the connection arguments is configured when working with fixed values:

```
char *argv1[5];
:
/* Configuration of the connection arguments for fixed values */
argv1[0] = "-aRFC_CALCULATOR";
argv1[1] = "-g10.10.34.131";
```

```
argv1[2] = "-xsapgw01";
argv1[3] = "-t1";
argv1[4] = NULL;
```

Working with fixed values, however, is not a common method and is used rarely during development because this variant is not easy to modify. If, for example, the IP address of the server changes, the program must be changed and compiled anew. Consequently, a configuration file is used with registered servers.

In a configuration file, the information for logging on to the SAP gateway is provided separately. In this way, the data for registration at the gateway can be changed without the need to modify and recompile the program. In our example, therefore, we will also work with one of these *SAPRFC.INI* files.

The *SAPRFC.INI* file for registering the server at the gateway of a specific application server has the following structure:

Argument	Meaning
DEST	Flags the start of a block with information for logging on to the SAP gateway (The name of the destination allows the program to identify which connection argument it should use)
TYPE	Type of connection to be made
PROGID	ID with which the server identifies itself to SAP
GWHOST	IP address of the server on which the SAP gateway is located (This is usually the application server)
GWSERV	The gateway ID

Table 3.16 Possible Arguments in an SAPRFC.INI File

For our server, the INI file could be as follows:

```
DEST        =RFC_CALCULATOR
TYPE        =R
PROGID      =RFC_CALCULATOR
GWHOST      =10.10.34.131
GWSERV      =sapgw01
RFC_TRACE   =0
```

The name *saprfc.ini* is set by SAP. The INI file must either be in the same directory as the executable program or the location must be given by the environment variable.

SAP provides a sample INI file together with the RFC SDK. It contains a detailed description of the different combinations for configuring the file. In Windows, it is located in the directory

C:\Program files\SAP\FrontEnd\SAPgui\rfcsdk\text

The following table shows the connection arguments needed by the array introduced above for working with an INI file:

Prefix	Meaning
-D	Name of the destination in the *saprfc.ini* file where the arguments for registering at the SAP gateway are located
-t	Activate or deactivate trace

Table 3.17 Connection Arguments for Working with an INI File

You can see that in the connection arguments for the server the destination is also transferred. The server searches the INI file for the name of the destination. When it finds an entry, it reads all values that come after the destination. It tries to log on to the SAP gateway with this information. Information is read until the next destination or until the end of the file. Information for several external servers can therefore be maintained in an INI file because each information block can be identified uniquely by the name of the destination. The structure of the array for working with an INI file has already been shown above in the `main()` function (see Listing 3.8).

After the array has been configured with the connection arguments, the function `RfcAccept` is called to which the array is transferred with the connection arguments. The `RfcAccept` function has the following interface:

Variable	Meaning
`**argv`	References to fields of the data type `char`. The connection arguments are located in these fields.
`RFC_HANDLE`	Data type of the return value. In this case, it is a connection handle.

Table 3.18 Interface of the RfcAccept Function

When the function has successfully been executed, you receive the connection handle as a return value.

3.7.3 Implementing the Message Loop

Once we have a valid connection with an R/3 System, we must create the message loop. The task of the message loop is to evaluate all messages sent from the SAP system to the server and to call the appropriate callback function. There are two types of message loops:

▶ Block mode

▶ Poll mode

Block mode means that the server is suspended until a message is found for it. *Suspended* means that the program will not have any CPU time allocated to it. The advantage of this procedure is that the server does not cause a load on the CPU while it's waiting for incoming messages.

In *poll mode,* the server constantly checks whether a message has come in for it. If the server has received a relevant message, the appropriate callback function is called. If it hasn't received a message, it runs another check for messages. This procedure offers the advantage that it can be used to create two message loops so that the server can also execute other tasks while waiting for a message from the R/3 System.

For our example, we selected block mode. It's implemented with the `RfcDispatch` function.

The interface of the `RfcDispatch` function is shown in the following table:

Variable	Meaning
handle	Connection handle; the return value of the function `RfcAccept`
RFC_RC	Data type of the return value

Table 3.19 Interface of the Function RfcDispatch

In our example, the function is integrated into a loop. The loop is ended only if an error occurs when forwarding the message or when executing the callback function.

```
/* Start message loop */
do{
    if((rc = RfcDispatch(hConnection)) != RFC_OK){
        if(rc != RFC_CLOSED){
            RfcLastErrorEx(&ErrorInfo);
            printf("%s\n", ErrorInfo.message);
```

```
        break;
    }
  };
}while(rc == RFC_OK);
```

Listing 3.9 Implementation of the Message Loop in Block Mode

3.7.4   Implementing the Server Services

The services of the external server are implemented using callback functions. A callback function must have the type RFC_ONCALL.

The function type RFC_ONCALL is defined as

```
RFC_RC (DLL_CALL_BACK_FUNCTION_PTR
                RFC_ONCALL) (RFC_HANDLE handle);
```

It must be recognized that the function type gets the connection handle as a transfer variable and has a variable of data type RFC_RC as a return value. The return value communicates whether the function was successfully executed. DLL_ CALL_BACK_FUNCTION_PTR sets the call convention—how the data will be administered on the stack when the function is called. For Windows, the call convention DLL_CALL_BACK_FUNCTION_PTR has the value __stdcall. You can see what value the call convention assumes for other operating systems in the file *saprfc.h*. Let's take a closer look at how to implement one of these callback functions for the function RFC_ADD.

Implementation of the callback functions always includes the following steps:

▶ Configuring the interface for exchanging data with the R/3 System

▶ Reading and sending the data from and to the R/3 System

▶ Implementing the logic

In addition, the callback function must be registered in the RFC API.

Configuring the interface to the R/3 System includes the definition of all parameters and tables that can be exchanged with an R/3 client. Technically, the implementation is again done using arrays of variables of type RFC_PARAMETER for individual parameters and structures, or using arrays of variables of type RFC_TABLE for tables. The configuration of an array of type RFC_PARAMETER has already been presented above with our external client.

For the external server, we need two integral import parameters and one integral export parameter. The import parameters are assigned the names IP_VALUE1 and IP_VALUE2 and the export parameter is named EP_RESULT. The technical descriptions for these parameters are stored in two arrays of type RFC_PARAME-TER. The description is configured in the same way as our client. The only difference is that the structure RFC_PARAMETER in the name field must now be given the name of the variable in our C program because our C program is now the server. The following program extract shows how the interface description is structured. The BuildSimpleParam function described above (see Listing 3.5) is once again used to set the values.

```
RFC_RC DLL_CALL_BACK_FUNCTION RFC_ADD(RFC_HANDLE
                                    hConnection)
{
    int iValue1 = 0,
        iValue2 = 0,
        iResult = 0;
    /* create only once, therefore static */
    static RFC_PARAMETER ImpParam[3],
                        ExpParam[2];
    . . .


/* Structure of the interface for the import
   parameter */
    ImpParam[0] = BuildSimpleParam("IP_VALUE1", TYPINT,
                            sizeof(RFC_INT), &iValue1);
    ImpParam[1] = BuildSimpleParam("IP_VALUE2", TYPINT,
                            sizeof(RFC_INT), &iValue2);
    . . .
}
```

Listing 3.10 Program Extract for Describing the Interface

After the interface to the R/3 System has been created, we can now ensure the receipt and sending of data from and to the R/3 System. Receipt of data is prompted by the function RfcGetData. The interface of the RfcGetData function is shown in the following table:

Variable	Meaning
handle	Connection handle that will be transferred to the callback function
parameters	Reference to an array of type RFC_PARAMETER that can contain only import parameters

Table 3.20 Interface of the Function RfcGetData

Variable	Meaning
tables	Reference to an array of type RFC_TABLE
RFC_RC	Data type of the return value that indicates whether the function has been executed successfully

Table 3.20 Interface of the Function RfcGetData (cont.)

The function RfcGetData contains a description for only those parameter types that can be exchanged with the R/3 System. If a parameter type is not found, the corresponding pointer is given the value NULL.

The function RfcSendData is used to send the data. The interface of the RfcSendData function is defined in the following table:

Variable	Meaning
handle	Connection handle that will be transferred to the callback function
parameters	Reference to an array of type RFC_PARAMETER that can contain only export parameters
tables	Reference to an array of type RFC_TABLE
RFC_RC	Data type of the return value that indicates whether the function has been executed successfully

Table 3.21 Interface of the RfcSendData Function

The interface of the function is therefore similar to the interface RfcGetData. The only difference is that in the pointer variables, field pointers are now transferred that contain a description of the parameters to be sent to the R/3 System. For the function RfcSendData, it is necessary to transfer a description for only those interface parameters that are exchanged with the R/3 System.

When calling the functions RfcGetData and RfcSendData, you should note that the two functions are called only after the descriptions of the import and export parameters have been created. Furthermore, the function RfcSendData is called only when the return values for the R/3 System have been determined.

Once the interface of the service function has been configured, we can continue with implementing the logic. Implementation of the logic also includes error handling. The function must indicate in its return value whether any errors occurred during its execution. The return value of the callback function is forwarded by the RfcDispatch function to the message loop. In this way, the message loop can react to errors. The variable rc of data type RFC_RC is defined in the callback function for error handling. The variable is returned by the callback function. Appropriate values of the enumeration data type RFC_RC are assigned to it.

The callback function RFC_ADD to be added may, therefore, in its complete form, be programmed as follows:

```
RFC_RC DLL_CALL_BACK_FUNCTION RFC_ADD
                              (RFC_HANDLE hConnection)
{
   RFC_RC rc = RFC_FAILURE;
   RFC_ERROR_INFO_EX ErrorInfo;
   int iValue1 = 0,
       iValue2 = 0,
       iResult = 0;
/* Array for the interface parameters */
   static RFC_PARAMETER ImpParam[3],
                        ExpParam[2];
   static int iCreated = 0;
   memset(&ErrorInfo, NULL, sizeof(RFC_ERROR_INFO_EX));
/* Structure of the import parameters */
   if(iCreated == 0){
      ImpParam[0] =
         BuildSimpleParam("IP_VALUE1", TYPINT,
                          sizeof(RFC_INT), &iValue1);
      ImpParam[1] =
         BuildSimpleParam("IP_VALUE2", TYPINT,
                          sizeof(RFC_INT), &iValue2);
/* Final identification */
      ImpParam[2].name = NULL;
/* Export-Parameter */
      ExpParam[0] =
         BuildSimpleParam("EP_RESULT", TYPINT,
                          sizeof(RFC_INT), &iResult);

/* Final identification */
      ExpParam[1].name = NULL;
      iCreated = 1;
   }
/* Get data from R/3 System */
   if((rc = RfcGetData(hConnection, ImpParam, NULL))
         != RFC_OK){
```

```
        RfcLastErrorEx(&ErrorInfo);
        printf("%s\n", ErrorInfo.message);
        return rc;
    }
/* Execute addition */
    iResult = iValue1 + iValue2;
/* Send result of calculation back to R/3-System */
    if((rc = RfcSendData(hConnection, ExpParam, NULL))
            != RFC_OK){
        RfcLastErrorEx(&ErrorInfo);
        printf("%s\n", ErrorInfo.message);
        return rc;
    }
/* Send success message back to the message loop */
    return RFC_OK;
}
```

Listing 3.11 Implementation of the Service Function RFC_ADD

Finally, the callback function in the server must be registered in the RFC API. Registration is necessary to notify the server which services to provide to the R/3 System. Registration is done using the function RfcInstallFunction. The interface of the function RfcInstallFunction is defined in the following table:

Variable	Meaning
functionname	Name under which the function will be known to the RFC Library and therefore also to the R/3 System
f_ptr	Address of the function
docu	Documentation on the function
RFC_RC	Data type of the return variable

Table 3.22 Interface of the Function RfcInstallFunction

Registration for the function RFC_ADD is as follows:

```
rc = RfcInstallFunction ("RFC_ADD", RFC_ADD, NULL);
```

RfcInstallFunction is called in the main() function before starting the message loop.

The function RfcInstallFunction also enables you to create a description for the callback function. This can be read in the R/3 System in maintenance for the

RFC destinations (Transaction SM59) when the server is logged on to the SAP gateway. Detailed documentation should therefore be available here for third parties. This can, for example, be stored in a separate file, from which the server reads the description. An improved `main()` function would contain the following additional elements:

```
...
char *argv1[5],
      Desc[1000];
FILE *pfDesc = NULL;
const char DescAdd[] =
          "C:\\Bookproject\\Chapter3\\Programs\\"\
          "SimpleRFCcalculator\\DescRfcAdd.txt";
/* Read documentation */
pfDesc = fopen(DescAdd, "r");
fread(Desc, 1000, 1, pfDesc);
fclose(pfDesc);
/* Register server function with documentation */
if((rc = RfcInstallFunction("RFC_ADD", RFC_ADD, Desc))
      != RFC_OK){
   RfcLastErrorEx(&ErrorInfo);
   printf("%s\n", ErrorInfo.message);
   return rc;
}
...
```

Listing 3.12 Additional Elements in the main() Function for Reading Documentation

In the `main()` function the data is now read from the *pfDesc* file in the `Desc` array. The array with the description of the callback function is transferred to the function `RfcInstallFunction`.

After registering the callback functions in the last step, we can start to compile our server and start the program. At this point, it should be able to log on to the specified R/3 System.

The registration of a function in the RFC Library as just described may seem somewhat curious to some readers. Therefore, we'll provide a very simple form as to how the registration and administration can be implemented. The method described should serve only to ease understanding and is not necessarily the same as that chosen by SAP. You can skip the rest of this section on first reading because it is unnecessary for first approaches to programming.

To administer functions with another software view, the following elements may be needed:

▶ A definition of function type

▶ Structure made up of two fields

▶ The symbolic name of the function is managed in one field, and the address of the callback function in the other.

▶ Field from variables of this structure data type

▶ Counting variable in which the number of callback functions is managed

▶ Function that enters the data in the field

▶ Function that executes the callback function using its symbolic name

For our example, we define the function type as a function to which no variables are transferred and that returns a variable of the data type int. The type definition would therefore be:

```
typedef int callbackfunc (void);
```

The structure for our example is:

```
typedef struct _FuncAdmin
{
    char* FuncName;
    callbackfunc *fptr;
} FUNCADMIN;
```

The global variable to determine the number of entries in our field is called iFuncCounter.

The function for inserting the data records is implemented as:

```
void SimRegisterFunc(char* FuncName,
                     callbackfunc *fptr)
{
    FuncAdmin[iFuncCounter].FuncName = FuncName;
    FuncAdmin[iFuncCounter].fptr = fptr;
    iFuncCounter++;
}
```

We can see that the interface of the SimRegisterFunc function is very similar to the interface for the function RfcInstallFunction. The transfer variable in both cases is a symbolic name for the callback function and its address.

Our `SimRegisterFunc` function enters the symbolic name of the callback function and its address in the array. In this way, the name and address of the callback function form a fixed logical unit.

If you want to finally execute the callback function using its logical name, you need a function that runs through the array with the callback functions and executes the appropriate callback function. It could be programmed like the `ExecuteRegisterFunction` function:

```
void ExecuteRegisterFunction(char* FuncName)
{
    for(int iCounter = 0; iCounter < iFuncCounter;
        iCounter++){
        if(strcmp(FuncAdmin[iCounter].FuncName, FuncName)
            == 0){
          FuncAdmin[iCounter].fptr();
          break;
        }
    }
}
```

3.7.5 Setting Up the Connection to the R/3 System

The first step to addressing our server from the SAP system is to maintain the data for connection to the server from the R/3 side. When maintaining the connection data, the technical properties of an RFC connection are brought together under a logical name. This logical name is given in every ABAP program. The procedure offers the advantage that the abundant connection data does not always have to be entered manually when developing the ABAP client. Maintenance of the connection data is done using Transaction SM59.

In the initial screen for this maintenance, you will first see a hierarchical list with the possible connection types (see Figure 3.10).

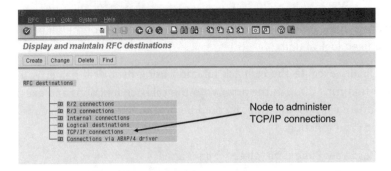

Figure 3.10 Initial Screen of Transaction SM59

We now want to create a connection to an external program, which corresponds to a TCP/IP connection. To create it, we position the cursor over **TCP/IP connections** and select the function **Create**.

The initial screen of the dialog for maintaining the connection data is displayed (see Figure 3.11). Here we enter a symbolic name for the RFC destination, the connection type, and a description. We enter "T" as the connection type. Connection type "T" stands for TCP/IP connections.

Figure 3.11 Initial Screen of the Maintenance Dialog

Once the data has been saved, a second maintenance screen appears in which it must be determined whether this is a registered or started server (see Figure 3.12). In addition, for a started server, the location of the server—the computer on which the server is located—is saved.

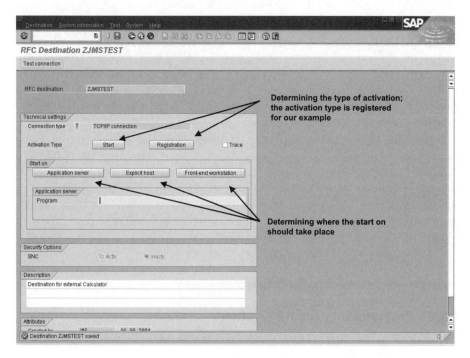

Figure 3.12 Maintenance Screen for Specifying the Server Type

We select the **Registration** function because we want to create a registered server. The last screen for maintaining the data for the registered connection is displayed (see Figure 3.13). In this screen template, we enter the name under which the server logs on to the SAP gateway in the **Program ID** field. It's important that the name entered here is identical to the name given in the *SAPRFC.INI* file on our server.

Once we have maintained this data, we can start our server and test the connection. We select **Test connection**. If everything is correct up to this point, we should have received a log showing the transfer time for the individual data packages. In this connection test, the default registered function `RfcPing` is usually executed.

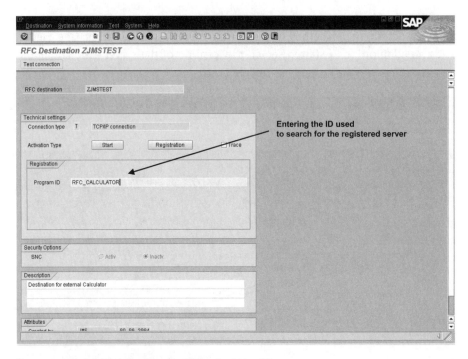

Figure 3.13 Maintaining the Program ID for Registered Servers

3.7.6 Programming the ABAP Client

For our test, an external server is accessed by ABAP through a report, which may be structured as follows:

```
REPORT  zcallrfccalculator message-id ZJMS.
CONSTANTS: gc_set(1) TYPE c VALUE 'X'.
DATA: lp_result TYPE i VALUE 0
    .
* Structure of the selection screen
PARAMETERS:  pa_value1 TYPE i DEFAULT 5
          , pa_value2 TYPE i DEFAULT 6
    .
START-OF-SELECTION.
* Call the function of the external server
CALL FUNCTION 'RFC_ADD' DESTINATION 'ZJMSTEST'
    EXPORTING ip_value1 = pa_value1
              ip_value2 = pa_value2
    IMPORTING ep_result = lp_result.

WRITE: / 'The result of the addition is: ', lp_result.
```

```
* Call the function of the external server
CALL FUNCTION 'RFC_SUB' DESTINATION 'ZJMSTEST'
     EXPORTING ip_value1 = pa_value1
               ip_value2 = pa_value2
     IMPORTING ep_result = lp_Result.
WRITE: / 'The result of the subtraction is: '
        lp_result.
```

Listing 3.13 Example Implementation of an ABAP Client for External Server

This program shows that a function of an external server is called in an ABAP program in exactly the same way as a normal function module in the R/3 system. In the CALL FUNCTION statement, the logical name of the connection is simply given with the addition DESTINATION. When calling the function, you should ensure that the names of the variables are identical to the names under which they are recorded in the function. The mirroring of the import and export parameters is also worth mentioning. The import parameters in our server become export parameters in the ABAP program and vice versa.

When the report is started, the user can enter two values in the selection screen and the result of the addition or subtraction will be displayed.

3.8 Frequent Errors on the Server Side

If we have done everything right up to now, two values will be added or subtracted by the server. If, however, your pocket calculator does not work correctly—contrary to expectations—the following troubleshooting notes may be helpful.

First, check what type of error has occurred. There are two types of errors:

▶ The ABAP program terminates with the error message *Server not registered*
▶ The program gets no result or an incorrect result

In the event of the first type of error, you should check whether the server was able to log on to your R/3 System and whether you can exchange data packages with the server. For this kind of checking, you should debug the server until the RfcAccept function is called. If the function returns a valid connection handle, you can at least log on to an SAP system with the connection arguments. If your program fails here, your array with the connection arguments was not created correctly.

If you get a valid connection handle, check whether you can exchange data with the server. To do so, start Transaction SM59 in the R/3 System and go to the maintenance screen for the connection that you have created. Once there, select the **Test connection** function. If the connection test was not run successfully, the connection data is incorrect. Frequent sources of error are:

▶ Different program ID in the SAP system and in the server's INI file

▶ Incorrect gateway

If you examine these possible sources of error carefully, you should be able to make a connection from your R/3 System to the server.

If your calculator does not calculate correctly—provided you have correctly implemented the logic for addition and/or subtraction—there is only one possible cause of error: The names of the import and export parameters are different in the server and in the R/3 System. Once again, carefully check the names with which you have entered the variables in the name field in structure RFC_PARAMETER, and also the names of the variables in the CALL FUNCTION statement in the ABAP program. Typing errors are often at fault. Unfortunately, in this case also, R/3 won't tell you that the variable with the name <name> does not exist; it simply ignores this error without sending an error message.

If you follow these notes on troubleshooting, you should be in a position to write a pocket calculator that can successfully exchange data with the R/3 System.

3.9 Functions Used

Here again is a summary of the new functions and structures used for our first server.

Function	Meaning
RfcAccept	Accept an incoming R/3 connection
RfcInstall-Function	Register a function under a name in the RFC Library
RfcDispatch	Function that waits for incoming messages from the R/3 system and returns only when it has received a message from an SAP system
RfcGetData	Read the data from the R/3 System
RfcSendData	Send the data to the R/3 System

Table 3.23 Functions and Structures of the Server

4 The Basics of RFC Programming

In the previous chapter, we developed simple external clients and servers that exchange data with the R/3 System. In this chapter, we'll take a closer look at the following aspects of the RFC Application Programming Interface (API):

▶ Type mapping

▶ Working with data aggregates

▶ Message loop

4.1 Type Mapping and Data Aggregates

One of Murphy's harshest computer laws is:

> *"Programming is like writing a novel. First you think of a few characters, then you have to see how you're going to get along with them."*

To help you avoid problems when working with data types in the future, the following sections should show you what aspects you need to bear in mind when transferring data types. Among other things, we'll look at:

▶ Problems when transferring strings

▶ Working with packed numbers

4.1.1 Generic Data Types

This section shows what a generic data type is and why it cannot be used in an RFC-enabled function module. As a starting point, we have a requirement to send the name of a customer from an R/3 System to an external program.

The experienced ABAP developer could simply declare an additional export parameter with data type c in the interface of the function module. But stop! When you then try to compile the function module with the definition of the parameter, the following odd error message appears: *Generic types are not permitted with RFC.*

What have you done wrong? It is, after all, okay to declare a variable with the data type c in a normal function module. To find an answer to this phenomenon, we'll have to look at a subroutine written in ABAP.

If an ABAP developer were asked to develop a subroutine to determine the length of a string, he or she would probably come up with something like this:

```
FORM write_string_length USING VALUE(ip_string) TYPE c.
  DATA: lp_size TYPE i.
```

```
        lp_size = strlen( ip_string ).
        WRITE: / 'The length of the string is: ', lp_size.
ENDFORM.
```

If two variables of type c are declared in an ABAP report, the previous subroutine can determine the length of the strings as is.

```
REPORT zprintstrlen.
DATA: Firstname(20) TYPE c VALUE 'Luke'
    , Surname(40)   TYPE c VALUE 'Skywalker'.
START-OF-SELECTION.
PERFORM write_string_length USING Firstname.
PERFORM write_string_length USING Surname.
```

It's amazing that the program works faultlessly. The standard size for type c, as defined in the interface of the subroutine, is one byte. It can therefore take up only one character. The variables Firstname and Surname are 20 or 40 characters in length, however. Nevertheless, the correct lengths of the Firstname and Surname are output.

This is because the variable of type c was not completely defined in the interface of the subroutine. The size of the variables is not specified. Interface parameters of this type are referred to as *generic parameters*. With a generic interface parameter, the SAP system completes the missing properties itself at runtime, when the properties of the data type of the variable, which is transferred to the subroutine at runtime, are adopted. The size of the interface parameter IP_STRING is therefore 20 bytes in one case and 40 bytes in another. In addition to type c, generic interface parameters also include numeric strings, packed numbers, and type x.

The principle used to complete missing type information is also used with interface parameters in function modules. A problem arises, however, if the function module is RFC-enabled. In an RFC call, only bytes are transferred between sender and recipient, but no information on data types. The sender or recipient of a byte sequence must therefore know how the sequence is to be interpreted. He or she can only know this if the number of the variables transferred and their size are known. If the recipient cannot supply this information, there is a danger that the byte sequence will be interpreted incorrectly and the data will be processed incorrectly. Consequently, all interface parameters of an RFC-enabled function module must be fully qualified, which means that the data type and size of the interface parameter are set uniquely.

There is no problem with an integer parameter. In ABAP, data type i has a fixed size of four bytes. With a true generic data type, however, the following possibilities exist to qualify it fully:

► A reference to a corresponding table or structure field that has the desired properties.
The interface parameter references the field of the table or structure with `LIKE`.

► A reference to a data element or a domain in the Data Dictionary.
In this case, the interface parameter references the data element or domain with the keyword `TYPE`.

4.1.2 The Character Data Types

The preceding section showed what you need to be aware of when declaring strings in the interface of a function module. Now, we'll look at the problems that can arise when transferring character strings.

The character data types include `RFC_CHAR`, `RFC_NUM`, `RFC_DATE`, and `RFC_TIME`. The last three data types listed are different from the `RFC_CHAR` type because the strings should only be numeric.

The transfer of a single character presents no problems. The client and server always send or receive the same character. The situation is different for character strings. The main problem that arises is that C/C++ and ABAP have different methods for identifying the end of a string.

In C/C++ a string is a sequence of characters ending in zero. A character string in C/C++ would therefore look like this internally:

The zero (\0) is used here to indicate the end of the character string. If it is not present, C/C++ does not distinguish the end.

The following rules apply to working with strings in C/C++:

► Strings must end with a zero.

► The size of the character field is the number of characters plus one, for the closing zero. If the first name should contain 30 characters, the corresponding character field will be 31 characters long.

► Character fields must always be initialized correctly to type with `NULL` because in general there is no automatic type-appropriate initialization in C/C++.

This is not the case for ABAP, however. The following rules apply in this case:

▶ The size of the string is determined only by the length of the value that is to be saved in it. A `Firstname` variable that should contain 10 characters is declared in ABAP as:

```
data: Firstname(10) type c.
```

▶ The initial value for a character string is always ' ' (space). This character corresponds to the value 20_{hex} in the ASCII table.

From these rules, we can draw the following conclusions:

▶ In ABAP and C/C++, strings that are to store values of the same length are assigned a different size because in C/C++ an extra byte is required for the closing zero.

▶ ABAP interprets the closing zero character as #. C/C++ however does not recognize the character ' ' (space) as an end-of-string marker.

This can lead to serious problems when strings have to be transferred between an SAP system and external C/C++ programs.

▶ When a string from a C/C++ client, initialized with a zero, is sent to an SAP system, the zero is interpreted as #, included in the ABAP string incorrectly, and later, written incorrectly to the database table.

▶ If, however, a string is sent from an SAP system to an external C/C++ server, the latter does not identify the end of the character sequence, because the ASCII character ' ' (space) does not correspond with the end-of-string flag in C/C++.

▶ The most serious problem, however, is the shift of bytes to the right (string is sent from a C/C++ program to the SAP system) or left (string is sent from the SAP system to an external C/C++ program), which results in an incorrect allocation of data.

To clarify the last point, let's assume that the first name and surname of a person are sent from an external C/C++ client to an R/3 System. The first name and surname are each five characters long. The C/C++ developer will create a structure in the program, defined as follows:

```
struct _PERSONALDATA{
   char Firstname[6],
        Surname[6];
}
```

The structure would be 12 bytes long. The corresponding ABAP definition would be as follows, however:

```
TYPES: BEGIN OF st_Personaldata
             , Firstname(5) TYPE c
             , Surname(5) TYPE c
       , END OF st_Personaldata.
```

The ABAP structure is therefore only 10 bytes. If an external client sends data of type Personaldata to the SAP system, it is dealt with as shown in Figure 4.1.

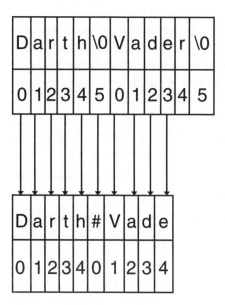

Figure 4.1 Byte Shift to the Right

We can clearly see the shift to the right. The sixth byte of the first name with the end of string flag \0 in the C/C++ client is moved to the first byte of the surname in the ABAP server and is interpreted there as #, whereas the fifth byte of the surname, with value r, does not even appear in the ABAP server. It has simply been cut out.

The problem of byte shifting is not limited to structures with character strings, but always arises when data has different sizes in the client and server.

So how can we solve the problems that arise when transferring strings and structures containing strings? The best way is to work with two string variables or structures in the C/C++ program. The first string variable satisfies the requirements of a string in a C/C++ program, while the second string variable complies with the requirements for a string in an ABAP program. This means:

▶ The string variable in the C/C++ format always has a field size that corresponds to the total length of the character string to be entered, plus one for the end of string marker.

▶ The string variable in the C/C++ format is always initialized with a zero.

▶ The string variable in the ABAP format always has a field size that is equal to the maximum length of the character string to be entered.

▶ The string variable in the ABAP format is always initialized with ' ' (space).

In an external client, the string variable in C/C++ format takes on all of the values to be transferred from the user. Before the data is transferred, the values are copied to the string in ABAP format. Conversely, for a C/C++ server, it applies that the string variable that satisfies the ABAP format requirements receives the character string first, and in a second step transfers the data to the string in C/C++ format.

This procedure ensures the following:

▶ There is no byte shifting, because the string to be sent to the SAP system has the same size in the C/C++ program as in the SAP function module.

▶ Incorrect values are not transferred for the zero end-of-string indicator. The string that is sent to the SAP system is already initialized with a space.

▶ The external client or server always detects the end of the character string.

4.1.3 Numeric Strings

Numeric strings are character strings that can contain only numbers. The data type n exists in ABAP for these strings. In an ABAP program, a check is run to determine whether a numeric value has been assigned to a variable of type n. If this is not the case, the program removes the non-numeric value and fills the variable with leading zeros. The following example should help to explain this:

```
REPORT ztestnumeric.
DATA: numeric(5) TYPE n.
START-OF-SELECTION.
numeric = '012A4'.
WRITE: / numeric.
```

The program generates the output 00124. The A was removed and the string was filled with leading zeros until the defined string length was reached.

Unfortunately there is no numeric data type in C/C++. Even the data type RFC_NUM in the RFC API is no more than an unsigned char, as you can see in the following extract from the header file:

```
typedef unsigned char  RFC_CHAR.
typedef RFC_CHAR       RFC_NUM
```

All ASCII characters can therefore be assigned to a variable of type RFC_NUM. This also includes the non-numeric characters. Two questions thus arise when transferring numeric strings:

▶ What happens when a non-numeric value is assigned to a variable of data type n in a function module?

▶ How can we ensure that an external client will also save only numeric values in a numeric field?

In answer to the first question, we will add the import parameter IP_NUMC, which is five characters long, to the interface of our function module Z_RFC_ADD. We will also add the parameter to the interface description in our external client. Furthermore, in the client program, we'll assign the value 012A4 to the parameter IP_NUMC. Finally, we'll activate the ABAP debugger by entering the value D in the TRACE field.

If we start our C program now, we can see in the ABAP debugger that the value 012A4 has been assigned to the variables IP_NUMC in the function module. The A is not deleted. Instead, the non-numeric value has been accepted in the SAP function module in a variable of data type n. This value has also been saved in a database table.

This result is not satisfactory. The following considerations should make the problem clearer. SAP frequently maintains a time stamp in its database tables; that is, the SAP system records the date and time of the last data modification. The date field has the type DATS. The DATS data type is a numeric field, eight bytes long. In a similar manner, the variable type is TIME. TIME is of type n and is six bytes long.

In the RFC API, the types RFC_DATE and RFC_TIME are available for transferring date and time values. They're defined as follows:

```
typedef RFC_CHAR       RFC_DATE[8]
typedef RFC_CHAR       RFC_TIME[6].
```

As mentioned above, the RFC_CHAR type is defined as:

```
typedef unsigned char RFC_CHAR .
```

Consequently, all ASCII characters can also be saved in variables of types RFC_ DATE and RFC_TIME. It is therefore possible to assign non-numeric values to time and date variables in the interface of a function module via an external client. These values are also saved incorrectly to a database table. This has far-reaching consequences. For example, it is no longer possible to determine what data record has been changed when. Therefore, it is necessary to ensure that only digits are saved in a variable of numeric type in an external client.

Unfortunately, the RFC API does not have an appropriate test function. You must develop your own. This is not difficult to do, as you can see in the following example:

```
int IsStringNumeric(char *Numc, char **pos)
{
   if(!Numc || !pos)
      return 1;
   *pos = Numc;
   while(*pos && **pos != '\0'){
      if(!isdigit(**pos))
         return 1;
      (*pos)++;
   }
   return 0;
}
```

Listing 4.1 Example of a Check for Non-Numeric Characters

The transfer values assigned to the function IsStringNumeric are the reference to the string to be checked and a reference to a pointer variable of type Char. In the latter named variable, if the string contains any non-numeric characters, the address of this character is returned; otherwise, the value is zero. The start address of the string to be checked is assigned to the variable pos. Subsequently, each character in the string is checked in a loop to determine whether it's a numeric character. The library function isdigit is used for this check.

4.1.4 The Case of Packed Numbers

Every ABAP programmer will already have worked with packed numbers at some stage in the form of variables of data type Quantity, Currency, or self-defined variables of data type p. These are very popular data types in ABAP. The value of a variable of a packed data type can be formatted—separators can be inserted for decimal places. For variables of data type float, this is not possible with no further preparation.

Thus, the value 1000.25 for a variable of type `float` is output as 1.0002500000000000E+03 and for a variable of type `p decimals 2` as 1,000.25.

When a variable of type `p decimals` has to be transferred a problem occurs, however: what is the appropriate counterpart to the `packed` type on the external program side? If you look at C/C++ types, you won't find a corresponding data type. We would therefore now like to explain what exactly packed numbers are and how they can be exchanged between an SAP system and an external program.

Packed numbers are actually just *Binary Coded Decimals* (BCD). A packed number is therefore presented in a field of data type `unsigned byte`, where each byte takes up to *two* decimal digits. This characteristic is made possible by the fact that in packed numbers each decimal digit is considered separately and transferred in binary representation (see Figure 4.2).

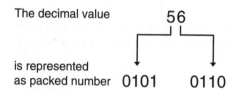

Figure 4.2 Change from Decimal to BCD Presentation

The groups of four binary numbers are also called *tetrads*. Each tetrad takes up four bits and the data type `Byte` has eight bits, so it is possible to have two tetrads in one byte (2 × 4 bits) and, thus, to manage two decimal numbers. Converting a binary coded number into a decimal number is then quite simple (see Figure 4.3).

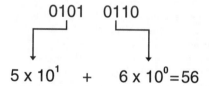

Figure 4.3 Conversion from BCD to Decimal Representation

Which converted tetrad is to be multiplied by which decimal power depends on the position of the tetrad in the byte array.

Just one small problem remains. The data type `unsigned byte` is defined in the file *saprfc.h* in the RFC API as:

```
typedef unsigned char rfc_byte_t.
```

It therefore does not manage binary numbers, only decimal numbers in the range 0 to 255 or characters in accordance with the ASCII character set. So the binary representation of packed numbers must—on the whole—still be converted into a decimal number. The procedure is presented in Figure 4.4.

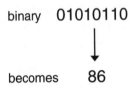

binary   01010110

becomes   86

Figure 4.4 Conversion of Decimal Value into a BCD Number

It should once again be stressed that the value 86 represents two binary coded numbers, namely 5 and 6.

Of course, as a developer you no longer have to create your own routines for converting packed numbers; rather, you can revert to the following functions of the RFC-API:

▶ RfcConvertCharToBcd
▶ RfcConvertBcdToChar

The function RfcConvertCharToBcd changes a number that has been transferred to it in the form of a string into a corresponding byte field. The interface of the function is:

Variable	Meaning
*in	Pointer to a string that contains the number to be converted. A decimal number should comply with the internal representation of a decimal number: algebraic sign first, decimal places separated with a dot.
in_len	Length of the string
*pdecs	Reference to the variable in which the number of decimal places is stored
*out	Reference to a field in which the BCD representation of the number is stored
out_len	Field byte size
int	Function return value

Table 4.1 Interface of the Function RfcConvertCharToBcd

The function returns a variable of data type int. From the value of the variables, the function informs the calling program of the execution status. The following values are returned:

Return Value	Meaning
0	Function was executed successfully
2	The size of the field for saving the BCD representation of the number is too small
3	The string to be converted does not contain a valid number
4	The string length is incorrect

Table 4.2 Return Values of the Function RfcConvertCharToBcd

The call for the function might look like this:

```
int main(int argc, char** argv)
{
    RFC_RC rc = RFC_OK;
    rfc_byte_t number[10];
    int iRC = 0,
        iDecimals = 2;
    iRC = RfcConvertCharToBcd(
                "1000.25", strlen("1000.25"),
                &iDecimals, number, sizeof(number));
    return (int)rc;
}
```

Listing 4.2 Calling the Function RfcConvertCharToBcd

The counterpart of function RfcConvertCharToBcd is RfcConvertBcdToChar. The function RfcConvertBcdToChar converts a byte field into the corresponding decimal representation of the number, whereby the decimal representation is returned in a string. The value in the string can then be assigned to a variable of type float using the function atof. The function RfcConvertBcdToChar has the following interface:

Variable	Meaning
*in	Field of type RFC_BCD with the BCD representation of the packed number
in_len	Field byte size
decs	Number of decimal places in the packed number
*out	Reference to a string in which the decimal representation of the packed number is returned

Table 4.3 Interface of the Function RfcConvertBcdToChar

Variable	Meaning
out_len	Size of string in bytes
int	Function return value

Table 4.3 Interface of the Function RfcConvertBcdToChar (cont.)

With the function `RfcConvertBcdToChar`, the return value also contains information on the status of the function execution. The function can return the following values:

Return Value	Meaning
0	Function was executed successfully
2	The string is not long enough to save the decimal representation of the packed number
3	The value in the BCD field does not represent a number
4	The size of the byte field is incorrect

Table 4.4 Return Values of the Function RfcConvertBcdToChar

The functions `RfcConvertCharToBcd` and `RfcConvertBcdToChar` are based on the functions `str2nbcd` and `nbcd2str` that are created from the RFC code.

If we take a look at the functions `RfcConvertCharToBcd` and `RfcConvertBcdToChar`, we can see that they convert a string to a packed number or they return the decimal form of a packed number in a string. The question arises whether it would not be better for the ABAP software component in question to convert a packed number into a string and transfer the string to the external software component. However, this would contradict the idea that the software components involved in a client-server relationship should largely be autonomous. In the spirit of autonomy, it is better if the software components exchange the data with its original data type—that is, the database data type. If one of the software components involved cannot process the data type, it must be responsible for converting it into a data type that it can process. It should not bank on a third-party software component doing the job.

4.1.5 Final Overview of Type Mapping

We'll conclude our discussion of type mapping with an overview of the mapping of RFC data types to ABAP data types and the mapping of RFC data types to frequently used database data types.

ABAP Data Type	Meaning	RFC Data Type
c	Character	RFC_CHAR
d	Date (presented in the format YYYYMMDD)	RFC_DATE
f	Floating point number (float)	RFC_FLOAT
i	Whole number (integer)	RFC_INT
n	Numeric string	RFC_NUM
p	BCD number	RFC_BCD
string	Character sequence (string)	Not allowed in function module interfaces
t	Time (presented in the format HHMMSS)	RFC_TIME
x	Byte (hexadecimal)	RFC_BYTE
xstring	Byte sequence (x string)	Not allowed in function module interfaces

Table 4.5 Mapping Between ABAP and RFC Data Types

Database Data Type	Meaning	RFC Data Type
ACCP	Posting period YYYYMM	RFC_CHAR
CHAR	Character string	RFC_CHAR
CLNT	Client	RFC_CHAR
CUKY	Currency key, referenced by CURR fields	RFC_CHAR
CURR	Currency field, stored as DEC	RFC_BCD
DATS	Date field (YYYYMMDD), stored as CHAR(8)	RFC_DATE
DEC	Calculation field or amount field with decimal point and +/- sign	RFC_BCD
FLTP	Floating point number with eight byte accuracy	RFC_FLOAT
INT1	1-byte integer	RFC_INT1
INT2	2-byte integer, only for length fields before LCHR or LRAW	RFC_INT2
INT4	4-byte integer	RFC_INT
LANG	Language key	RFC_CHAR
NUMC	Numeric string	RFC_NUM
QUAN	Quantity field, stored as DEC	RFC_BCD

Table 4.6 Mapping Between Database and RFC Data Types

Database Data Type	Meaning	RFC Data Type
RAW	Uninterpreted sequence of bytes	RFC_BYTE
TIMS	Time field (HHMMSS), stored as CHAR(6)	RFC_TIME
UNIT	Unit key for QUAN fields	RFC_CHAR

Table 4.6 Mapping Between Database and RFC Data Types (cont.)

4.2 Working with Structures

Up to now, our external client and server programs were interwoven very simply as they exchanged only simple data types with the R/3 System. Unfortunately, in the real world it is rare that only individual variables are exchanged. Usually one or more data records (structures) are sent. Next, we'll explain how data records can be exchanged.

The transfer of a structure is presented using an example program. The objective is to transfer a customer master data record from an R/3 System to an external program. The customer number, for which the master data is to be read from the R/3 System and transferred to the client, is entered in the client program.

For the SAP part of the example, we'll use the function module Z_RFC_GET_SINGLE_CUSTOMER, which was presented above. We therefore need to develop only the external program. For an external program to exchange a structure variable with a function module, the following extra steps must be carried out in the program:

▶ A structure definition must be created in the program. The definition of the structure must correspond to the structure definition in the R/3 System.

▶ The description of the structure configuration must be registered in the RFC API.

▶ The structure variable must be declared as a parameter in the description of the interface for the data exchange.

Based on our example, this means that we create the structure _RSCUSTOMERSAP. It has the same configuration as the database table ZKNA1JMS in the Data Dictionary. The structure is used to exchange customer master data with the R/3 System. Due to the problem with strings explained above, we'll also use a second structure definition. The structure _RSCUSTOMEREXT has the same fields as the structure _RSCUSTOMERSAP, but the CHAR fields are all one byte bigger to make room for the end-of-string indicator \0. The structure _RSCUSTOMEREXT is used to further process the data received. The structure _RSCUSTOMERSAP is defined as:

```
typedef struct _RSCUSTOMERSAP
{
    RRC_CHAR CLIENT[3];
    RFC_CHAR CUSTNO[10];
    RFC_CHAR NAME1[35];
    RFC_CHAR COUNTRY1[3];
    RFC_CHAR CITY01[35];
    RFC_CHAR ZIPCD[10];
    RFC_CHAR STREET[35];
    RFC_INTEXPSALES;
    RFC_CHAR CURR[5];
    RFC_CHAR TELF1[16];
    RFC_CHAR TELFX[31];
} RSCUSTOMERSAP;
```

Listing 4.3 Definition of the Structure _RSCUSTOMERSAP

Next, we have to create a description of the structure configuration and register it in RFC API. Creating a structure description involves entering a description of the technical properties for each field in the structure. The technical properties are taken from the structure in the Data Dictionary. The description is stored in an array of type RFC_TYPE_ELEMENT2. This type is defined in the RFC-API as:

Field	Meaning
name	Name of the field in the Data Dictionary structure in the R/3 System
type	Field type; here you must enter a value of counting type RFC_TYPE
length	Field byte size
decimals	Number of decimal places
offset	Distance of the field from the beginning of the structure in bytes

Table 4.7 Configuration of the Structure RFC_TYPE_ELEMENT2

The offset for a field can be calculated as follows:

Offset ~current field~ = Offset ~predecessor~
+ byte size for the data type of the preceding field

Provided the structure in the external program is based on a structure in the Data Dictionary, the following options exist to determine the byte size of the data type:

- ▶ The byte size of the underlying data type for each field in a structure or table can be found in the field `INTLEN` in the database table DD03L

- ▶ In the Data Dictionary, you can use the menu **Utilities · Runtime object display** to get an overview of the properties of the fields in a structure or table, among other things. You can see the byte size of the data type in the column ABAP length (see Figure 4.5).

Furthermore, the offset for a field can also be taken directly from the runtime object for a Data Dictionary element. It can be read from the column `Offset`.

Thus, the entry for the field `NAME1` of structure `_RSCUSTOMERSAP` is as follows:

```
RFC_TYPE_ELEMENT2 DESC_RS_CUSTOMER_SAP[11]
DESC_RS_CUSTOMER_SAP[2].name =      "NAME1"
DESC_RS_CUSTOMER_SAP[2].type =      TYPC
DESC_RS_CUSTOMER_SAP[2].length =    35;
DESC_RS_CUSTOMER_SAP[2].decimals = 0;
DESC_RS_CUSTOMER_SAP[2].offset   =
                   DESC_RS_CUSTOMER_SAP[1].offset
                 + DESC_RS_CUSTOMER_SAP[1].length;
```

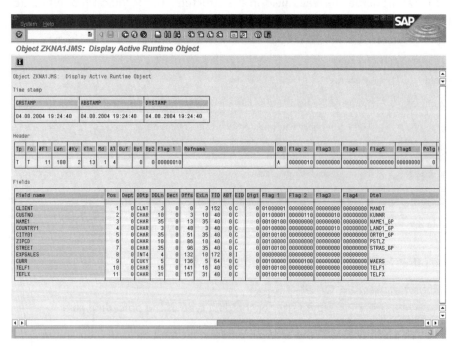

Figure 4.5 Runtime Object of Table ZKNA1JMS

The size of the array corresponds to the number of fields in the structure. Our array has to save 11 descriptions, because the table ZKNA1JMS has 11 fields. The following additional function can help to simplify the creation of the structure description:

```
RFC_TYPE_ELEMENT2 BuildTableElement(char* pName,
                                    int    iType,
                                    int    iLength,
                                    int    iDecimals
                                    int    iOffset)
{
    RFC_TYPE_ELEMENT2 Element;
    Element.name     = pName;
    Element.type     = iType;
    Element.length   = iLength;
    Element.decimals = iDecimals;
    Element.offset   = iOffset;
    return Element;
};
```

Listing 4.4 Additional Function to Fill the Structure RFC_TYPE_ELEMENT2

For the field NAME1 in table ZKNA1JMS, the function call would be as follows:

```
DESC_RS_CUSTOMER_SAP[2] = BuildTableElement("NAME1",
                    TYPC, 35, 0,
                    ( DESC_RS_CUSTOMER_SAP[1].offset
                   + DESC_RS_CUSTOMER_SAP[1].length) );
```

After you've configured the field description, you must register it in the RFC API. You can do this by using function RfcInstallStructure2. Values for the following variables must be transferred to the function:

Variable	Meaning
name	Name of the structure with which the description is linked
elements	Address of the array with the description of the field structure
entries	Number of elements in the field

Table 4.8 Interface of the Function RfcInstallStructure2

Variable	Meaning
pTypeHandle	Reference to a variable of type RFC_TYPEHANDLE The variable takes on the type handle with which the RFC API is linked to the field description.
RFC_RC	Return value of the function that indicates the status of the execution

Table 4.8 Interface of the Function RfcInstallStructure2 (cont.)

If the function RfcInstallStructure2 was executed successfully, the handle in the variables pTypeHandle will be the one with which the RFC API linked the structure description.

Finally, the structure variable RSCustomerSAP of type RSCUSTOMERSAP must be declared in the interface description. This is done by entering the structure variable in the array ExpParam. The array accepts all variables for which our program can receive data from the R/3 System. It's important that we now transfer the type handle, determined with function RfcInstallStructure2, to the field type in the structure RFC_PARAMETER.

If the client program calls up the function module Z_RFC_GET_SINGLE_CUSTOMER in the R/3 System now, the customer master data record will be in the structure variable RSCustomerSAP.

The following listing is an extract from the program GetCustomerSAP. Once again it shows the steps required to create a structure variable as exchange parameter.

```
RFC_RC GET_CUSTOMER_FROM_SAP(RFC_HANDLE hConnection,
                     RFC_ERROR_INFO_EX *pErrorInfo)
{
   / *Declaration of variables to accept the
     data from or send to SAP */
   :
   RSCUSTOMERSAP RSCustomerSAP;
   /* Declaration of the array for the import and
     export parameters */
   RFC_PARAMETER ImpParam[2]
               , ExpParam[2]
                 ;
   /* additional declarations for structure */
   RFC_TYPEHANDLE  Tabletype;
   RFC_TYPE_ELEMENT2 DESC_RS_CUSTOMER_SAP[11];
   :
   /*  Create Description of
```

```
        the Structure _RSCUSTOMERSAP */
    DESC_RS_CUSTOMER_SAP[0] = BuildTableElement
                                    ("CLIENT", TYPC, 3, 0, 0);
        :
    /* Register the structure in the RFC API */
    if(( rc = RfcInstallStructure2
            ("IS_CUSTOMER_DATA", DESC_RS_CUSTOMER_SAP,
            11, &Tabletype)) != RFC_OK){
        RfcLastErrorEx(pErrorInfo);
        return RFC_FAILURE;
    };
    /* Announce the structure variable as export
     parameter */
    ImpParam[0] = BuildSimpleParam("IS_CUSTOMER_DATA",
    /* Transfer table type of function
    RfcInstallStructure2 */
                            Tabletype,
                            sizeof(RSCUSTOMERSAP),
                            &RSCustomerSAP);
```

Listing 4.5 Creating a Structure as Import Parameter

You may point out (and rightly so) that creating the description of the field structure manually would be very time-consuming for large tables and structures. For this reason, we have a solution for automating this task in Chapter 6. Here, however, we would like to illustrate why this work is inevitable, especially in more complex system environments. To do so, we must again examine the mapping of the ABAP type system on the RFC system, as previously described.

▶ The ABAP type system is provided by the SAP Application Server and is therefore platform-independent on an abstract level.

▶ The platforms on which, for example, the clients are executed, have somewhat different forms regarding the internal presentation of data. This includes, of course, the size of the individual data types (for example, 32-bit platforms have a four-byte Long type) and the requirements for the alignment of data. A platform may require, for example, that integer values are always aligned to four byte or even eight-byte limits.

For the area of network programming, which is what RFC development really is, there is also the so-called *Endian* problem. The fundamental decision here, which is made on the hardware level of a platform, pertains to the arrangement of individual bytes within a multi-byte variable, for example, a four-byte integer. On many platforms, the form selected may at first seem strange, as it is the one in which the "least significant" byte appears first in the memory ("little endian"). This is the case in Intel processors in the x86 range, for example. Other CPUs, however, such as the SUN Sparc series, save the most significant and highest value byte in first place in the memory. This at first inconspicuous fact can, however, be significant when transferring mixed data types, such as structures. The following example first shows the big-endian representation of a structure from an integer variable (here with the value 4) and a character variable (value 'a'):

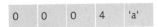

Each field corresponds to a byte. In a little-endian environment, the corresponding layout in the memory would be:

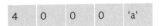

Converting this type of simple structure from a little-endian system to a big-endian system can only be done, obviously, if information on memory layout is also supplied. This is precisely the information that is supplied when logging a structure on to the RFC API.

4.3 Working with Internal Tables

Internal tables are used if several data records are to be exchanged between an external program and an SAP function module. This is frequently the case. Consequently, knowing how to work with internal tables is also important for RFC programming.

To demonstrate how to work with internal tables, we will develop a module that is in a position to send new customer master data to the function module Z_RFC_CREATE_NEW_CUSTOMER. The function module updates the data record to the database table ZKNA1JMS.

Let us first consider the design of the module. The module should manage customer master data records, including transfer of same to the R/3 System. It should therefore encapsulate the structure of the interface for exchanging data with the SAP function module internally. The module must also provide operations for manipulating the data records from the outside. These functions for manipulating the data records are the actual interfaces of this module. The module must also make the definition of the structure of the data records available. The definition informs the program parts—that call the module operations—how the data records to be transferred should look. Finally, we need an operation that transfers the data to the SAP system.

Here, we'll focus on the realization of functions in C to ensure consistency with what has been presented up to now. Use of C++ would stand to reason here. You can find a corresponding implementation in C++ on the Web site for this book at *www.sap-press.com*.

A design draft could look like this:

```
/* Public functions */
  RFC_RC Initialization(void);
  RFC_RC AppendCustomer(RSCUSTOMEREXT  *pCustomerExt,
                        RFC_ERROR_INFO_EX *pErrorInfo);
  RFC_RC InsertCustomer(char *CUSTNO,
                        RSCUSTOMEREXT *pCustomerExt,
                        RFC_ERROR_INFO_EX *pErrorInfo);
  RFC_RC UpdateCustomer(char *CUSTNO,
                        RSCUSTOMEREXT *pCustomerExt,
                        RFC_ERROR_INFO_EX *pErrorInfo);
  RFC_RC DeleteCustomer(char *CUSTNO,
                        RFC_ERROR_INFO_EX *pErrorInfo);

  RFC_RC GetCustomer(char *CUSTNO,
                     RSCUSTOMEREXT* pCustomerExt,
                     RFC_ERROR_INFO_EX *pErrorInfo);
  RFC_RC SendDataToSAP(RFC_HANDLE *phConnection,
                       RFC_ERROR_INFO_EX *pErrorInfo);
  int GetIndexOfCustno(char *CUSTNO);
  int  GetNumberOfRS(void)
      {return ItFill(m_TableParam[0].ithandle);};

/* Internal module functions */
  void InitialMembers(void);
  void CreateInterface(void);
  RSCUSTOMERSAP ConvertDataFromExtToSAPFormat(
                        RSCUSTOMEREXT *pCustomerExt);
  RSCUSTOMEREXT ConvertDataFromSAPToExtFormat(
                        RSCUSTOMERSAP *pCustomerSAP);
/* Internal module members */
/* for the table parameters */
  static RFC_TABLE m_TableParam[2];
```

```
/* Administration of customer number and table index */
typedef struct
{
    char Custno[11];
    int iTableIndex;
}RSINDEXCUSTNO;
/* Array for administration of the customer number and its
   index in the internal table */
RSINDEXCUSTNO RSIndexCustno[600];
```

Listing 4.6 Definitions of Components of the Module CreateCustomerSAP for Exchanging Customer Master Data

The listing above differentiates between public and in-module functions and variables. By "in-module," we want to convey that the functions cannot be used by a client that uses the module. If this approach was implemented under Windows as DLL, in-module functions would not be included in the definition file. The definition file would be:

```
; RfcCreateCustomer.def definition file for
; exported functions
LIBRARY      "RfcCreateCustomer"
DESCRIPTION  "Library functions for customer attachment"

EXPORTS
    Initialization
    AppendCustomer
    InsertCustomer
    UpdateCustomer
    DeleteCustomer
    GetCustomer
    SendDataToSAP
    GetIndexOfCustno
    GetAnzRS
```

Listing 4.7 Definition File under Windows for the Module CreateCustomerSAP

In the design above, the tables to be exchanged are encapsulated in the array m_TableParam. The Initialization function is used to initialize the module. It calls the functions InitialMembers and CreateInterface internally to initialize the module. The function CreateInterface configures the description of the interface to the SAP function module. It is more convenient for the client to access the customer master data using the customer number. Therefore the in-module variable `RSIndexCustno` is inserted. The variable refers to the structure `RSINDEXCUSTNO`. The assignment of customer numbers to the corresponding table index is managed in the structure. It is therefore possible that the customer number is transferred to the interface of the functions `Append-Customer`, `InsertCustomer`, `UpdateCustomer`, `DeleteCustomer` and `GetCustomer`, which implement access to the data records. The function `SendData-ToSAP` offers the possibility of sending data to the SAP system. Finally, the table index for a customer can be determined by the function `GetIndexOfCustno`.

4.3.1 Creating an Internal Table in an External Program

All functions of the RFC API for working with internal tables are defined in the file *sapitab.h*. This file should therefore also be included in an external program that works with internal tables.

To create an internal table in an external program, you must perform the following step:

▶ Reserve memory space for the internal table. The data records are saved in the memory area requested.

▶ Create and register the structure configuration of the table in the RFC API.

▶ Insert the table parameter in the interface description for the data exchange.

The allocation of memory is done with the function `ItCreate`. Values must be transferred to the function for the following variables:

Variable	Meaning
name	Name to identify the internal table in trace files
leng	Structure byte size, which is determined by using the `sizeof` operator
occu	Number of data records for which memory space will be required when a data record is inserted into the internal table for the first time Memory size = number of data records * structure byte size
memo	Only used internally by SAP, must be filled with 0
ITAB_H	The handle of the table is the return value of the function

Table 4.9 Interface of the Function ItCreate

If the function `ItCreate` was executed successfully, it returns the handle to the internal table. The handle forms a symbolic link to the memory space that has been reserved for the data records. Figure 4.6 illustrates its significance.

It becomes clear that the external program does not administer the memory area with the data records of the internal table directly. Only the RFC API has this access to the memory area. If the external program wants to access data records in this memory area, this can be done only by using the functions of the RFC API. The external program must transfer the table handle with which the RFC API identifies the memory area.

The counterpart of the function ItCreate is the function

```
int SAP_API ItDelete (ITAB_H itab)
```

The ItDelete function deletes all information relating to the internal table identified by the table handle (see Figure 4.6). The function releases the memory space occupied by the data records again. The entry for the administration information on the internal table is deleted after this. Once the function has been executed, the table handle can no longer be used.

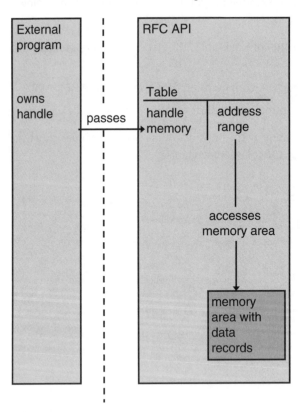

Figure 4.6 Significance of the Table Handle

If you want to release only the memory space taken up by the data records in the internal table, you should use the following RFC API function:

```
int SAP_API ItFree (ITAB_H itab)
```

It releases only the memory space occupied by the data records; however, the administration information of the internal table is not deleted. The internal table can still be used, for example, to add new rows.

Once the internal table has been created, the next step is to register the description of the structure configuration in the RFC API. Creating the description of the field structure for tables and registering it is the same as the procedure for structures described in the previous section. We will therefore not repeat it.

Finally, we still have to add the internal table to the interface description for data exchange. All tables that are to be exchanged with the SAP system are managed in an array of type RFC_TABLE. This type is a structure of the RFC API. It has the following configuration:

Field	Meaning
name	Name of the tables in the function module interface
nlen	Length of the table name
type	Handle to the description of the structure configuration with which the table is linked (the handle is determined by using the function RfcInstallStructure2)
leng	Structure byte size
ithandle	Table handle—return value of the function ItCreate
itmode	Type of data transfer between SAP system and external program
newitab	Flag to indicate that the table was created using the RFC API

Table 4.10 Configuration of the Structure RFC_TABLE

For our example, the structure RFC_TABLE is given the following values in the function CreateInterface:

```
m_TableParam[0].name     = "IT_CUSTOMER_DATA";
m_TableParam[0].nlen     = strlen("IT_CUSTOMER_DATA");
m_TableParam[0].type     = Tabletype;
m_TableParam[0].leng     = sizeof(_RSCUSTOMERSAP);
m_TableParam[0].itmode   = RFC_ITMODE_BYREFERENCE;
m_TableParam[0].ithandle =
```

```
ItCreate("IT_CUSTOMER_DATA", sizeof(_RSCUSTOMERSAP),
         100, 0);
```

Listing 4.8 Configuration of the Interface Description for the Table IT_CUSTOMER_DATA

The transfer method for the internal table is specified by the value in the `itmode` field. The following values can be given here:

Value	Meaning
RFC_ITMODE_BY-REFERENCE	Transfer is done as pass by reference (Changes to the table content are transferred to the client)
RFC_ITMODE_BY-VALUE	Transfer is done as pass by value (Changes to the table content are not transferred to the client. This type of transfer is used only internally in SAP.)
RFC_ITMODE_KEEPALIVE	This type of transfer is used only internally in SAP

Table 4.11 Possible Values for the Field itmode

4.3.2 Administration of Data Records in an Internal Table

This section describes how the data records in an internal table might be managed by the RFC API. Although the developer no longer has to worry about programming the administration, it is still necessary to know something about the inner workings of internal tables in order to work properly with them.

An internal table must be in a position to manage data records with different configurations and of different sizes. After all, not only customer master data can be sent to the SAP system, but also order data, which will certainly have a different structure than customer master data. Managing data with different configurations using a shared program interface is best done in a field of data type void*–a pointer of type void, which is characterized by the fact that it can save the address of a variable with any data type. Therefore, it's exactly the data type we are looking for.

A function to initialize an array of type void* could be programmed as presented below.

```
typedef void* PVOID;
PVOID *ArrayAnyType;
int iRSSize = 0;
void CreateArrayAnyType(int iNoOfArgu, int iSizeOfRS)
{
    ArrayAnyType = (void**)malloc(iNoOfArgu);
```

```
    iRSSize = iSizeOfRS;
    for(int iArgC = 0; iArgC < iNoOfArgu; iArgC++){
        ArrayAnyType[iArgC] = NULL;
    }
}
```

Listing 4.9 Function to Initialize an Array of Type void*

The transfer variable received by the function `CreateArrayAnyType` is the number of data records to be created and the byte size of the data record that is to be stored in it. It creates a field of pointers of type `void*`. The pointers of type `void` later include the address of the newly reserved memory space for the individual data records. The byte size of the data record is also saved in the global variable `iRSSize`. Finally, the content of the field is initialized with the value `NULL` in a loop.

If we replace the variable `iNoOfArgu` with the variable `occu` and the variable `iSizeOfRS` with the variable `leng` of the function `ItCreate`, then it becomes apparent that the function `CreateArrayAnyType` simulates the function `ItCreate` in the RFC API. Only the variable `name` is missing because no entries are written in a trace file. Assuming that data records of the type `RSCUSTOMERSAP` are to be saved, the call for the function `CreateArrayAnyType` would be as follows:

```
CreateArrayAnyType(10, sizeof(RSCUSTOMERSAP));
```

The functions `InsertRS` and `GetRS` represent the saving and reading of data records in the array.

```
void* InsertRS(int iIndex)
{
    return ArrayAnyType[iIndex] = calloc(1, iRSSize);
};
void* GetRS(int iIndex)
{
    return ArrayAnyType[iIndex];
};
```

The function `InsertRS` receives the index to identify the field in which the address of the newly required memory space should be administered. It reserves memory for the data record to be created using the function `calloc`. The address of the memory location is returned so that the caller of function `InsertRS` can manipulate the content of the location. Calling the function looks like this:

```
RSCUSTOMERSAP *pCustomer = NULL;
pCustomer = (RSCUSTOMER*)InsertRS(2);
```

The function InsertRS is also similar to the function ItInsLine in the RFC API, which will be discussed at a later stage.

Finally, the function GetRS represents access to a data record. Access is made using the index to identify the field in which the address of the data record is saved. The function GetRS returns the address of the memory location. This function also resembles the function ItGupLine in the RFC API.

To summarize this information:

▶ An internal table can be compared to an array of type void*

▶ The creation of an internal table can be compared to a request from the memory for the array of type void*

▶ The addresses of the memory locations where the data records are kept are administered in the array

▶ You can access the address of a data record via the index

▶ A new data record is inserted in the field in such a way that memory is reserved for the data record at runtime. The address of the memory location is saved in the variable of type void*. This is an element of the array of type void* and can be addressed using its index.

4.3.3 Reading and Writing Data Records in an Internal Table

In Section 4.3.2, we simulated the administration of an internal table to help us better understand the concept *internal table*. Now we'll examine more closely the RFC API features for managing data records in internal tables. Once again we'll return to our module CreateCustomerSAP, which has the task of administering customer master data.

The module provides operations for accessing customer master data. These are the functions AppendCustomer, InsertCustomer, UpdateCustomer, Delete-Customer, and GetCustomer. The functions AppendCustomer and InsertCustomer insert new customer master data in the internal table. The difference between the two functions is that AppendCustomer adds the new data record to the end of the internal table whereas InsertCustomer inserts the data record at a specific position. The UpdateCustomer function updates an existing data record and DeleteCustomer deletes a data record. GetCustomer simply restores the customer master data. These functions are implemented by the RFC API functions for managing data records in internal tables.

To implement the methods `AppendCustomer` and `InsertCustomer`, the RFC API functions `ItAppLine` and `ItInsLine` are required. The definition of the function `ItAppLine` is

```
void* SAP_API ItAppLine(ITAB_H itab);
```

The function `ItAppLine` adds a data record at the end of an internal table. As a transfer parameter, it needs only the table handle to identify the internal table to which the data record should be attached. If memory space can be reserved for the data record, the function returns the address of the memory location. If the allocation of memory space fails, the return value is `NULL`.

The function `ItInsLine` inserts a data record at a specific position. The interface of the function `ItInsLine` is displayed in the following table:

Variable	Meaning
itab	Table handle to identify the table in which the data record is to be inserted
line	Position at which the data record is to be inserted
void*	Return type of the function—address of the reserved memory space

Table 4.12 Interface of the Function ItInsLine

The `AppendCustomer` function of module `CreateCustomerSAP` is created as follows, using the function `ItAppLine`:

```
RFC_RC AppendCustomer(RSCUSTOMEREXT    *pCustomerExt,
                      RFC_ERROR_INFO_EX   *pErrorInfo)
{
/* Check if pointers are valid */
   if(!pCustomerExt || !pErrorInfo)
      return RFC_FAILURE;
   void *pRow = NULL;
/* add new empty row to the internal table */
   if(!(pRow = ItAppLine(m_TableParam[0].ithandle))){
      RfcLastErrorEx(pErrorInfo);
      return RFC_FAILURE;
   }
/* Transfer data in SAP format
   and copy data to the memory location
   identified by pRow */
   memcpy(pRow,
       &(ConvertDataFromExtToSAPFormat(pCustomerExt)),
```

```
        sizeof(_RSCUSTOMERSAP));
    return RFC_OK;
}
```

We will not show the implementation of the other functions. They're implemented in the same way and can be seen in the program `CreateCustomerRFC` on the Web site for this book.

Changing and deleting data records is done using the functions `ItGupLine` and `ItDelLine` of the RFC API. The interface of the function `ItGupLine` is:

Variable	Meaning
itab	Table handle to identify the table in which the data record is located
line	Index of the position where the data record is located
void*	Function return type; address of the memory location where the data record is located

Table 4.13 Interface of the Function ItGupLine

The function `ItGupLine` returns the address of the memory location of the data record. This means that the content of the memory location can be changed by the calling program.

The function to delete data records in an internal table is `ItDelLine`. The interface of the function `ItDelLine` is displayed in the following table:

Variable	Meaning
itab	Table handle to identify the table in which the data record to be deleted is located
line	Index of the position where the data record is located
int	Function return type, the value of which indicates whether the operation was executed successfully Values are interpreted as follows: Return value = 0: execution successful Return value > 0: data record does not exist Return value < 0: unknown error

Table 4.14 Interface of the Function ItDelLine

When a data record is deleted, all of the records that come after it move forward one place. If an internal table has three data records and the second record is deleted, then what was the third data record now becomes the second.

Read access to the data record is achieved using the function `ItGetLine`. The interface of the function `ItGetLine` is displayed in the following table:

Variable	Meaning
itab	Table handle to identify the table in which the data record to be read is located
line	Index of the position where the data record is located
void*	Function return type—it contains the memory address of the data record

Table 4.15 Interface of the Function ItGetLine

According to SAP documentation, the function `ItGetLine` should allow only a read access to the data record in the internal table. A modification of the memory content of the returned memory location should not have an effect on the internal table. This is not the case, however. The function `ItGetLine`, like the function `ItGupLine`, returns the memory address where the original data record is located in the internal table. A change to the content of the memory location thus also affects the content of the internal table. To work correctly, the function `ItGetLine` would have to copy the content of the memory location in a newly requested memory area and return the address of the new memory area.

The following function is used to copy the data record from an internal table in another memory area:

```
int SAP_API ItCpyLine  (ITAB_H itab, unsigned line, void *dest)
```

The data record to be copied is identified by the field `line`. The destination of the copy procedure is specified in the `dest` field. The table handle `itab` determines the internal table to be addressed.

The RFC API counterpart of the function `ItCpyLine` is as follows:

```
int SAP_API ItPutLine (ITAB_H itab, unsigned line, void* src)
```

The function copies the content of the memory area identified by `src` to the data record addressed by `line`. The table is once again identified by the table handle.

The number of data records in an internal table is determined with this function:

```
unsigned SAP_API ItFill (ITAB_H itab)
```

It receives the handle of the table as an argument. The function returns the number of data records in the table identified by the handle.

The following function is used to determine how much memory space is required for each data record in the internal table:

```
unsigned SAP_API ItLeng (ITAB_H itab)
```

The table handle is transferred to it to identify the internal table, and the function returns the memory requirement.

4.3.4 Overview of the Functions for Internal Tables

The following table shows the functions for working with internal tables. These functions are ordered alphabetically.

Function	Meaning
ItAppLine	Add a row to an internal table
ItCpyLine	Copy the content of a data record from an internal table to a memory area specified by dest
ItCreate	Create an internal table
ItDelete	Delete an internal table including the administration information
ItDelLine	Delete a data record from the internal table
ItFill	Number of data records in the internal table
ItFree	Delete all data records from an internal table. The administration information remains intact.
ItGetLine	Return of the memory address of a data record in the internal table
ItGupLine	Return of the memory address of a data record in the internal table
ItInsLine	Insert a data record in the internal table at the position specified by the index
ItLeng	Byte size of a data record to be saved
ItPutLine	Copies the content of the memory location src to the data record identified by the index

Table 4.16 Functions for Working with Internal Tables

4.4 The Message Loop

The *message loop* is a basic component of every external server. In this section, we'll take another look at the possibilities for programming it.

In our first server in Chapter 3, we mentioned that there were two possible methods for programming a message loop:

1. Block mode
2. Poll mode

Block mode was explained in the last chapter (see Section 3.7.3). Here, we'll present the programming of a message loop in poll mode. The RFC API offers two functions for programming a message loop in this mode:

▶ RfcListen

▶ RfcWaitForRequest

The difference between the two functions is that the function RfcListen checks only whether a message has been received from the SAP system, and then immediately returns with the result. There are three possible return values, with the following meanings:

Return Value	Meaning
RFC_OK	A message has arrived from an SAP system
RFC_RETRY	There are no messages
RFC_FAILURE	Error in communication between the SAP system and the RFC server

Table 4.17 Possible Return Values for the Function RfcListen

The disadvantage of the function RfcListen is that because it returns immediately, it must constantly verify whether a message has arrived from the SAP system. The executing process must therefore listen constantly and is not suspended, which increases system load. If you want proof of this, look at the CPU usage of a program that executes a message loop with the function RfcListen in Windows Task Manager.

It is better to use the RfcWaitForRequest function. The interface of the function RfcWaitForRequest is displayed in the following table:

Variable	Meaning
handle	Connection handle
wtime	Time interval during which it should wait for incoming messages from the SAP system

Table 4.18 Interface of the Function RfcWaitForRequest

The length of time that it should wait for messages from the R/3 System is also assigned to the function. The thread is suspended for the duration of this time interval. It is therefore not allocated any CPU time, so the load on the system is kept low. The time interval is given in seconds. The return values for the function RfcWaitForRequest are the same as those for the function RfcListen.

Let's look at the programming for a message loop in poll mode:

```
do{
    rc = RfcWaitForRequest(hConnection, 1);
    switch(rc){
        case RFC_RETRY:{
            rc = RFC_OK;
            break;
            }
        case RFC_OK:{
            if((rc = RfcDispatch(hConnection)) != RFC_OK){
                RfcLastErrorEx(&ErrorInfo);
                printf("%s\n", ErrorInfo.message);
                }
            break;
            }
    case RFC_FAILURE:{
        RfcLastErrorEx(&ErrorInfo);
        printf("%s\n", ErrorInfo.message);
        break;
        }
}while(rc == RFC_OK);
```

Listing 4.10 Message Loop in Poll Mode

A message loop in poll mode is essentially made up of a DO-WHILE loop. The DO-WHILE loop is run through as long as the loop control variable rc has the value RFC_OK. Within the loop, the function RfcWaitForRequest is called. Rfc-WaitForRequest checks whether a message has been sent by the SAP system and returns with the result of the check.

The result of the query is evaluated in a case statement. If there is a message, the RfcDispatch function is called which, for its part, addresses the callback function. We must emphasize that RfcWaitForRequest checks only whether there is a message. It does not activate the callback function. The same is true for RfcListen.

One frequent argument against suspending a process is that requests from the SAP system are no longer executed immediately. However, it's hard to support this argument when you see how brief the maximum time lapse is before a request from an SAP system is executed. In our example, this time lapse is one second. In real time, this is completely irrelevant for most uses.

If suspending the processes for an interval of one second is not acceptable, you can reduce this time using the function RfcListen in conjunction with an operating-system function for suspending the process. With Linux, for example, there are the functions sleep, for suspending in the seconds range, and nanosleep, for suspending at nanosecond level. In Windows programming, the function SLEEP is frequently used in this case. The SLEEP function suspends a thread for n milliseconds. The modification of the message loop is as follows:

```
do{
    rc = RfcListen(hConnection);
    switch(rc){
        case RFC_RETRY:{
/* Suspend process for 300 milliseconds */
            Sleep(300);
            rc = RFC_OK;
            break;
        }
    :
}
```

Listing 4.11 Suspending the Process in a Message Loop if There Are No Messages from the SAP System

Finally, if we consider the programming effort produced by a message loop in poll mode, it is apparent that it isn't significantly higher than it would be with a message loop in block mode. Now we can see that message loops in poll and block mode are on a par with each other.

4.5 Alternatives for Logging on to an R/3 System

We will now once again demonstrate different possibilities for logging on to the R/3 System. We'll look at:

▶ Working with a configuration file
▶ Load balancing
▶ Function RfcOpen

4.5.1 Working With a Configuration File

With an external client, you can also work with the configuration file *saprfc.ini*. If you want to use a configuration file, you must include the following argument in the string with the connection arguments for the function RfcOpenEx:

```
dest=<Reference to entry in the file saprfc.ini>
```

With this value, the function RfcOpenEx reads the data for the connection from the file, and all other system-specific logon data in the string with the connection data is ignored. The following example shows how the file *saprfc.ini*, for logging on to a particular application server, should be structured. Instead of the IP address of an application server, incidentally, a complete SAP router string can also be used.

```
DEST=RFCSERVER
TYPE=A
ASHOST=10.10.34.131
SYSNR=01
RFC_TRACE=0
ABAP_DEBUG=0
USE_SAPGUI=0
```

There are several options for configuring the file *saprfc.ini*. To read up on all options, a sample file is provided with the RFC software development kit (SDK). In Windows, this file is located in the directory *C:\Program files\SAP\FrontEnd\ SAPgui\rfcsdk\text*.

The connection arguments for using the file *saprfc.ini* are transferred to the function RfcOpenEx as follows:

```
char ConParam[] = "DEST=RFCSERVER CLIENT=099 "\
                  "USER=<User> PASSWD=<Password> "\
                  "LANG=DE ABAP_DEBUG=0
memset(&ErrorInfoEx, NULL,
      sizeof(RFC_ERROR_INFO_EX_EX));
if((hConnection = RfcOpenEx(ConParam, &ErrorInfoEx))
               == RFC_HANDLE_NULL){

  printf("%s\n", ErrorInfo.message);
  rc = RFC_FAILURE;
}
return rc;
```

4.5.2 Working with Load Balancing

There are two alternatives for using load balancing:

► Using a configuration file
► Directly specifying the IP address of the server on which the message server is located

The configuration file is called *SAPMSG.INI*. The name of the server on which the message server of the SAP system is located is stored in this file. In Windows, the file is located in the directory *C:\WINNT*. The following table shows how the connection arguments should be specified when using load balancing, if working with the file *SAPMSG.INI*:

Argument	Meaning
r3name	The name of the R/3 System In addition to the name, the address of the computer on which the message server is located must also be given in the file *SAPMSG.INI*.
group	Optional specification of the logon group

Table 4.19 Structure of the Connection Arguments for Load Balancing Using SAPMSG.INI

If the connection is made via an SAP router, the value for the argument r3name must be structured as follows:

```
r3name=<Name of the SAP Router><R/3 system name = Reference to an
entry in the file SAPMSG.INI>
```

The specification for the R/3 name refers to an entry in the file *SAPMSG.INI*, which is located on the SAP router.

SAP also allows you to work with a configuration file to specify the SAP router. The name of the file is *SAPROUTE.INI*. In Windows, this file is also located in the directory *C:\WINNT*. If working with two configuration files, the value for the argument r3name should be structured as follows:

```
r3name=<Reference to SAP router in the file SAPROUTE.INI>
<R/3 system name = Reference to entry in the file SAPMSG.INI>
```

If working without a configuration file, you must specify the following connection arguments:

Argument	Meaning
r3name	Name of the R/3 System
mshost	Address of the server on which the message server is located
group	Optional specification of the logon group

Table 4.20 Structure of the Connection Arguments for Load Balancing Without the Use of SAPMSG.INI

If the connection is created via an SAP router, the name of the SAP router must also be prefixed in the argument mshost.

4.5.3 Working with the RfcOpen Function

In Chapter 3, the function RfcOpenEx was used to log on to the R/3 System. We will now present its precursor RfcOpen. Although the function is no longer used in new projects, it is still supplied by SAP.

The advantage of the function RfcOpen is that the connection data is stored in structures; therefore, via the names of the structure fields, the type of information in question is immediately obvious. Furthermore, work is done in dialog boxes with input fields. In this case, a structure offers the advantage of linking the input field directly with the structure field, something that would not be possible with a string alone.

The function RfcOpen uses two structures to specify the connection data. The user-dependent connection data is stored in the first structure and the system-independent data is stored in the second structure.

The structure for the user-dependent connection data is RFC_OPTIONS. It has the following fields:

Fields	Meaning
destination	Reference to entry in the file *saprfc.ini*
mode	Method of connection
connopt	Reference to structure with the system data for the connection
client	Client
user	User
password	User's password

Table 4.21 Configuration of the Structure RFC_OPTIONS

Fields	Meaning
language	Logon language
trace	Activate trace

Table 4.21 Configuration of the Structure RFC_OPTIONS (cont.)

The user-specific logon data is stored in the fields `client`, `user`, `password`, and `language`. The `trace` field is used to activate logging in a trace file of the functions called and data sent.

The `mode` field is used to control which structure variable in the `connopt` field is referenced. The structure variable contains the system data. Typically, two modes are used:

Mode	Additional Structure
RFC_MODE_R3ONLY	RFC_CONNOPT_R3ONLY
RFC_MODE_VERSION_3	RFC_CONNOPT_VERSION_3

Table 4.22 Frequently Used Modes for the Structure RFC_OPTIONS

In this section, we'll examine the option RFC_MODE_VERSION_3, because it supports load balancing. With the option RFC_MODE_VERSION_3, the system data is transferred to a structure variable of type RFC_CONNOPT_VERSION_3. The structure of RFC_CONNOPT_VERSION_3 is as follows:

Field	Meaning
hostname	IP address of the application server, if it is necessary to log on to a specific application server
sysnr	System number
use_load_balancing	Indicator to determine whether load balancing should be used for logon (if the value is not zero, load balancing is used)
lb_host	IP address of the application server on which the message server runs
lb_system_name	System number
lb_group	Logon group to which you would like to log on
use_sapgui	Indicator to determine whether the SAP GUI should be active

Table 4.23 Fields of the Structure RFC_CONNOPT_VERSION_3

The field `use_load_balancing` in the structure `RFC_CONNOPT_VERSION_3` determines that the IP address of the application server—on which the message server is running—must be specified in field `lb_host`. If the distributed R/3 System actually consists of several application servers, and they are not arranged in a logon group, the default logon group `NULL` must be entered in the field `lb_group`. Furthermore, data in the fields `hostname` and `sysnr` are not taken into account once the `use_load_balancing` option has been set.

5   Troubleshooting

According to Murphy's computer laws, programming is the process by which errors are incorporated into a program and debugging is the process by which they are removed. In the previous chapters, we saw how errors can occur. Now, we'll look at ways to eliminate them. In this chapter—in addition to the ABAP Debugger—we'll show you several SAP test programs so that you don't have to develop a program for tests.

5.1   The ABAP Debugger

For developers of an external client, it is advantageous to know how to work with the ABAP Debugger because it can help you learn why data is not processed in the way you had envisioned.

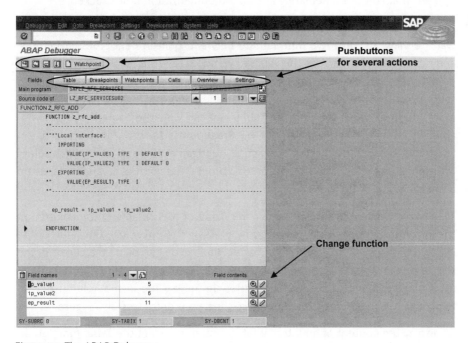

Figure 5.1 The ABAP Debugger

Before you can work with the ABAP Debugger, the SAP GUI must be installed on the computer.

We will now explain the most important functions of the ABAP Debugger. In Figure 5.1 you will see that it has a debugger application toolbar and another bar with pushbuttons. The functions on these two toolbars are used most frequently. The functions in the application toolbar control program execution during the debugging process. We can differentiate between the following types of program execution:

- **Single-step** execution (function key **F5**) executes exactly one program statement. It branches to called modularization units (subroutines or function modules), so that these units can also be executed step by step.

- **Step-over** execution also executes the current command (function key **F6**). If the current command is a call for a modularization unit, however, it does not branch to this unit but steps over it.

- **Continue** (function key **F8**) ends single-step execution. The program is executed up to the next breakpoint or until the end of the program.

- With **Return** (function key **F7**), the current modularization unit is executed completely. Program execution stops in the calling program at the first statement that comes immediately after the modularization unit checked.

In the pushbutton bar, you can, among other things, select which variable you want to view. In ABAP we differentiate between built-in data types, structures, and table types. You can see the value of variables referring to a built-in data type or a structure type when you select the **Function** fields. This is also the standard setting of the ABAP Debugger. To display the content of variables with a table type, you must select the function **Table**. You can view the content of eight variables or a table at the same time. The **Breakpoints** function allows you to set additional breakpoints during the actual debugging process. The **Watchpoints** function allows you to halt execution of a program as soon as a variable takes on a specific value.

To view the value of a variable, enter the name of the variable in the column on the left. After you confirm your entry by pressing the **Enter** key, the value of the variable is displayed. In addition to manual input, you can place the cursor in the source text on the variable and then double click on it. The value of a variable in the Debugger can also be changed. Enter the new value in the column on the right, and use the **Change** function to confirm your entry (see also Figure 5.1).

To display the content of an internal table, you must select the **Table** function. In this window (see Figure 5.2), you must first enter the name of the internal table and confirm your entry.

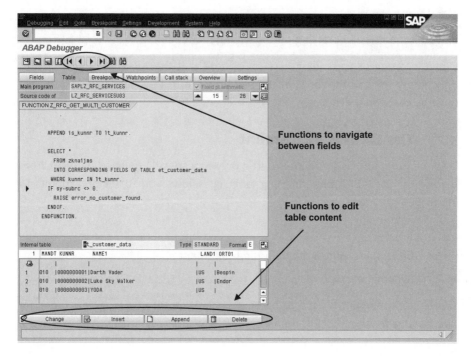

Figure 5.2 ABAP Debugger—Table View

Often, the monitor is not wide enough to display all the fields of the internal table. If this is the case, the Debugger offers scroll options. You can go to:

▶ The first field in the internal table

▶ The next field to the left

▶ The next field to the right

▶ The last field in the internal table

In addition to displaying the table contents, the ABAP Debugger has the following options for working with internal tables:

▶ Change the content of table rows

▶ Insert new rows

▶ Append new rows

▶ Delete rows

To change the content of a field in an internal table, proceed as follows:

▶ Position the cursor on the table field

▶ Double-click on the field

- ▶ Enter the new value
- ▶ Confirm entries by pressing on the **Change** function

When inserting or appending new rows, note that the ABAP Debugger creates only empty rows. If the fields of the new row are to be given values, each field must be changed individually.

5.2   The BREAK Statement

Often, a program has to be interrupted only at a specific point to debug it from that point. The ABAP programming language allows you to set breakpoints to interrupt a program.

There are two possibilities:

- ▶ Set a breakpoint using a programming statement
- ▶ Set a dynamic breakpoint

The BREAK statement is used to hardcode a breakpoint in a program. There are two variants for the BREAK statement:

- ▶ BREAK-POINT
- ▶ BREAK ⟨USER⟩

On arriving at the BREAK statement, an ABAP program is halted and the ABAP Debugger is activated. The difference between the two statements is that the BREAK ⟨USER⟩ statement is user-dependent—unlike the BREAK-POINT statement. With the BREAK ⟨USER⟩ variant, the program is interrupted only if the user specified in the USER option has executed the program.

The BREAK ⟨USER⟩ statement is the most frequently used form of the BREAK statement because it can be used to stop a program without interrupting other users with the breakpoint. This is particularly advantageous when working with production systems.

Dynamic breakpoints can be used at different points in time and therefore have different validity periods.

The ABAP Editor enables you to set a dynamic breakpoint. The breakpoint is set using the menu options **Utilities · Breakpoints · Set**. When you start the program, execution will be interrupted at the breakpoint. The breakpoint is only valid as long as the user is logged on to the R/3 System, however. If the user logs off of the system and later logs on again to the same system, all dynamic breakpoints are deleted. This form of the breakpoint is particularly recommended for debugging SAP and ABAP programs to check, for example, what value specific variables have.

The second possibility for setting a dynamic breakpoint is to do so within the actual debugging session. Position the cursor on the program line in which program execution should next be interrupted. Then set a breakpoint by double-clicking on the program line. The activity of the breakpoint is limited to the current debugging process, however. When you start the program again, the breakpoint is deleted. This variant is particularly recommended if the debugging session should skip certain program parts.

5.3 The Gateway Monitor

The SAP Gateway Monitor is a tool for displaying all external programs that are registered with the SAP Gateway. The RFC Trace can also be activated here. The RFC Trace will be discussed in the next section.

The Gateway Monitor is started using Transaction SMGW. The list of the current external clients is displayed by default in the initial screen (see Figure 5.3).

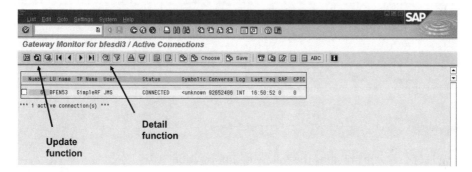

Figure 5.3 Gateway Monitor—List of External Clients

The list provides the following information:

▶ Name of the computer on which the external client is located

▶ Name of the program

▶ Name of the user who has logged on

▶ The connection status

▶ Symbolic destination
The key for reading the connection data from table TXCOM for CPI-C connections

▶ Time of last request
The time when the client last activated an SAP function module

▶ Conversation ID

▶ Protocol used

▶ Execution status
  NULL indicates successful execution.

To view additional details, position the cursor on the desired connection and then execute the details function. In the detail view, among other things, you will receive information about the SAP function modules activated and the data exchanged.

To display the servers registered on the SAP Gateway, you must execute the **Logged on clients** function in the **Goto** menu.

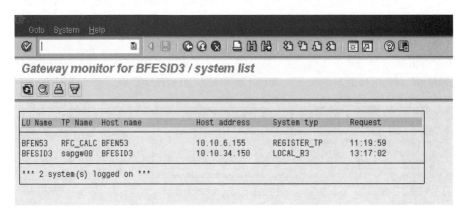

Figure 5.4 Gateway Monitor—List of External Servers

The list of servers provides the following information:

▶ Name of the computer on which the external server is located

▶ Name under which the external system logged on to the SAP Gateway

▶ Name of the computer

▶ IP address of the computer

▶ Type of registration

▶ Time at which the R/3 System last executed a server function

5.4   The RFC Trace

The *Remote Function Call Trace* is a recording of all RFC-based interactions between an R/3 System and an external system. The information is saved in a file. The RFC Trace provides information about:

▶ The way in which the external program is logged on to or registered with the SAP Gateway

▶ Functions executed

▶ Values sent

The RFC Trace can be activated in the R/3 System and also in the external program.

In an external server there are three alternatives for activating the RFC Trace:

▶ When working with an INI file, a value not equal to zero must be set for the argument `RFC_TRACE`.

▶ When transferring the connection arguments using the command line, you can set any value for the option `t`. The value `0` (i.e., `-t0`) also activates the RFC Trace. If you want to deactivate the RFC Trace, you must transfer the `' '` (space) value. It looks like this:

```
argv1[2] = "-xsapgw01";
argv1[3] = " ";
argv1[4] = NULL;
```

▶ The `Trace` indicator can be set when maintaining the RFC destinations—Transaction SM59. If the indicator is set, an RFC Trace is created for the external server. The Trace is also created if the server is already logged on to the gateway. Furthermore, in the SAP system, this indicator overrides the external server options for creating the RFC Trace—this means that the RFC Trace is created even if the server has not allowed for this option.

For an external client, how the RFC Trace is activated depends on the function used for creating the connection:

▶ If using the `RfcOpenEx` function, the option `ABAP_DEBUG` is transferred in the connection string with the value one.

▶ If the older function `RfcOpen` is used, in the `trace` field of the structure `RFC_OPTIONS`, a value not equal to zero must be specified.

The Trace file created is saved in the program directory of the external server or client. The name of the file depends on the operating system.

On Windows NT-based operating systems, the name of the Trace file starts with "RFC." This is followed by the process ID of the client program.

Activation of the RFC Trace from the SAP system occurs in the SAP Gateway Monitor. Activation and deactivation occur via the menu **Goto · Trace · External pro-**

grams · **Activate** or **Deactivate**. The functions for the RFC Trace are accessed via the menu **Goto · Trace · Gateway**. The functions are shown in Figure 5.5.

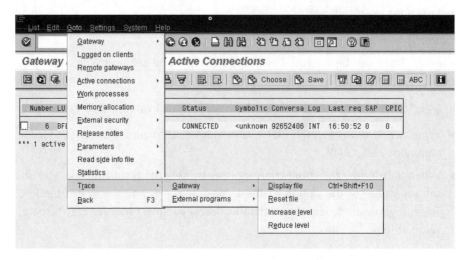

Figure 5.5 RFC Trace—Functions in the Gateway Monitor

The extent of the recording is controlled using the functions **Increase level** and **Reduce level**. The levels available are 0 to 3. The higher the level, the more information is logged. You should note that the values sent between programs are logged only with trace level 3. The Trace file is initialized using the **Reset file** function. A reset can be useful for targeted troubleshooting. The **Display file** function displays the Trace file.

In addition to activating the RFC Trace using the Gateway Monitor, you can also activate an RFC Trace using Transaction ST05. This variant is useful for testing first conclusions and is explained in Section 5.4.3.

5.4.1 Structure of the Trace File for an External Client

We'll present the configuration of the Trace file for an external client and server. As an example, we'll use our client from Chapter 3. The client should calculate the sum of the values 77 and 88 by activating the function module Z_RFC_ADD in the R/3 System.

The communication process for an external client with the R/3 System undergoes three phases:

▶ The client logs on to the SAP Gateway (one-off operation)

▶ The data is sent to the SAP function module

▶ The data is read from the SAP function module

Steps two and three are repeated each time the client activates a function module in the R/3 System. Each of the phases named are executed by a function of the RFC Application Programming Interface (API) and for every RFC API function executed during a cycle, an entry is written to the Trace file. Every entry in the Trace file has the following structure:

▶ RFC API function executed

▶ Values with which the function was executed

▶ The values are in the memory extract that comes after the function. With RFC API functions that exchange data directly with the R/3 System, the structure of the interface is also logged.

▶ Return value, which indicates the status of the execution

In our external client, the connection is made using the function RfcOpenEx. The values for the connection are stored in the connection string. The information pertaining to these values appears first in the Trace file. On examination of the Trace file, one thing that stands out is that the password is replaced by the value :) secret (:. Therefore, in a very simple way, you can ensure that third parties can never get the user name and password from a trace.

The function module Z_RFC_ADD is activated by the function RfcCallReceiveEx. Internally, the function RfcCallReceiveEx uses the function RfcCallEx to send data and the function RfcReceiveEx to read data. The next display in the Trace file is information on the functions.

The following is recorded for the function RfcCallEx:

▶ The function module activated

▶ The structure of the interface for data export

▶ The values exported

The values sent to the R/3 System can be found in a memory extract, where they are presented in hexadecimal form and in the corresponding ASCII characters. For the variable IP_VALUE2, we send the value 88. The hexadecimal for 88 is 58. The corresponding ASCII character is X. This value can therefore also be found in the Trace file (see Figure 5.6).

Finally, the return value of the function RfcCallEx is displayed. In our example, this is RFC_OK.

The same information is displayed for function RfcReceiveEx as for RfcCallEx. The details of the SAP function module activated are, of course, not included. The return value of the function RfcCallEx is also RFC_OK.

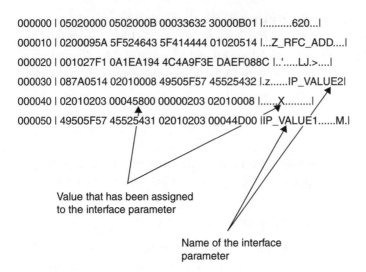

```
000000 | 05020000 0502000B 00033632 30000B01 |.........620...|
000010 | 0200095A 5F524643 5F414444 01020514 |...Z_RFC_ADD....|
000020 | 001027F1 0A1EA194 4C4A9F3E DAEF088C |..'.....LJ.>....|
000030 | 087A0514 02010008 49505F57 45525432 |.z......IP_VALUE2|
000040 | 02010203 00045800 00000203 02010008 |.....X.........|
000050 | 49505F57 45525431 02010203 00044D00 |IP_VALUE1......M.|
```

Value that has been assigned
to the interface parameter

Name of the interface
parameter

Figure 5.6 Extract from the Trace File for an External Client

Finally, the return value of the function `RfcCallReceiveEx` is logged. It has the value `RFC_OK` only if the functions `RfcCallEx` and `RfcReceiveEx` were previously executed without any errors.

5.4.2 Structure of the Trace File for an External Server

The Trace file of an external server differs only slightly from the form described above.

As an example, we'll use the external pocket calculator from Chapter 3, and we will assume that we want to add the values 77 and 88. For the addition, the function `RFC_ADD` is activated in the server.

A communication process for the R/3 System with an external server comprises four phases:

▶ Registering the server with the SAP Gateway (one-off operation)

▶ Receiving the message

▶ Reading the data

▶ Sending the data

Phases two to four are repeated every time the R/3 System sends a message. As was the case for the external client, each of the phases named is executed by a function of the RFC API. An entry is also made in the Trace file for every function executed during the cycle. In principle, every entry in the Trace file has the same structure as an entry for an external client. The following should be noted, however:

- ▶ The memory extract for the data sent to the server comes after the function RfcDispatch.

- ▶ Next, the callback function to which the message from SAP was forwarded is logged.

  >>>> [1] Dispatch call to:RFC_ADD

- ▶ For the function RfcGetData, only the structure of the interface for the data import is displayed. Also listed are the interface parameters for which values were actually received. The values themselves can be seen in the memory extract that comes after the function RfcDispatch.

- ▶ The structure of the information block for function RfcSendData again corresponds to the structure mentioned above. It consists of the name of the function, the structure of the interface for the data export, the memory extract for the values sent, and the return value of the function.

- ▶ Finally, the return value of function RfcDispatch comes after the message loop.

5.4.3 Traces Using Transaction ST05

As explained above, within an R/3 System, the RFC Trace can also be activated using Transaction ST05. The RFC Trace created with the transaction does not contain as much information as a Trace file, but it does show at first glance which function modules are executed in the R/3 System and which functions are executed by the R/3 System. It is particularly helpful during the development phase because, when running tests, the first question to be answered is, "Was the function executed?"

Figure 5.7 shows the initial screen for Transaction ST05. The user can specify what type of trace he or she wants to create. For an RFC Trace, select the option **RFC trace**.

An RFC Trace is recorded in four steps:

- ▶ Activate the trace with the function **Trace on**
- ▶ Execute the RFC actions
- ▶ Deactivate the trace using the function **Trace off**
- ▶ Display the list of traces executed using the function **Trace list**. When the function is executed, you can enter the selection criteria—for the trace to be displayed—in a dialog box. By default, the criteria is initialized with the values for the last trace executed by the user.

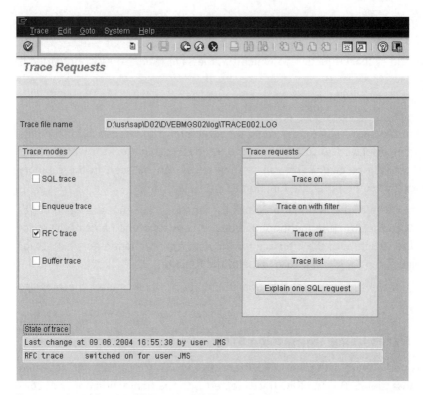

Figure 5.7 Initial Screen of Transaction ST05

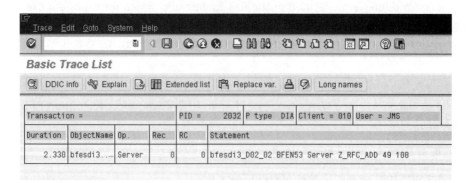

Figure 5.8 Trace with Transaction ST05

The trace shown in Figure 5.8 shows the results when the function module Z_RFC_ADD was executed in the R/3 System by an external client. In the initial list, you get the following information for an RFC Trace:

- The **Duration** column shows the time taken for the execution.

- In the **ObjectName** column you find the name of the instance on which the function module was executed. If the instance name is not known, a ? will be displayed.

- The value in the **Operation** column in an RFC Trace determines whether the R/3 System was the client or the server for the RFC executed. The value `Server` lets you know that the R/3 System was the server.

- Record number. This value is not required for an RFC Trace.

- The **RC** column contains the return value of the executed statement.

- The **Statement** column contains a string that, for an RFC Trace, consists of the name of the local computer that executed the RFC call, the name of the application server (if known), the nature of the client-server relationship regarding the R/3 System, the name of the function module executed, and the number of bytes sent and received.

5.5 The RFC Generator

The RFC Generator is a tool developed by SAP. It allows you to generate test programs for the interface of an RFC-enabled function module to call the function module. The test programs can be generated in C/C++ and in Visual Basic.

If the RFC Generator is used in this way, the test program is considered an external client that activates the SAP function module. There is also an option to create a test program for an external server that is activated by the R/3 System. For this, you create a "Dummy function module" in the SAP R/3 System. The function module has the same interface as the external server should. Furthermore, in the attributes of the function module, the processing type must be set to **Remote-enabled module**. The RFC Generator is then started. But instead of an external client, you will now get a sample program for an external server.

To start the RFC Generator, you must call the Function Builder—Transaction SE37. Note that the call must be made for the function module for which you want to create the test program. The functions for the RFC Generator can then be reached via the menu **Utilities · RFC interface** (see Figure 5.9).

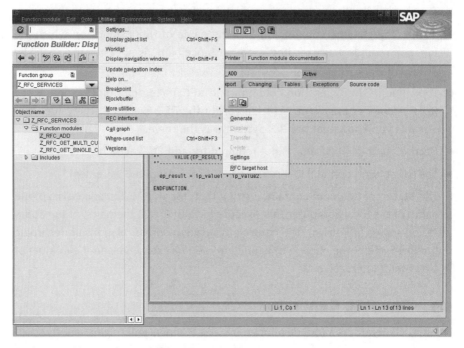

Figure 5.9 Functions of the RFC Generator

The most frequently used functions are **Settings** and **Generate**. You can define the following by using the **Settings** submenu (see Figure 5.10) in the menu **Utilities · RFC interface**:

▶ If an example code should be generated for a client or a server

▶ In which language the example should be created

▶ In which file the program is saved

Use the **Generate** function to create the program and the source code files for the program.

However, there is one restriction associated with using the RFC Generator. The creation of the example program will fail if there are also parameters in the interface that have a number (integer, for example) as their data type. Program generation will be terminated with the error message *Error reading the structure of parameter IP_VALUE1 (Activate structure)*. If the parameter has a data element as its data type, however, and if that data element refers to a number data type, there will be no problem creating an example program.

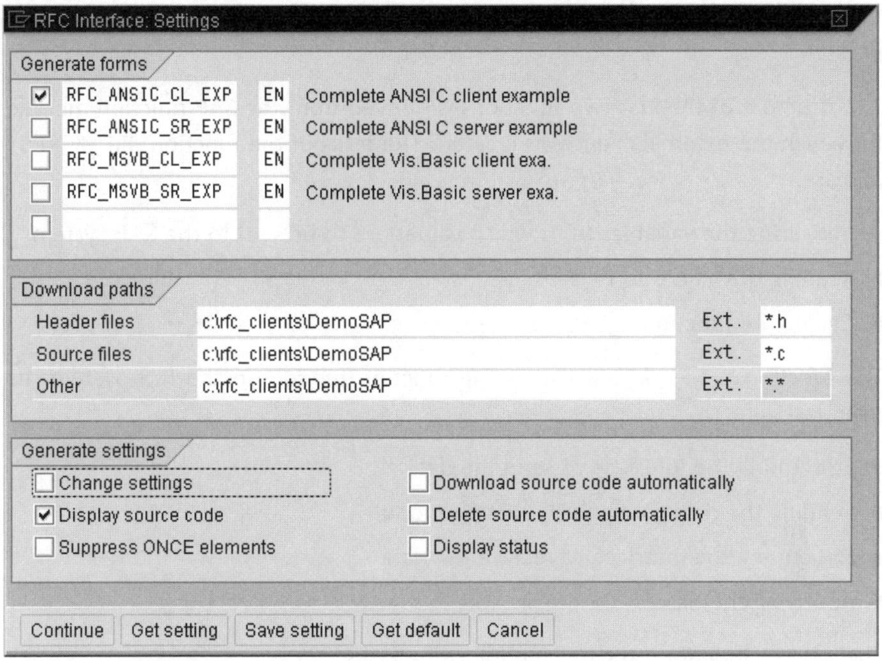

Figure 5.10 Options for the RFC Generator Settings

Now, let's take a closer look at the structure and functioning of the programs generated and the macros for setting the values to be transferred. We'll consider only C/C++ programs.

5.5.1 Structure of the Client Program Generated

To help you visualize the SAP test programs, an external client and server were generated for the SAP function module Z_RFC_ADD. Under Windows, the SAP test programs are console applications. They offer the user the possibility of entering values interactively using a command prompt.

The client test program contains the following functions or macros:

- cll_z_rfc_add
- z_rfc_add
- INS
- OUT (macro)
- OUTS
- LOG

- ► `logon`
- ► `main`

The structure of the first two functions is derived from the SAP function module for which the external client was created. The tasks of the function `CLL_Z_RFC_ADD` are:

- ► Initializing the variables from which values are to be sent to the SAP System
- ► Reading the values to be sent
- ► Calling the function `Z_RFC_ADD`

The function `Z_RFC_ADD` activates the function module in the R/3 System. Its main tasks are:

- ► Structuring the interface to send the data
- ► Sending the data to the SAP function module
- ► Structuring the interface to receive the data
- ► Receiving the data

The `main()` function executes the following tasks:

- ► Opening the INPUT, OUTPUT, and LOG file. The INPUT file prepares the data for logging on to the R/3 System. It must also provide the values for the interface parameters of the function module. The reason for this lies in the functioning of `INS`, which will be described below.
- ► Offering a menu from which the user can select a processing type.
- ► Executing the functions `Logon`, `CLL_Z_RFC_ADD`, and `Logoff`.

The client generated always processes an entire send operation. A send operation consists of the actions log on, send and receive data, and log off. Therefore, an open connection cannot be used for several send operations.

The `OUT` macro and the `OUTS` function control the output of data on the screen and in the file.

The `INS` function reads the values for logging on to the SAP system and for the send operation from the INPUT file, or requests it directly from the user. It first checks whether a file has been specified. If it has, the necessary information is read from the file; otherwise, it is requested from the user. If you're working with an INPUT file, this file must contain all the necessary information. If a request fails, the user will not be asked for information. Instead, the program will terminate with an error message. The information in an INPUT file usually has the following structure:

```
Name of information=Value
```

If you want to work with an INPUT file structured according to the previous example, you should modify that part of the INS function that reads the values from the INPUT file, as shown below, because the original program sequence encounters considerable problems when trying to read the values from an INPUT file.

```
/* Additional pointer */
char *pAdress = NULL;
:
if(infile){
/* Read input file and compare with event */
   do{
       if(!(fgets(str,1024,infile))){
           OUT("error reading input file",0);
           exit(1);
       };
   }while(!(strstr(str, subtopic)));
/* Transfer value */
   str = _strrev(str);
   pAdress = strchr(str, '=');
   *pAdress = '\0';
   str = _strrev(str);
/* Remove new line character */
   if((pAdress = strchr(str, '\n')))
       *pAdress = '\0';
```

Listing 5.1 Modified Reading of Data from the INPUT File

In this program sequence, the INPUT file is scanned until a line is found that provides the values for the information specified in the field subtopic. Once the line with the information has been found, the part in the line that specifies the type of information read is removed. The following steps are executed for this:

▶ Reverse the character string—if the character string has the structure

'IP_CUSTNO=0000000135'

then, after being reversed, it has the structure

'5310000000=ONTSUC_PI'.

▶ After this, the equals sign is replaced by the end of string identifier \n so that the string variable now has the value

`'5310000000'`

▶ The content of the string variable is once again reversed, so that it now has the correct value

`'000000135'`

The LOG function logs all procedures during program execution. The data is written to a file specified by the command field.

The logon function, finally, activates logon to the R/3 System.

5.5.2 Structure of the Server Program Generated

The server test program is essentially made up of the following functions or macros:

▶ srv_z_rfc_add
▶ z_rfc_add
▶ INS
▶ OUT (macro)
▶ OUTS
▶ LOG
▶ main

The functions INS, OUTS, LOG, and the macro OUT are identical to the client generated, so we will not discuss them any further. For the INS function in particular, what was said in the previous section regarding the use of the INPUT files is also relevant here.

The function SRV_Z_RFC_ADD has the following tasks:

▶ Configuring the interface to exchange data with the R/3 System
▶ Receiving values from the R/3 System
▶ Sending values to the R/3 System
▶ Calling the function Z_RFC_ADD

The tasks of the function Z_RFC_ADD are as follows:

▶ Calling the macros and functions to output the values received
▶ Reading the values to be sent

The `main` function basically executes the following tasks:

▶ Opening the INPUT, OUTPUT, and LOG file

▶ Making the callback functions known to the RFC API

▶ Structuring the message loops in blocking mode

The server program created by the SAP system can be used only as a started server. If you also want to use the program as a registered server, you must adjust the program accordingly in the `main` function (see also Chapter 3).

5.5.3 Macros for Setting and Reading Values

The programs created by the SAP system have the following macros:

▶ SETCHAR/GETCHAR

▶ SETNUM/GETNUM

▶ SETDATE/GETDATE

▶ SETTIME/GETTIME

▶ SETBYTE/GETBYTE

▶ SETINT/GETINT

▶ SETFLOAT/GETFLOAT

The task of the macros is to prepare the values, according to type, that are to be sent to or received by the SAP system. The macros SETNUM, SETDATE, and SET-TIME in particular are somewhat problematic. Their task consists of preparing the numeric values to be sent according to type. Unfortunately, type-related preparation is limited to the addition of a preceding or closing zero. There is no check to determine whether the string contains only numeric characters. The problems that can arise as a result are addressed in greater detail in Section 4.1.3's discussion of numeric strings.

The macros GETBYTE and SETBYTE are used to convert packed numbers into a string and vice versa. The calls for functions nbyte2str and str2nbyte are hidden behind them. These functions are equivalent to the functions RfcConvertBcdToChar and RfcConvertCharToBcd that we introduced in Chapter 4.

5.6 SAP Test Programs

SAP also delivers some test programs in combination with the RFC software development kit (SDK). The test programs are external servers and clients. All test programs supplied can be found in Windows in the directory:

C:\Programs\SAP\FrontEnd\SAPgui\rfcsdk\bin

SAP also provides the source codes for the programs. They're located in the directory:

C:\Programs\SAP\FrontEnd\SAPgui\rfcsdk\text

With Windows, all test programs are developed as console applications. It is possible to transfer several optional parameters to them when called.

The following programs are external servers for the R/3 System:

▶ `rfcexec.exe`

▶ `srfcserv.exe`

▶ `trfcserv.exe`

The following programs function as external clients:

▶ `sapinfo.exe`

▶ `startrfc.exe`

▶ `srfctest.exe`

▶ `trfctest.exe`

Given that with console applications you can transfer parameters only if they're started with a DOS prompt, we recommend that you create batch files to use the programs. You'll see how the batch files for calling the test programs should be structured with the example of the program `srfctest.exe`.

```
@rem So that you know which program is started
@echo Start the program srfctext.exe from SAP
@echo off
rem Change to the program directory of srfctest
cd c:\
cd Programs
cd SAP
cd Frontend
cd SAPgui
cd rfcsdk
cd bin
srfctest.exe
@echo on
pause
```

Listing 5.2 Batch File to Start the SAP Program srfctest.exe

Initially, it's apparent that there's a switch to the program directory in which the SAP test programs are located, and then the appropriate SAP test program is executed. Finally, processing is interrupted by the PAUSE command to look at the results of the program. The output of the command sequence to change to the program directory is suppressed by the echo on and echo off commands.

Next, we'll examine the program startrfc.exe, because it can also prove useful for more complex tests.

The startrfc.exe program allows for the targeted testing of function modules in the R/3 System, including the transfer of values. It functions as a client of the R/3 System. The program can be used if it is started with the option -? in the command line.

To test an SAP function module specifically with the program startrfc.exe, four information blocks must be transferred to the command line.

▶ The first block contains all information about the function module to be called, including the values that are to be transferred.

▶ The second block contains information on the R/3 System to be activated.

▶ The third block is optional. It can be used to activate the RFC trace and the debugging of ABAP programs.

▶ The fourth block contains the user-specific logon data.

The information listed above is transferred to the command line with the following identifiers:

Identifier	Meaning
-F⟨name of FM⟩	Name of the function module is transferred with the prefix -F
-E⟨parameter⟩=⟨value⟩	The export parameter is transferred with the prefix -E. Each export parameter must be transferred with a leading -E. For the function module Z_RFC_GET_SINGLE_CUSTOMER from Chapter 3, the variable IP_CUSTNO would be transferred as: -EIP_CUSTNO=0000000001
-T⟨name⟩	Name of the table to be transferred
-3	A connection to the R/3 System should be opened
-h⟨I.P.⟩	IP address of the application server
-s⟨number⟩	System number
-debug	Activate the ABAP debugger; optional

Table 5.1 Identifiers to Call Up a Function Module Using the Program startrfc.exe

Identifier	Meaning
`-t`	Activate the RFC trace; optional
`-u<name>`	User ID
`-p<value>`	Password
`-c<client>`	Client to which one wants to log on
`-l<ID>`	Logon language

Table 5.1 Identifiers to Call Up a Function Module Using the Program startrfc.exe (cont.)

The different items of information are separated from each other with a " " (space) character.

The potential to send and receive tables to and from SAP function modules is particularly interesting. If tables are to be sent or received, the following details are necessary:

Parameter	Meaning
`-T<name>`	Name of the table to be transferred
`<width>,`	Structure byte size
`r=<file>`	Name of the file from which the values to be sent must be read
`w=<file>`	Name of the file in which the values received are written

Table 5.2 Details for Sending and Receiving Tables

We shall now present the sending and receiving of tables using a modification of the function module Z_RFC_GET_SINGLE_CUSTOMER. The goal of the modification is to read several customer master data records and pass the customer numbers on to an internal table. In the first step, the function module Z_RFC_GET_SINGLE_CUSTOMER is copied to the function module Z_RFC_GET_SINGLE_CUSTOMER_V1. We add the table parameters IT_KUNNR and ET_CUSTOMER to the interface of the function module Z_RFC_GET_SINGLE_CUSTOMER_V1. In the first table, the customer numbers for which master data records are to be read are transferred; in the second table, the customer master data records are returned. The function module Z_RFC_GET_SINGLE_CUSTOMER_V1 is programmed as shown in Figure 5.11.

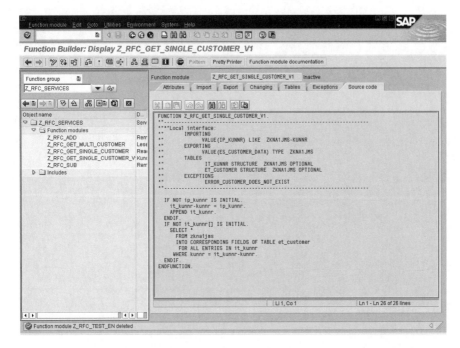

```
Function module  Edit  Goto  Utilities  Environment  System  Help                               SAP

⊘                           ▯  ◁ 🖫  © © ©  🖳 🕅 🕅  🕄 🕄 🕄 🕄  🖾 🖾  ⑦ 🖳

Function Builder: Display Z_RFC_GET_SINGLE_CUSTOMER_V1

← →  🥸 🥸 🖼  🖓 ·  🖼 🖓  🚣 🖳 🔲 🔳  ⬤  Pattern   Pretty Printer   Function module documentation
```

Function group			Function module	Z_RFC_GET_SINGLE_CUSTOMER_V1	Inactive
Z_RFC_SERVICES	▾	🗞	Attributes	Import	Export	Changing	Tables	Exceptions	Source code

```
Object name                        D...
▽ 🗀 Z_RFC_SERVICES               Serv
  ▽ 🗀 Function modules
      Z_RFC_ADD                    Rem
      Z_RFC_GET_MULTI_CUSTOMER     Less
      Z_RFC_GET_SINGLE_CUSTOMER    Rea
      Z_RFC_GET_SINGLE_CUSTOMER_V  Kun
      Z_RFC_SUB                    Rem
  ▷ 🗀 Includes
```

```
FUNCTION Z_RFC_GET_SINGLE_CUSTOMER_V1.
*"----------------------------------------
*"*"Local interface:
*"  IMPORTING
*"     VALUE(IP_KUNNR) LIKE  ZKNA1JMS-KUNNR
*"  EXPORTING
*"     VALUE(ES_CUSTOMER_DATA) TYPE  ZKNA1JMS
*"  TABLES
*"     IT_KUNNR STRUCTURE  ZKNA1JMS OPTIONAL
*"     ET_CUSTOMER STRUCTURE  ZKNA1JMS OPTIONAL
*"  EXCEPTIONS
*"     ERROR_CUSTOMER_DOES_NOT_EXIST
*"----------------------------------------

  IF NOT ip_kunnr IS INITIAL.
    it_kunnr-kunnr = ip_kunnr.
    APPEND it_kunnr.
  ENDIF.
  IF NOT it_kunnr[] IS INITIAL.
    SELECT *
      FROM zkna1jms
      INTO CORRESPONDING FIELDS OF TABLE et_customer
      FOR ALL ENTRIES IN it_kunnr
      WHERE kunnr = it_kunnr-kunnr.
  ENDIF.
ENDFUNCTION.
```

```
                                         LI 1, Co 1              Ln 1 - Ln 26 of 26 lines

🥚 Function module Z_RFC_TEST_EN deleted                                            ◁
```

Figure 5.11 Configuration of the Function Module Z_RFC_GET_SINGLE_CUSTOMER_V1

To inform the program `startrfc.exe` that the customer numbers must be read from a file, the command line must be enhanced as follows:

`-TIT_CUSTNO,193,r=<Path and name of the file>`

After the name of the table parameter comes the size of the structure in bytes. The latter is determined from the Data Dictionary. This is done by simply adding the sizes of the individual fields in the structure. The size of the fields in bytes can be seen in the **Length** column. You can see the column in the **Fields** view of the Data Dictionary for the table or structure (see also Section 2.2.5). At the end comes the name of the source file. It is specified after the prefix `r`.

If

`-TET_CUSTOMER,193,w=<Path and name of the file>`

is added to the command line, the customer master data read will be written to a file. If the `w` option is not used, the data records read will be output to the screen.

The observations in this chapter should help you to eliminate even the most difficult of problems. If not, perhaps Murphy can be of assistance again:

In every program, errors tend to turn up at the opposite end from where you start looking for them.

6   Advanced Techniques

In Goethe's poem, "The Sorcerer's Apprentice," we read:

"The old sorcerer has vanished, for once has gone away!
Spirits called by him, now banished, my commands shall soon obey!"

In this chapter, we want to extend RFC Application Programming Interface (API) skills so that in future we can also work "magic" with it. We'll include the following aspects:

▶ Return calls from the server

▶ Automatic generation of a field description

▶ Transactional servers and clients

▶ Parallel processing

Parallel processing is often important beyond the area of RFC-based client-server programming.

6.1   Return Calls from the Server

Sometimes the server requires additional information from the client to carry out its tasks. If, for example, in an external warehouse management system it is discovered that an article needed for a customer order is no longer in stock, the external server needs information on how to proceed with this purchase order item. The server must request additional information from the client. To request this information, the server activates a function in the client that provides the information. This technique, which reverses the "normal" data flow between client and server, is referred to as *callback*. This situation is illustrated in Figure 6.1.

A return call from an external server to an R/3 client does not present any problems, provided that the server is executed synchronously. The callback function simply calls the RFC API functions for activating R/3 function modules internally. The functions are as follows:

▶ RfcCallEx and RfcReceiveEx

▶ RfcCallReceiveEx

We will demonstrate how a callback would be made from an external server to an R/3 System using the example of our pocket calculator. It should now also offer division of two values. For this, the function RFC_DIV is added to the server. It is the same as the function RFC_ADD in many ways. As a first step, it is sufficient to copy the function RFC_ADD to the function RFC_DIV and replace the addition with the division. The additions required for a callback to an R/3 function module will be illustrated below.

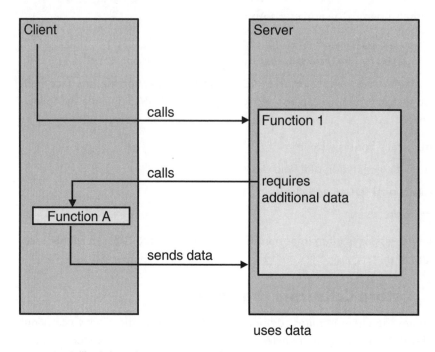

Figure 6.1 Callback from the Server to the Client

Division by zero is not allowed. The server will therefore need information on what to do should such an exception arise. We will define that if the divisor is zero, the external pocket calculator will activate a function module in the R/3 System that will require the user to enter a valid divisor.

Entering this permitted divisor is an interactive process. Interactive processes are done in dialog mode, so the SAP GUI must be installed on the computer on which the server is running. The solution presented here is mainly didactic; in practice, callback functions are not interactive.

We will look at how to create the function module Z_RFC_GET_NEW_DIVISOR. This requires two steps:

▶ Creating the interface of the function module

▶ Implementing the logic of the function module

The interface of the function module is very simple. It is made up of just the export parameter EP_NEW_DIVISOR, of data type i.

After defining the interface, we can realize the logic of the function module. It consists of a loop that is run through as long as the variable EP_NEW_DIVISOR has the value zero. The SAP function module POPUP_TO_GET_ONE_VALUE is called in the loop. It generates a dialog box for entering a value and is very useful because it allows for the generation of dialog boxes with no prior knowledge of dialog programming. The interface of the function module is as follows:

Parameter	Direction	Meaning
textline1	Importing	Text for providing additional information for the user Output comes in the first line of the dialog box
textline2	Importing	Meaning same as textline1, but the text is output in the second line
textline3	Importing	Meaning same as textline1, but the text is output in the third line
titel	Importing	Title of the dialog box
valuelength	Importing	Number of characters in the field
answer	Exporting	Function executed by user
value1	Exporting	Value entered by user

Table 6.1 Interface of the Function Module POPUP_TO_GET_ONE_VALUE

When setting the value for the parameter VALUELENGTH, you should bear in mind that the number of characters that can be in the field, not the byte size, will be transferred. A variable of data type INT4, for example, is 4 bytes. The largest value that can be saved in the variable is 4294967296. The value has 10 characters. This value should be transferred to the interface of the function module.

Furthermore, the export parameter VALUE1 has the data element PVARFIELD as its data type. The data element is a character field with 30 characters. As a result, the direct allocation of the parameter EP_NEW_DIVISOR with data type INT4 to the parameter VALUE1 at runtime would lead to a type conflict and program crash. To eliminate this problem, the temporary variable LP_NEW_DIVISOR is introduced. It has the data element PVARFIELD as data type and, after calling the function module POPUP_TO_GET_ONE_VALUE, its value is assigned to the parameter EP_NEW_DIVISOR. Taking what was just said into consideration, the logic for the function module Z_RFC_GET_NEW_DIVISOR would look like this:

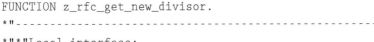

```
FUNCTION z_rfc_get_new_divisor.
*"----------------------------------------------------------
*"*"Local interface:
```

```
*"   EXPORTING
*"      VALUE(EP_NEW_DIVISOR) TYPE   I
*"   EXCEPTIONS
*"       ERROR_INVALIDATE_DIVISOR
*"------------------------------------------------------------
  DATA: lp_new_divisor TYPE pvarfield
          .
  WHILE ep_new_divisor = 0.
    CALL FUNCTION 'POPUP_TO_GET_ONE_VALUE'
          EXPORTING
               textline1     = 'Division by zero is not allowed '
               textline2     = 'Please enter a new operator'
*              textline3     = ' '
               titel         = 'Error'
               valuelength   = 10
          IMPORTING
*              answer        =
               value1        = lp_new_divisor
          EXCEPTIONS
               title_too_long = 1
               OTHERS         = 2
                 .
    ep_new_divisor = lp_new_divisor.
    IF ep_new_divisor = 0.
      MESSAGE i208(00) WITH text-t02.
    ENDIF.
  ENDWHILE.
ENDFUNCTION.
```

Listing 6.1 Function Module for Entering a Valid Divisor

In this listing, we can also see the execution of the ABAP statement MESSAGE. It is used to output messages. A message is displayed—in our example—if the user enters zero as the divisor.

Finally, the function module Z_RFC_GET_NEW_DIVISOR is activated. If we test the function module in the development environment of the SAP system, the resulting display should look something like that shown in the dialog boxes below (see Figures 6.2 and 6.3).

Figure 6.2 Error Message if the Divisor is Zero

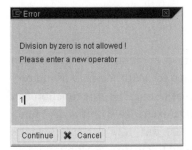

Figure 6.3 Dialog Box to Enter the Divisor

Once the additional function module has been created in the R/3 System, we can continue with the enhancement of the server. The following steps must be executed in the server:

▶ Implement a function to activate the function module in the R/3 System

▶ Add a check for the value of the divisor in the callback function RFC_DIV

The function GetNewDivisor is developed to activate the function module in the R/3 system. The function is realized as follows:

```
RFC_RC GetNewDivisor(RFC_HANDLE hConnection,
                     int        *piNewDivisor)
{
   RFC_RC rc = RFC_FAILURE;
   RFC_PARAMETER ImpParam[2];
   RFC_ERROR_INFO_EX ErrorInfo;
   char *pException = NULL;
   memset(&ErrorInfo, NULL, sizeof(RFC_ERROR_INFO_EX));
   ImpParam[0] = BuildSimpleParam
                     ("EP_NEW_DIVISOR", TYPINT,
                       sizeof(RFC_INT), piNewDivisor);
   ImpParam[1].name = NULL;
   if((rc = RfcCallReceiveEx(
            hConnection, "Z_RFC_GET_NEW_DIVISOR",
```

```
                NULL, ImpParam, NULL, NULL, &pException))
            != RFC_OK){
        RfcLastErrorEx(&ErrorInfo);
        printf("%s\n", ErrorInfo.message);
        return rc;
    }
    return RFC_OK;
}
```

Listing 6.2 The Function GetNewDivisor

In the interface of the function GetNewDivisor, in addition to the connection handle, a pointer to the new divisor is also transferred. With the help of the previously imported function BuildSimpleParam (see Listing 3.9), the function first configures the description of the interface for data exchange with the SAP function module. Because the function module Z_RFC_GET_NEW_DIVISOR exports only the parameter EP_NEW_DIVISOR, we only need to create a description for an importing parameter. The connection with the pointer variable piNewDivisor is made here. The function module Z_RFC_GET_NEW_DIVISOR is then activated by calling the function RfcCallReceiveEx.

Finally, a check must be made in the callback function RFC_DIV to see if the divisor sent by the R/3 System is zero, and if so, the GetNewDivisor function must be called. The following listing shows a variant for the implementation:

```
RFC_RC DLL_CALL_BACK_FUNCTION RFC_DIV(
                            RFC_HANDLE hConnection)
{
    int iDivisor = 0;
    :
    if(iDivisor == 0){
        if((rc = GetNewDivisor(hConnection, &iDivisor))
                == RFC_OK)
            iResult = iValue1 / iDivisor;
        else
            iResult = -99999999;
    }else{
        iResult = iValue1 / iDivisor;
    }
    :
}
```

Listing 6.3 Implementation of the Callback Function RFC_DIV

We can see that the function sends the value -99999999 back to the R/3 System to indicate an error in function `GetNewDivisor`. It would also be possible to send an exception. Sending an exception will be described in Section 6.5.

Now, if we activate the function `RFC_DIV` in our report `ZCALLRFCCALCULATOR` and enter the value zero for the divisor, we should be presented with a dialog box and asked to enter a divisor not equal to zero. Figure 6.4 once again illustrates the relationship between the R/3 client and the pocket calculator.

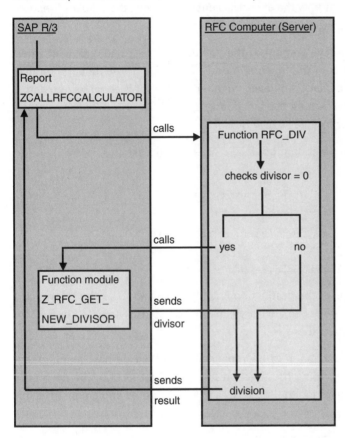

Figure 6.4 Pocket Calculator Callback to the R/3 Client

Having presented callback for an external server, we now take a look at a callback from an R/3 server to an external client. For this we will once again use the division of two numbers as an example. This time, however, the program `RFCCalcu-latorClient` requests the R/3 System to divide two values.

The following steps must be carried out for our example:

► Add the function module Z_RFC_DIV, which executes the division, to the function group Z_RFC_SERVICES.

► Add the callback function RFC_GET_NEW_DIVISOR to the client. It requests a new divisor.

The situation is practically the same as in the previous example. The only difference lies in the fact that now the external client implements the callback function, which is activated by the R/3 server.

Let us start with the development of the function module Z_RFC_DIV. Its interface is identical to that of the function module Z_RFC_ADD. The function module Z_RFC_DIV must also check, however, whether the divisor is equal to zero and, if so, make a callback activating the function RFC_GET_NEW_DIVISOR in the client. This requires the user to enter a new divisor.

Programming for the function module Z_RFC_DIV looks like this:

```
IF ip_value2 = 0.
   CALL FUNCTION 'RFC_GET_NEW_DIVISOR'
                 DESTINATION 'BACK'
        IMPORTING ep_new_divisor = ip_value2.
ENDIF.
EP_RESULT = IP_VALUE1 / IP_VALUE2.
```

The SAP server thus uses the destination BACK for the callback to the external client. This RFC destination is an auxiliary construction specially created by SAP for the objectives described above.

Finally, the callback function must be implemented in the external client and registered in the RFC API using the function RfcInstallFunction. Based on the above example, the function RFC_GET_NEW_DIVISOR can be implemented as follows:

```
RFC_RC DLL_CALL_BACK_FUNCTION
          RFC_GET_NEW_DIVISOR(RFC_HANDLE hConnection)
{
   RFC_RC rc = RFC_OK;
   int iDivisor = 0;
   RFC_PARAMETER ExpParam[2];
   RFC_ERROR_INFO_EX ErrorInfo;
   ExpParam[0] = BuildSimpleParam(
                     "EP_NEW_DIVISOR", TYPINT,
```

```
                            sizeof(RFC_INT), &iDivisor);
  ExpParam[1].name = NULL;
  if((rc = RfcGetData(hConnection, NULL, NULL))
         != RFC_OK){
     RfcLastErrorEx(&ErrorInfo);
     printf("%s\n", ErrorInfo.message);
     return rc;
  }
  do{
     printf("%s\n", "Division by zero is not "\
                      "allowed!");
     printf("%s", "Please enter a new "\
                    "operator: ");
     scanf("%i", &iDivisor);
  }while(iDivisor == 0);
  if((rc = RfcSendData(hConnection, ExpParam, NULL))
         != RFC_OK){
     RfcLastErrorEx(&ErrorInfo);
     printf("%s\n", ErrorInfo.message);
     return rc;
  }
  return RFC_OK;
}
```

Listing 6.4 The Function RFC_GET_NEW_DIVISOR

You can see that the function RFC_GET_NEW_DIVISOR is configured in the same way as a callback function in a regular external server. Finally, there is an extract from the main() function, to show how the callback function is registered.

```
int main (int argc, char** argv)
{
   ...
/* Registering the callback function in the client */
   rc = RfcInstallFunction("RFC_GET_NEW_DIVISOR",
                           RFC_GET_NEW_DIVISOR, NULL);
   ...
}
```

You will find the full program CallbackFromSAPServer on the Web site for this book at *www.sap-press.com.*

6.2   Automatic Creation of a Structure Description

In previous chapters we have learned how to create a structure or table description tion manually and register it in the RFC API. The manual creation of the field structure was used to demonstrate what the field structure actually is. In practice, the manual creation of the field structure has not been used for a long time now, because the procedure is very prone to errors (just think of complex tables such as VBAK or VBAP). The RFC API does, of course, offer a very good solution to determine mine information about the configuration of ABAP Data Dictionary (AD) structures at a program's runtime.

Two RFC API functions are needed to dynamically determine information on the structure of AD elements:

▶ RfcGetStructureInfoAsTable

▶ RfcExidToRfcType

The function RfcGetStructureInfoAsTable determines the actual description of the element configuration. The function RfcExidToRfcType is an auxiliary function that determines the RFC data type that corresponds to an ABAP data type.

The interface of the function RfcGetStructureInfoAsTable is:

Variable	Meaning
hRfc	Connection handle
StructName	Name of the AD structure
pItabStruct	Handle for the table that contains the description of the structure configuration
pItabHeads	Handle for the table with information on the hierarchy of fields, if AD elements of ABAP type 2 are accessed. See also the comment on ABAP type 1 below
pTypeKind	Return value that identifies the type of AD element
	Values are interpreted as follows:
	RFCTYPE_STRUCTURE: AD element is a structure
	RFCTYPE_TABLE: AD element is a table
pB1SLen	Size of the structure in systems in which the value is determined by calculating one byte per character field
pB2SLen	As pB1SLen, but calculated with two bytes per character field
pB4SLen	As pB1SLen, but calculated with four bytes per character field

Table 6.2 Interface of the Function RfcGetStructureInfoAsTable

Variable	Meaning
pSId	Identifier for the structure
exception	String for error messages
RFC_RC	Return type of the function

Table 6.2 Interface of the Function RfcGetStructureInfoAsTable (cont.)

When using this function, you should note that internally it requires memory space for the table in which the data related to the structure of the AD element is managed. The calling program must release the memory space again once the table is no longer required. This is done using the function ItDelete, to which the table handle is transferred. Furthermore, the use of the function is allowed only for structures and tables that comply with what is known as *ABAP type 1*. This restriction means that the fields of the AD structure are not mapped onto the following C data types: RFCTYPE_ STRING, RFCTYPE_XSTRING, RFCTYPE_XMLDATA, or RFCTYPE_ITAB.

The variable pItabStruct is of the type ITAB_H. In it, the function Rfc-GetStructureInfoAsTable returns the handle to the table in which the information on the structure is recorded. If the handle is used in the functions for accessing the data records in a table, information is provided on the structure of the fields in the AD structure. The data records have the structure of structure RFC_U_FIELDS. This is defined in the RFC API as:

Field	Meaning
Tabname	Name of the AD structure
Fieldname	Field name
Position	Position in the structure
Exid[1]	Identifier for the ABAP data type
Decimals	Number of decimal places
Offset_b1	Offset in the structure Here the offset is calculated with one byte for every Character
Length_b1	Field byte size, whereby one Character is one byte
Offset_b2	As Offset_b1, but here, two bytes per Character are calculated
Length_b2	As Length_b1, but in this case a Character is two bytes in size

Table 6.3 Structure of RFC_U_FIELDS

Field	Meaning
Offset_b4	As Offset_b1, but here, four bytes per Character are calculated
Length_b4	As Length_b1, but in this case a Character is four bytes

Table 6.3 Structure of RFC_U_FIELDS (cont.)

The information on the structure of the AD element is almost sufficient to fill the structure RFC_TYPE_ELEMENT2. All we need now is information for the C data type, which is to be stored in the type field of structure RFC_TYPE_ELEMENT2.

The C data type is determined using the function RfcExidToRfcType. The identifier for the ABAP Dictionary is transferred to the interface of the function, and it returns the corresponding RFC data type. The definition of the function RfcExidToRfcType is:

Variable	Meaning
Exid	Identifier of the ABAP data type
pType	Reference to a variable with the data type RFCTYPE, in which the RFC data type is returned
RFC_RC	Return type of the function

Table 6.4 Interface of the Function RfcExidToRfcType

The allocation of ABAP data type to a C data type—and thus also an RFC data type—is recorded in the table RFCTA in the R/3 System.

The GetFieldDesc function shown below comes from the program CreateStructDesc and reveals how the structure of AD tables and structures can be determined at runtime using the functions described above:

```
RFC_RC GetFieldDesc(RFC_HANDLE hConnection,
                    char* pTableName, char *pDDName,
                    RFC_TABLE *pTableParam,
                    RFC_TYPE_ELEMENT2 **pColDesc,
                    RFC_ERROR_INFO_EX *pErrorInfo)

{
   RFC_RC rc = RFC_OK;
   ITAB_H hTStructDesc = RFC_HANDLE_NULL,
          hTHeader     = RFC_HANDLE_NULL;
   RFCTYPE DDType;
```

```
   RFC_STRUCT_TYPE_ID TypID;
   rfc_char_t *pException = NULL;
   unsigned int iStructSize1B = 0,
                iStructSize2B = 0,
                iStructSize4B = 0;
/* for new table */
   RFC_TYPEHANDLE Tabletype = 0;

/* Determine the field structure */
   if((rc = RfcGetStructureInfoAsTable(
                   hConnection, pDDName,
                   &hTStructDesc, &hTHeader, &DDType,
                   &iStructSize1B, &iStructSize2B,
                   &iStructSize4B, &TypID, &pException))
         != RFC_OK){
      RfcLastErrorEx(pErrorInfo);
      return rc;
   }
   unsigned int iAnzRS = ItFill(hTStructDesc);
   RFCTYPE CType = (RFCTYPE)0;
   RFC_U_FIELDS *pFieldDesc = NULL;
   if(!(*pColDesc = (RFC_TYPE_ELEMENT2*)calloc(
                   iAnzRS, sizeof(RFC_TYPE_ELEMENT2)))){
      strcpy(pErrorInfo->message, E_MEM_ALLOC);
      return rc;
   };
/* Create the array of type
   RFC_TYPE_ELEMENT2 from the information provided by
    RfcGetStructureInfoAsTable */
   for(int iRowCounter = 1; iRowCounter <= iAnzRS;
       iRowCounter++){
      pFieldDesc =
         (RFC_U_FIELDS*)ItGetLine(
                      hTStructDesc, iRowCounter);
/* Determine RFC data type for ABAP data type */
      if((rc = RfcExidToRfcType(
             pFieldDesc->Exid[0], &CType)) != RFC_OK){
         RfcLastErrorEx(pErrorInfo);
         printf("%s\n", pErrorInfo->message);
         ItDelete(hTStructDesc);
```

```
                  ItDelete(hTHeader);
                  free(*pColDesc);
                  return rc;
              }
          (*pColDesc)[iRowCounter - 1] = BuildTableElement(
                  pFieldDesc->Fieldname, CType,
                  pFieldDesc->Length_b1, pFieldDesc->Decimals,
                  pFieldDesc->Offset_b1);
          }
/* Register structure description with the
   RFC API */
   if((rc = RfcInstallStructure2(pTableName, *pColDesc,
                                 iAnzRS, &Tabletype))
           != RFC_OK){
      RfcLastErrorEx(pErrorInfo);
      ItDelete(hTStructDesc);
      ItDelete(hTHeader);
      free(*pColDesc);
      return rc;
   }
/* Release handle for tables hTStructDesc, hTHeader
   again */
   ItDelete(hTStructDesc);
   ItDelete(hTHeader);
/* Enter table parameter for the array in
   the table parameter */
   pTableParam->name    = pTableName;
   pTableParam->nlen    = strlen(pTableName);
   pTableParam->type    = Tabletype;
   pTableParam->leng    = iStructSize1B;
   pTableParam->itmode  = RFC_ITMODE_BYREFERENCE;
   if((pTableParam->ithandle =
           ItCreate(pTableName, iStructSize1B, 100, 0))
       == ITAB_NULL){
      strncpy(pErrorInfo->message,
           E_NOT_ENOUGH_MEM, strlen(E_NOT_ENOUGH_MEM));
      free(*pColDesc);
      return rc;
   }
```

```
/* If everything worked out: */
   return rc;
}
```

Listing 6.5 Structure of the Function GetFieldDesc for Determining AD Information at Runtime

The function `GetFieldDesc` is divided into three areas:

▶ Determining the structure information using the functions described above

▶ Transferring the information in an array of type `RFC_TYPE_ELEMENT2`, including registration with the RFC API

▶ Creating the table as an interface parameter in the array `pTableParam`

In so doing, information is transferred to the interface of the function regarding the name of the table in the interface of the function module (`pTableName`) and the name of the Data Dictionary element (`pDDName`). The necessary data can then be determined. If the function was executed successfully, the description of the structure configuration is returned to the calling program in the array `pColDesc`. For productively used applications, the following aspects should also be extended in the function:

▶ Checking whether all interface variables (pointer variables in particular) have been given valid values.

▶ Using the function for creating structures. The function `GetFieldDesc` is currently limited to the creation of table parameters, which limits its application.

Finally, we show what the call for function `GetFieldDesc` looks like:

```
int main(int argc, char** argv)
{
   RFC_RC rc = RFC_OK;
   RFC_ERROR_INFO_EX ErrorInfo;
   RFC_HANDLE hConnection = RFC_HANDLE_NULL;
   RFC_TABLE TableParam[2];
   RFC_TYPE_ELEMENT2 *TabDesc = NULL;
   char ConParam[] =
           "CLIENT=099 USER=<User> PASSWD=<Password> "\
           "LANG=EN ABAP_DEBUG=0 "\
           "ASHOST=10.10.34.131 SYSNR=01";

   . . .
   GetFieldDesc(hConnection,
           "ET_CUSTOMER_DATA", "ZKNA1JMS",
           &TableParam[0], &TabDesc,
```

```
                    &ErrorInfo);
    ...
    return rc;
}
```

Listing 6.6 Calling the Function GetFieldDesc

6.3   Transactional Remote Function Calls

Up to now, we have always sent the data synchronously from a client to a server. The R/3 System took on both client and server roles. If the connection to the server failed, the client could just send the data again, as soon as the connection became available. For a pocket calculator, this procedure does not present any problems.

But what happens if, for example, we call one or more functions on a server that in turn update data to a database? In this case, the procedure outlined above would mean that, in some cases, data would be written to a database in duplicate because the client sends the data twice. This can have unacceptable results. Imagine if the data sent are production orders for a production line, and there is a danger of duplicate production.

We therefore need a solution that ensures that certain procedures are transferred and executed only once. The following aspects are usually important, too:

▶ Encapsulating logically related RFC calls in a *logical unit* (Logical Unit of Work, or LUW)

▶ Status management for the LUW

▶ Implementation that ensures that the server updates or revokes the data sent with an LUW all together, for example, on a database

Transactional RFCs (tRFC) are used to realize these requirements. In a transactional RFC, the client groups the RFC calls in a program sequence in a logical unit and sends them to the server together. At the same time, status management is carried out in the client for the LUW. An external client must implement all relevant aspects for tRFC management itself. This includes, as mentioned, status management and repeating the tRFC if the connection to the R/3 System fails the first time. When developing the server, no function in the server can execute a separate or standalone database commit or rollback. This is done for all RFC functions together by a central function. It is always executed at the end of a sequence of RFC calls. This ensures that the data records in an LUW are always updated together. The main area of use for transactional RFCs is database changes in external systems. Figure 6.5 illustrates the processes inside a transactional RFC.

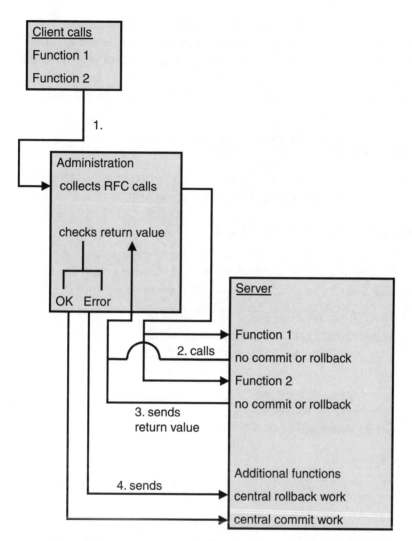

Figure 6.5 Flowchart of a Transactional RFC

The tRFC thus provides the basis on which the principles of atomicity and consistency can be realized (see also the ACID principle, as explained in Chapter 7). You should note, however that the programmer may have to do additional work in the tRFC environment to achieve the above mentioned aspects. For this reason, we shall present the programming of an external transactional RFC server and client in more detail. Section 6.4 looks at the expansion of the transactional RFCs to queue RFC calls.

We will add one more general remark on the structure of the tRFC here: The "at least once" rule for the tRFC must also apply if the server requested is not currently available. There must then be a delayed send. One way to implement this type of logic is to use a process specifically for this purpose that takes the data to be sent from temporary storage, for example, a database table. This procedure is applied in the SAP system.

6.3.1 The R/3 System as tRFC Client

In this section, we'll present the development of an R/3 client for initializing tRFC calls and see how these calls are managed in the R/3 System.

The Development of a tRFC-R/3 Client

In the previous section, we saw that for a tRFC, the client frequently groups all RFC calls together in an LUW and then carries out status management for the LUW. To group function calls together in an LUW, we must enhance the report ZCALLRFCCALCULATOR from Chapter 3 as follows:

```
CALL FUNCTION 'Z_RFC_ADD' IN BACKGROUND TASK
                          DESTINATION 'ZTESTJMS'
      EXPORTING
          IP_VALUE1 = PA_VALUE1
          IP_VALUE2 = PA_VALUE2.
CALL FUNCTION 'Z_RFC_SUB' IN BACKGROUND TASK
                          DESTINATION 'ZTESTJMS'
      EXPORTING
          IP_VALUE1 = PA_VALUE1
          IP_VALUE2 = PA_VALUE2.
COMMIT WORK.
```

Listing 6.7 Transactional Call for Functions Z_RFC_ADD and Z_RFC_SUB from Report ZCALLR-FCCALCULATOR

The call for the functions Z_RFC_ADD and Z_RFC_SUB is done in the report with the option IN BACKGROUND TASK. With this option, the RFC calls are not executed synchronously, but are grouped in an LUW executed by a separate process. The LUW is closed with the command COMMIT WORK. When executing the RFC calls, only RFC calls with the same DESTINATION should be grouped in the same LUW.

Managing tRFC Calls

The report ZCALLRFCCALCULATOR can now execute tRFC calls thanks to the enhancements above. Given that transactional RFCs are executed by a separate process, the data in an LUW must first be buffered in database tables until the process that executes the RFC calls is started. As part of this process, the LUW is linked with a transaction ID (TID) so that the data belonging to the LUW can always be clearly identified. We describe the current form of the TID (SAP Release Basis 6.20 or lower) because it can aid understanding and may sometimes be helpful for debugging. Please note, however, that the inner structure of the TID can change on the SAP side and is not determined exactly by the API.

The TID is currently structured as follows in the SAP system:

▶ Eight-digit computer ID
▶ Four-digit process ID
▶ Eight-digit time stamp
▶ Four-digit counter

A TID would thus look like that shown in Figure 6.6.

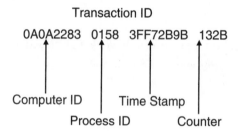

Figure 6.6 Structure of the Transaction ID

The RFC function calls linked with an LUW and the data to be sent are managed in the following tables:

▶ ARFCSSTATE
▶ ARFCSDATA

The ARFCSSTATE table manages the header data for a tRFC and the ARFCSDATA table manages the RFC functions to be called and the data to be sent (see Figure 6.7).

So only erroneous or as yet unexecuted LUWs are managed in the tables. As soon as an LUW is executed successfully, the data is deleted from the tables for the LUW. This ensures that an LUW can never be sent through the R/3 System twice.

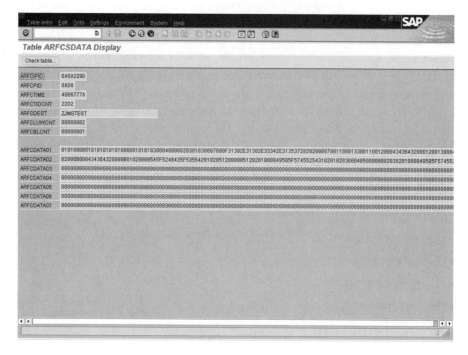

Figure 6.7 Data Record in Table ARFCSDATA in the Detail View

The tRFCs that contain errors, or that have not been executed yet are displayed in Transaction SM58 (transactional RFC). If Transaction SM58 is executed, a list is created that includes the following information, among other things:

► R/3 user that created the LUW

► Function calls that belong to the LUW

► Destination of the tRFC

► Date and time when the LUW was created

► Execution status

► Transaction ID

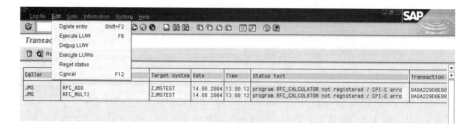

Figure 6.8 List of Transactional RFCs Not Yet Executed

All important functions for editing an LUW that has not yet been executed can be accessed using the **Edit** menu (see Figure 6.8). These include:

▶ **Execute LUW**
The R/3 System tries to execute the RFC functions of the selected LUW. If the call is successful, the LUW is deleted from the list; otherwise, the display is updated to show the errors.

▶ **Execute LUWs**
The R/3 System tries to execute the RFC calls for all LUWs.

The list of erroneous or not yet executed tRFCs can also be controlled using the QOUT Scheduler, which is described in Section 6.4.

6.3.2 Programming a Transactional RFC Server

We will now describe how an external transactional RFC server is developed using the RFC API.

We have already explained that the functions of a transactional server cannot execute separate data changes. Instead, the server must offer two additional functions that will—depending on the execution status of the preceding functions—centrally execute the data validation (for example, with a database commit) or displacement (for example, with a database rollback). These functions are executed by the R/3 client at the end of a sequence of function calls. In a tRFC server, the following additional functions must be implemented:

▶ onCheckTIDEx

▶ onCommitEx

▶ onRollbackEx

▶ onConfirmTIDEx

The functions onCommitEx and onRollbackEx are responsible for the central updating or central retraction of data(base) changes. The functions onConfirm-TIDEx and onCheckTIDEx must also be realized. The task of the function onCheckTIDEx is to check the TID received. If the server has already processed the TID, it can inform the R/3 client of this, whereupon the R/3 System will not execute any further RFC function calls. The function onCheckTIDEx can return the following values:

Return value	Meaning
0	The transaction ID has not yet been received from the server and the associated function calls should be executed now
1	The function calls linked with the transaction ID have already been executed and may not be edited further
< 0	Indicates an internal error

Table 6.5 Return Values for the Function onCheckTIDEx

Figure 6.9 illustrates the process for checking the TID.

The function onCheckTIDEx, allows for a double-check of the TID. The external tRFC server can also store received TIDs and, before executing an LUW, check to see whether it has received the data already. LUW management in the R/3 System can thus be enhanced with the tRFC server.

The interface of function onCheckTIDEx should look like this:

```
int DLL_CALL_BACK_FUNCTION FuncName (
                    RFC_TID TID,
                    RFC_HANDLE hConnection)
```

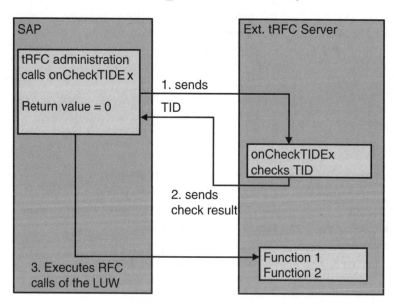

Figure 6.9 Checking the Transaction ID in the Server

The data type RFC_TID is defined as follows in the RFC API:

```
#define RFC_TID_LN  24 /* Offset of (ARFCSDATA, arfcdest) */
typedef rfc_char_t RFC_TID[RFC_TID_LN+1].
```

This is a data type with a 25-character long `character` field.

With the specification `DLL_CALL_BACK_FUNCTION`, we once again have a call convention that must be equated with the call convention `__stdcall` under Windows NT and its successor Windows 2000. This macro is empty on Unix-based systems.

The function `onCommitEx` should be defined as follows:

```
int DLL_CALL_BACK_FUNCTION FuncName (
                RFC_TID TID,
                RFC_HANDLE hConnection)
```

The database commit, for example, can be executed within the function. The function should return the value zero if the data is updated successfully, and a value not equal to zero if the action failed.

The counterpart of the function `onCommitEx` is the function `onRollbackEx`. Its interface should be structured as follows:

```
int DLL_CALL_BACK_FUNCTION FuncName (
                RFC_TID TID,
                RFC_HANDLE hConnection,
                int bValidateHandle)
```

The function executes the rollback if errors occurred.

At the end of a tRFC, the function `onConfirmTIDEx` is activated by the R/3 system. The function interface should be realized as follows:

```
void DLL_CALL_BACK_FUNCTION FuncName (
                RFC_TID TID,
                RFC_HANDLE hConnection)
```

This function indicates to the server that the current LUW was executed successfully, so the server can delete the administration data for the LUW from its tables.

The four functions are registered with the RFC API using the function

`RfcInstallTransactionControl2`

The interface of the function is as follows:

Variable	Meaning
onCheckTIDEx	Address of the callback function for checking the transaction ID
onCommitEx	Address of the callback function for confirming the data (for example, database commit)
onRollbackEx	Address of the callback function for rejecting the data (for example, database rollback)
onConfirmTIDEx	Address of the callback function for confirming the execution of the LUW

Table 6.6 Interface of the Function RfcInstallTransactionControl2

The function `RfcInstallTransactionControl2` does not return any value. The creation of the callback functions and their registration are presented below in their simplest form. The logic of the callback functions is not significant; normally the logic for writing record sets to the database is implemented in here, and of course other output forms can be used instead of `MessageBox`:

```
/* Functions for transactional RFC */
int DLL_CALL_BACK_FUNCTION RfcOnCheckTIDEx(
                                RFC_TID TransactionID,
                                RFC_HANDLE hConnection)
{
   int rc = RFC_OK;
   MessageBox(NULL, "Check TID passed!", "Message", MB_OK);
   return rc;
};
int DLL_CALL_BACK_FUNCTION RfcOnCommitEx(
                                RFC_TID TransactionID,
                                RFC_HANDLE hConnection)
{
   MessageBox(NULL, "Commit LUW passed!", "Message", MB_OK);
   return RFC_OK;
};
int DLL_CALL_BACK_FUNCTION RfcOnRollbackEx(
                                RFC_TID TransactionID,
                                RFC_HANDLE hConnection,
                                int bValidateHandle
{
   MessageBox(NULL, "Rollback LUW passed!",
            "Message", MB_OK);
   return RFC_OK;
```

```
};
void DLL_CALL_BACK_FUNCTION RfcOnConfirmTIDEx(
                                    RFC_TID TransactionID,
                                    RFC_HANDLE hConnection)
{
   MessageBox(NULL, "Confirm TID passed", "Message", MB_OK);
   return;
};
int main(int argc, char** argv)
{
:
/* Registering the functions for transaction checks */
   RfcInstallTransactionControl2(
                       RfcOnCheckTIDEx, RfcOnCommitEx,
                       RfcOnRollbackEx, RfcOnConfirmTIDEx);
:
}
```

Listing 6.8 Example of the Use of RfcInstallTransactionControl2

This listing is an extract from the program TRFCCALCULATOR, which you will find on the Web site for this book. The program just shows how the interfaces of functions for transaction checks should look and how they are registered. Absolutely no logic is realized with regard to database management of the TID. During execution of the functions, only one message is displayed. It shows which step of the transaction check is currently being executed.

Once the check functions for a transactional RFC have been implemented and registered, as a last step, the callback functions have to be adjusted in the server. Callback functions from tRFC servers cannot return values to the client. The reason for this is that the program context in which the RFC call was initiated can no longer exist at the moment of execution. This is obvious if you see that transaction function calls were made asynchronously in a separate task and not by the initiating program itself. The program that initiated the RFC calls is no longer active at the time of execution. The context in which any possible return values could be usefully evaluated is thus also lost. It would serve no purpose for a transactionally executed function to return values. This is why the function RfcSendData is called in the functions RFC_ADD and RFC_SUB as shown below:

```
if((rc = RfcSendData(hConnection, NULL, NULL))
        != RFC_OK){
   RfcLastErrorEx(&ErrorInfo);
```

```
    printf("%s\n", ErrorInfo.message);
    return rc;
}
```

The pointer variables that receive the description of the interface structure for the export are set at NULL.

6.3.3 Transactional RFC Client

Having developed an external tRFC server, let us now take a look at the development of an external tRFC client for the R/3 System. A tRFC client must also ensure that the function modules to be executed in the R/3 System are executed only once.[1] The tRFC client must therefore also carry out its own status management for the transactions. This is usually done by creating appropriate database tables. The RFC API does not, of course, provide any functions for this task.

With the following functions and the database table ARFCSTATE however, the RFC API provides considerable support for the development of tRFC clients. With the elements listed below, the R/3 system internally prevents the function modules linked with an LUW from being executed twice:

Function RFC API	SAP function module	Meaning
RfcCreateTransID	API_CREATE_TID	Generate the TID
RfcIndirectCallEx	ARFC_DEST_SHIP	Check and execute the LUW
RfcConfirmTransID	API_CLEAR_TID	Delete successfully executed transaction from the administration tables

Table 6.7 Functions of the RFC API for the Development of tRFC Clients

The function RfcCreateTransID generates a unique TID for the LUW. The interface of the function is as follows:

Variable	Meaning
handle	Connection handle
tid	Reference to a variable of type RFC_TID. The transaction ID is returned in the variable.

Table 6.8 Interface of the Function RfcCreateTransID

---

1 Remember that the tRFC ensures this only "at least once."

The key function of the RFC API for a tRFC client is `RfcIndirectCallEx`. It has the following interface:

Variable	Meaning
handle	Connection handle
function	Name of the SAP function module to be executed
exporting	Array of type RFC_PARAMETER with a description of the technical properties of the export parameters
tables	Array of type RFC_TABLE with a description of the tables to be sent
tid	Transaction ID assigned to the LUW

Table 6.9 Interface of the Function RfcIndirectCallEx

The function `RfcIndirectCallEx` has two tasks:

▶ To check if the transaction has been successfully executed in the R/3 System
▶ To execute the function module linked to the transaction

The `RfcIndirectCallEx` function in the R/3 System activates the function module `ARFC_DEST_SHIP` to check whether the transaction has already been successfully executed in the R/3 System. It checks the TID sent and, depending on the result, permits the execution of the transaction or not. Checking the TID involves two main steps:

1. First, it is necessary to find out if this is a new transaction. For this, the function tries to write the TID to the table `ARFCRSTATE` using the `INSERT` command. If it cannot insert it, this means that the transaction has already been sent to the SAP system once.

2. In the second step, the status of the transaction is checked in the function. The status gives information on how the transaction was executed in the R/3 System. If the status has the value `FINISHED`, the transaction has already been successfully executed in the R/3 System and it will not be possible to execute the transaction again. For this, the value of the control variable `SKIP` is set to X.

Once the function belonging to an LUW has been executed successfully, the transaction is usually marked accordingly in the client so that it cannot be sent to the R/3 System again. It is also no longer necessary to manage the TID in table ARFCRSTATE. As a result, after the successful execution of an LUW, the tRFC client should call the RFC API function `RfcConfirmTransID`. The task of this function is to delete the administration data for the transaction from the R/3 System. The interface of the function is as follows:

Variable	Meaning
handle	Connection handle
tid	ID of the transaction for which the administration data is to be deleted from table ARFCRSTATE

Table 6.10 Interface of Function RfcConfirmTransID

We will now show how the above mentioned functions work together, using enhancements to program RFCCalculatorClient from Chapter 3. In the Compute function, the SAP function module is activated, depending on the calculation type selected. The statements for the addition are changed as follows:

```
RFC_RC Compute(RFC_HANDLE hConnection,
            RFC_ERROR_INFO_EX *ErrorInfo,
            int *piValue1, int *piValue2, int *piResult)
{
   RFC_RC rc = RFC_FAILURE;
   RFC_TID TID;
   static RFC_PARAMETER ImpParam[2],
                     ExpParam[3];
   static iBool iCreated = iFalse;
   char cOperation,
        *pException = NULL,
        FTid[] = "C:\\Private\\Bookproject\\Chapter\\"\
                 "Chapter6AdvTech\\Programs\\"\
                 "TRFCClient\\TestID.txt",
        *pDummy = NULL,
        cAnswer = ' ';
   FILE *pFTid = NULL;
   memset(TID, NULL, sizeof(RFC_TID));
   :
   _flushall();
   printf("%s\n", "Please enter the operation!");
/* Call SAP function*/
   switch(cOperation = (char)getchar()){
      case '+':{
         _flushall();
/* Determine the source of origin for the TID */
         printf("%s\n",
                "New TID or TID from the file");
         if((cAnswer = (char)toupper(getchar())) ==
```

```
                   'Y'){
/* Get new TID from SAP and save in file */
            if((rc = RfcCreateTransID(
                    hConnection, TID)) == RFC_OK){
/* Save new TID in file */
                pFTid = fopen(FTid, "w");
                fwrite(TID, strlen(TID), 1, pFTid);
                fclose(pFTid);
            }else{
                RfcLastErrorEx(ErrorInfo);
                break;
            }
/* Read TID from file */
        }else{
            pFTid = fopen(FTid, "r");
            fread(TID, sizeof(RFC_TID) - 1, 1, pFTid);
            fclose(pFTid);
            TID[24] = NULL;
        }
/* Activate the function */
        if((rc = RfcIndirectCallEx(hConnection,
                "Z_RFC_ADD", ExpParam, NULL, TID))
                == RFC_OK){
            printf("%s\n", "Confirm TID?");
            _flushall();
/* Check if TID must be confirmed and carry out
   confirmation */
            if((cAnswer =
                (char)toupper(getchar())) == 'Y')
                RfcConfirmTransID(hConnection, TID);
            _flushall();
/* Error occurred while executing the LUW =>
   Error message */
        }else{
            RfcLastErrorEx(ErrorInfo);
        }
        _flushall();
        break;
    }
```

Listing 6.9 Adjusting the Logic for the Addition to Execute a tRFC

As a result of the changes presented above, the following can be controlled in a tRFC client:

▶ Whether a new TID is to be created by the R/3 System for the transaction or whether an existing TID is to be used

▶ newly generated TID is stored in a file.

▶ Whether the successful execution of the TID has been confirmed with the SAP system

We will also activate an RFC trace (Transaction ST05) in the R/3 System for each RFC call to see if the function module Z_RFC_ADD has been executed.

For the first execution of the transaction, we let the R/3 System generate a new TID and execute it with this. As to whether the successful execution of the transaction should be confirmed in the R/3 System, the answer is no. Thus, in our file we have a TID that is already marked as successful in the R/3 System. If at the end we finally consider the content of the RFC trace, we can see, as expected, that the function module Z_RFC_ADD has been executed successfully (see Figure 6.10).

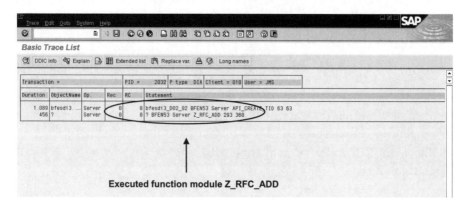

Figure 6.10 RFC Trace for a tRFC Client

We now execute a transactional RFC for the second time, but this time we use the TID that is located in the file. We don't create a new TID. If you look at the trace, you will see that the function module Z_RFC_ADD was not executed, which is also as we expected.

Of particular interest is that the function RfcIndirectCallEx also returns the value RFC_OK, although the function module was not executed. In this case, it would be more useful to have a return code that indicates that the TID is already recorded in the R/3 System as having executed successfully.

6.4   Queue RFCs

Queue RFCs represent an enhancement of the transaction concept in terms of serialization. The abbreviated name for a queue RFC call is qRFC.

The tRFC guarantees the appropriate administration of an individual LUW (updating all data together, status management, and so on). But it reaches its limits if several LUWs have to be sent to the recipient in a particular order. Let us assume, for example, that order header and item data are sent to the server in two separate transactions. It would not be very useful to send the order item data before the header data.

If the tRFC were used in this situation, this sequence could not be guaranteed. This is because every process executed by an LUW tries to send data to the recipient as soon as possible. The results of other tRFCs are not taken into account. Each tRFC is considered in isolation. Thus, in the scenario outlined above, it may happen that the tRFC with the order header data cannot be executed, but the order item data is sent without any problems. The recipient receives the item data before the header data and cannot process it. Consequently, in LUWs in which the different data contents depend on each other, you need to enhance the transaction concept in such a way that it guarantees that transactions with interdependent content are always sent to the recipient in a specific order.

One possibility for meeting this requirement is to form logical communication channels. In this case, transactions with interdependent content are assigned to the same communication channel and sent to the recipient in the order in which they are entered in the channel.

Figure 6.11 illustrates this principle. Reports 1 to 3 do not communicate directly with the server; rather they line up their LUW in the exit queue in qRFC management. The incoming LUWs are executed by qRFC management in sequence.

Before a transaction is sent to the recipient, the processing status of the transaction immediately before it is checked. If the previous transaction was executed successfully, the current transaction is sent; otherwise, it is not. In this way, the first transaction in a queue that is not executed successfully ends the processing of all subsequent transactions. Processing is continued only when the erroneous transaction has been sent successfully.

Logically, this serialization is sometimes useful. Before using the qRFC, however, you must be clear that, as a result of the queuing, the parallelism still possible with tRFC in certain circumstances is completely or partly waived. It is a good idea to balance the simply realized functionality and performance.

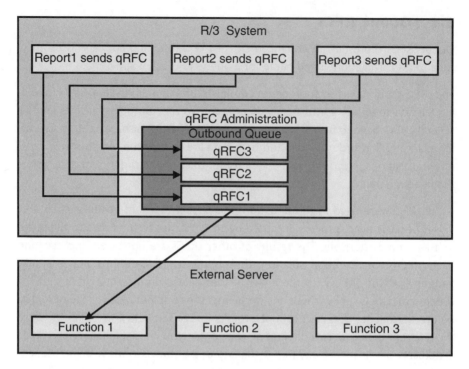

Figure 6.11 Principle of Queue RFC Calls

The concept of qRFC calls was first introduced by SAP with Release 4.6A. It is still, therefore, a relatively new concept that will be further developed in the future. In the next sections, we will take a closer look at these aspects of qRFC calls:

▶ Administration of qRFCs

▶ Development of a qRFC client in the R/3 System

▶ Development of an external qRFC client

6.4.1 Administration of qRFCs in the R/3 System

qRFC administration is a tool in the SAP system for managing the inbound and outbound queues. It is divided into two important areas. The first area involves the setting up and monitoring of outbound channels and is covered by the QOUT Scheduler. The second area involves the setting up and monitoring of inbound channels and is covered by the QIN Scheduler. The qRFC administration is started using Transaction SMQE.

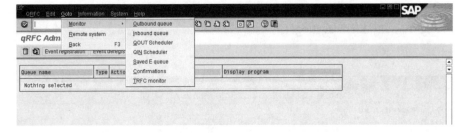

Figure 6.12 Initial Dialog of qRFC Administration

Open the menu **Goto · Monitor** (see Figure 6.12) to see a selection of functions that can be used to branch to the individual administration sub-areas.

We will take a closer look at the following sub-areas:

► Outbound queue

► Inbound queue

► QOUT Scheduler

► QIN Scheduler

The functions **QOUT Scheduler** and **QIN Scheduler** are used to branch to the administration of the outbound and inbound channels. The menu options **Outbound queue** and **Inbound queue** are used to branch to lists to display status and detailed information on the outbound and inbound queues in question. Here, you'll find information on the transactions in the corresponding queues that have not yet been processed.

The QOUT Scheduler

In the QOUT Scheduler, you determine ("register") which destination—previously created using Transaction SM59—is to be used for qRFC calls. These outbound queues are typically used if the SAP system wants to communicate with external servers.

Note that the destination itself is not an outbound queue. The outbound queue is created and assigned to a registered destination in the ABAP program that initiates the qRFC call. Internally, the program assigns a logical name for the outbound channel and concurrently executes the RFC calls that are assigned with the outbound channel (see the example of an ABAP-qRFC client in Listing 6.10).

The following functions are available for registering a destination in the QOUT Scheduler:

- ▶ Registration
- ▶ Register without activating
- ▶ Deregistration

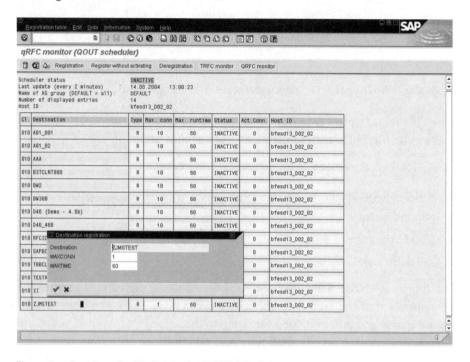

Figure 6.13 Register a Destination in the QOUT Scheduler

The first two functions are used to define the destinations to which the qRFC calls can be sent. The difference between the two functions is that in the second case the outbound channels assigned to the destination are not activated at the outset. Therefore, all qRFC calls to this destination will be saved in the outbound queue and not sent to the external server. The **Deregistration** function is used to deactivate an active destination so that the qRFC calls will no longer be forwarded to the external server. The **Registration** function can also be used to activate an inactive destination.

The **QRFC monitor** function branches to the list of outbound channels. Here you can get an overview of the transactions in the individual outbound queue that have not yet been processed successfully. With the **TRFC monitor** function, you can switch to an overview of the tRFC calls that have not yet been executed.

The **Registration** function can be executed in the QOUT Scheduler to register a destination for qRFC calls. In the maintenance dialog shown in Figure 6.13, you must enter the following information:

- Name of the destination to be registered
- In the field **MAXCONN,** the number of work processes that will be used to transfer the LUWs is specified
- The value in the **MAXTIME** field specifies how much time the QOUT Scheduler can allow for the LUWs in an outbound queue to be processed by the external server in one run. This limitation is to ensure that an individual queue does not spend too much time on processing.
- The **NO_TRFC** field (not shown in Figure 6.13) is an optional, undocumented parameter

If you position the cursor on a registered destination and execute the **QRFC monitor** function, you can branch to the overview of the outbound queue to which the destination is assigned (see Figure 6.14).

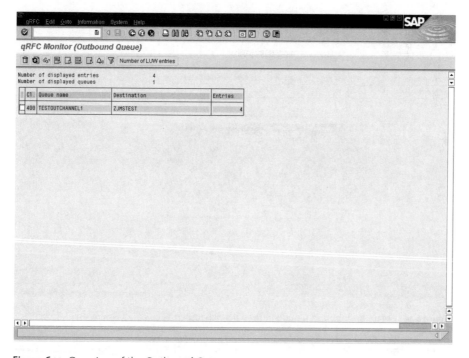

Figure 6.14 Overview of the Outbound Queue

You can see the number of transactions that have not yet been processed by the external server in the **Entries** column. You can also select an outbound queue and go to its detail view. There you can see the individual LUWs in the outbound queue.

The QIN Scheduler

If you select the **QIN Scheduler** function in qRFC Administration, you will branch to administration for the inbound channel. Inbound channels are used by external clients if they want to send qRFC calls to the R/3 System.

The following functions are also available in administration for managing an inbound queue (see Figure 6.15):

▶ Registration

▶ Register without activating

▶ Deregistration

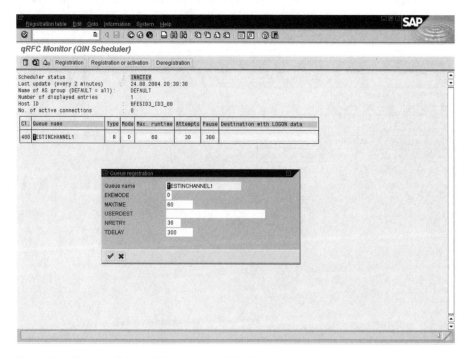

Figure 6.15 Create an Inbound Queue in the QIN Scheduler

They are the same as the functions in the QOUT Scheduler. If you select the **Registration** function, the maintenance dialog shown in Figure 6.15 for creating an inbound channel is displayed. Here you have to specify only the name of the inbound channel; all other fields will already be filled with the appropriate default values. Frequently, the execution type in the **EXEMODE** field is changed from Dialog (D) to Background (B) processing.

If you double-click on an inbound channel, the qRFC inbound screen is displayed. The registered inbound queues are displayed here in the form of a list, including their status information. The value in the **Entries** field is interesting: It lets you know how many as yet unprocessed transactions there are in an inbound queue. By double-clicking on an inbound channel, you can also view the transactions in it.

For further information on the qRFC Manager, see *http://help.sap.com*.

6.4.2 Developing a qRFC Client in the R/3 System

The development of a qRFC client in the R/3 System is very simple. Before calling the function to be executed remotely, you have to call only one function module. It is used to determine which outbound queue the tRFC calls are assigned to and that's it; a tRFC has just become a qRFC.

The R/3 System provides the following four function modules for assignment:

▶ `TRFC_SET_QUEUE_NAME`

▶ `TRFC_SET_QUEUE_LIST`

▶ `TRFC_SET_QUEUE_RECEIVER_LIST`

▶ `TRFC_QUEUE_INTIALIZE`

The function module `TRFC_SET_QUEUE_NAME` is used if all qRFC calls are assigned to the same outbound channel. It is the easiest to use and is also used in our example. The interface of the SAP function module `TRFC_SET_QUEUE_NAME` is as follows:

Parameter	Meaning
`QNAME`	Name of the outbound channel to which the qRFC calls are assigned
`NOSEND`	Indicates that the qRFC call should not be sent
`TRFC_IF_SYSFAIL`	Un-executed qRFCs are converted into a tRFC
`CALL_EVENT`	ID of an event that should be triggered after execution of the LUW in the R/3 System

Table 6.11 Interface of the Function Module TRFC_SET_QUEUE_NAME

Import parameters two to four are optional and both have the default value SPACE. You need to be careful if using the import parameter `TRFC_IF_SYSFAIL`. If it is assigned the value `X`, a qRFC call is converted into a normal tRFC call if it is not executed correctly. The result is that the outbound channel will no longer be blocked and all qRFC calls will be independent of the status of the one before them in the queue. This type of outbound channel should be used only to optimize performance. It is not possible to use it for serialization.

For a program to be able to send qRFC calls, it must contain the following program schema:

▶ Determining the name of the outbound queue—this is done, among other things, by executing the function module TRFC_SET_QUEUE_NAME

▶ Executing all RFC calls

▶ Closing the LUW with the statement COMMIT WORK

We will implement the program schema in our report ZCALLRFCCALCULATOR, so that it can send qRFC calls. We also want to test the qRFC Administration of the SAP system a little. For this, before creating a qRFC call, the user must decide whether the qRFC should be sent.

Consequently, the following elements are added to the report ZCALLRFCCALCULATOR:

▶ A loop that will continue until the user ends it with the function **Cancel** in a dialog box

▶ A dialog box to control program flow

▶ A call for the function module TRFC_SET_QUEUE_NAME

The dialog window provides the following functions for the user:

▶ **Send qRFC** causes qRFC administration of the R/3 System to try to execute the RFC call

▶ **Block qRFC** means that the qRFC is not sent, but is only queued in the corresponding outbound queue

▶ **Cancel** ends the loop and thus the report

The following program extract shows how these requirements are implemented in the report ZCALLRFCCALCULATOR.

```
   WHILE lp_answer <> gc_quit.
*  Check if new LUW must be created and if the new
*  LUW should be blocked
     CALL FUNCTION 'POPUP_TO_DECIDE'
          EXPORTING
*                DEFAULTOPTION     = '1'
                 textline1         = ' '
                 textline2         = ' '
```

```
*          TEXTLINE3          = ' '
           text_option1       = 'Send qRFC'
           text_option2       = 'Block qRFC'
           icon_text_option1 = 'ICON_OO_EVENT'
           icon_text_option2 = 'ICON_BREAKPOINT'
           titel              = 'Message'
*          START_COLUMN       = 25
*          START_ROW          = 6
*          CANCEL_DISPLAY     = 'X'
      IMPORTING
           answer             = lp_answer
           .
    CASE lp_answer.
      WHEN gc_send.
        CALL FUNCTION 'TRFC_SET_QUEUE_NAME'
            EXPORTING
                 qname              = 'TESTOUTCHANNEL1'
                 nosend             = ' '
*                 trfc_if_sysfail   = ' '
*                 call_event        = ' '
            EXCEPTIONS
                 invalid_queue_name = 1
                 OTHERS             = 2.
        IF sy-subrc <> 0.
           MESSAGE i208(00) with
                        'Unable to set Queue Name'.
             EXIT.
        ENDIF.
      WHEN gc_block.
        CALL FUNCTION 'TRFC_SET_QUEUE_NAME'
            EXPORTING
                 qname              = 'TESTOUTCHANNEL1'
                 nosend             = 'X'
*                 trfc_if_sysfail   = ' '
*                 call_event        = ' '
            EXCEPTIONS
                 invalid_queue_name = 1
                 OTHERS             = 2.
        IF sy-subrc <> 0.
           MESSAGE i208(00) with
```

```
                             'Unable to set Queue Name'.
              EXIT.
           ENDIF.
        ENDCASE.
        IF lp_answer <> gc_quit.
* Call the RFC function RFC_ADD
           CALL FUNCTION 'RFC_ADD' IN BACKGROUND TASK
                                    DESTINATION 'ZJMSTEST'
                 EXPORTING ip_value1 = pa_value1
                           ip_value2 = pa_value2
                              .
           COMMIT WORK.
        ENDIF.
     ENDWHILE.
```

Listing 6.10 R/3 qRFC Client

By modifying ZCALLRFCCALCULATOR, we can test the behavior of qRFC calls in a targeted way.

For the first attempt, the external server, which provides the function RFC_ADD, is not active. We implement the report ZCALLRFCCALCULATOR and will try to execute a couple of qRFC calls. As expected, nothing happens. All qRFC calls are queued in the outbound queue TESTOUTCHANNEL1. If you look at the content of the queue TESTOUTCHANNEL1 in the qRFC monitor, you will find all buffered RFC calls there. You may get the impression that the blocked qRFC calls are no different from tRFC calls, but this would be a mistake. To illustrate this, we will activate the program TRFCCALCULATOR. We will now try to execute a qRFC call from among the buffered qRFC calls. Nothing happens! This is, as explained, the decisive difference between a tRFC and a qRFC. The tRFC would execute the call without a problem because it is in no way dependent on other LUWs. The qRFC does allow for dependencies and executes the buffered calls in the sequence in which they entered the queue.

The second attempt should show that the sending of qRFC calls is interrupted once the execution of one qRFC call fails. Once again we execute the program ZCALLRFCCALCULATOR and activate the server TRFCCALCULATOR. In addition, the outbound queue TESTOUTCHANNEL1 must be initialized. If we select the **Send** function, the server confirms receipt of the LUWs in the message windows that were implemented in the functions for transaction control (see development of a tRFC server in Section 6.3.2). If we select the function **Block qRFC**, the server is silent because it has not received the LUW. If we then execute the function **Send**

qRFC again, however, the new transactions will not be sent to the server either—the server will not display a message window. This shows that once the first call in the channel fails, all qRFC calls for an outbound queue are blocked. In this case a tRFC would also behave differently. It would send the subsequent RFC calls.

The concept of the qRFC was presented as a 1:1 ratio between client and server because the development of this type of relationship is easier to implement. But the possibilities of the qRFC are not limited to a 1:1 relationship. Between client and server there can well be m:n relationships, whereby the performance of qRFCs can be improved. For example, a client can make requests to several servers. You should also consider the following observation: Practical experience shows that even qRFC with all the possibilities it offers does not relieve the developer of the duty to design distributed calls carefully.

6.4.3 Developing an External qRFC Client

Having seen the development of a qRFC client, we will now finally look at the development of an external qRFC client.

The RFC API provides the function `RfcQueueInsert` for this development. It replaces the function `RfcIndirectCallEx` which we saw when developing external tRFC clients. The functions `RfcCreateTransID` and `RfcConfirmTransID` can also be used here in the normal way. The interface of the function `RfcQueueInsert` is:

Variable	Meaning
`handle`	Connection handle
`function`	Name of the SAP function module to be executed
`exporting`	Array of type `RFC_PARAMETER` with a description of the technical properties of the export parameters
`tables`	Array of type `RFC_TABLE` with a description of the tables to be sent
`qname`	Name of the inbound queue to which the qRFC calls are to be assigned
`qcount`	Counter that can be used to determine the sequence for processing the LUWs At press time, the function has not yet been realized
`tid`	Transaction ID to which the LUW is assigned

Table 6.12 Interface of the Function RfcQueueInsert

To test a qRFC call from an SAP function module using an external client, we will execute the following steps:

- Create the inbound channel TESTINCHANNEL1 in the QIN Scheduler
- Copy the sources of the TRFCClient to a QRFCClient and replace the RFC API function RfcIndirectCallEx with the function RfcQueueInsert

Adjustments in the program QRFCClient are limited—as mentioned—to calling the function RfcQueueInsert in the function Compute. The modifications can be seen in the following listing:

```
switch(cOperation = (char)getchar()){
    case '+':{
/* Logic for creating the TID is identical to that
   of the program TRFCClient */
  :
/* Call the function RfcQueueInsert to execute
   a qRFC */
        if((rc = RfcQueueInsert(
                    hConnection, "Z_RFC_ADD",
                    ExpParam, NULL,
                    "TESTINCHANNEL1", 0, TID)) ==
              RFC_OK){
          printf("%s\n", "Confirm TID");
          _flushall();
          if((cAnswer = (char)toupper(getchar()))
                  == 'Y')
            RfcConfirmTransID(hConnection, TID);
          _flushall();
        }else{
          RfcLastErrorEx(ErrorInfo);
        }
        _flushall();
        break;
    }
```

Listing 6.11 Adjustments to the Compute Function for Executing a qRFC Call

The function RfcQueueInsert activates the inbound channel TESTINCHANNEL1 in the R/3 System. We are now in a position to send the qRFC calls to the R/3 System. The qRFC behavior is demonstrated with the following tests:

- Sending qRFC calls to an active inbound channel
- Sending qRFC calls to a registered but not active inbound channel

- Repeated sending of an LUW which has already been successfully executed in the R/3 System

- Sending several qRFC calls with the same TID to the same inbound channel in a program sequence

Furthermore, before executing each qRFC call, an RFC trace is activated in the R/3 System to determine whether the appropriate function modules were executed.

To execute the first scenario, we start the program QRFCClient and send a qRFC call as normal. After sending, the inbound queue TESTINCHANNEL1 in the qRFC Manager is empty. Even if the processing type has been changed from "Dialog" to "Batch processing" for the inbound channel, the inbound queue in a test system is usually empty because the load of work processes in this type of system is very low—and you are working on a test system, right? Doubts regarding the execution of the qRFC in the R/3 System can be dispelled using the RFC trace. The execution of the function module Z_RFC_ADD is recorded there.

For the second attempt, we will deactivate the inbound channel with the **Deregistration** function in the QIN Scheduler. We will then send some qRFC calls to the R/3 System again. If you look at the contents of TESTINCHANNEL1 now, you'll see our qRFC calls. At first glance, the result corresponds with our expectations. If we take a closer look at the inbound queue, however, we see that qRFC administration in the R/3 System works with its own TID allocation. The SAP internal TID cannot automatically be accessed by the client—for example using function RfcQueueInsert.

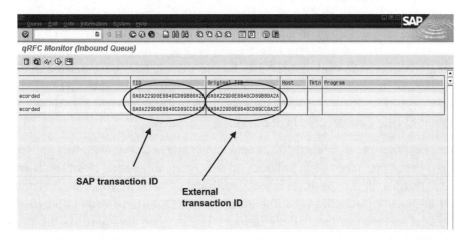

Figure 6.16 Assigning an External TID to SAP Internal TID in the Monitor for Inbound Queues

Figure 6.16 shows that the R/3 System always considers the TID of the client to be an external TID, even if the TID has previously been requested from the R/3 System using the function `RfcCreateTransID`. The client must therefore determine under which TID the R/3 System manages the LUW. Unfortunately, there is currently no easy option for this. The key of the table `TRFCQSTATE`, in which the SAP TID assignment for the TID of the external client is to be found, is the TID of the R/3 System, which the client still does not know. The only way for an external client to determine the SAP TID is to read all LUWs in the inbound queue `TESTINCHANNEL1` and then determine the SAP TID for its TID. The R/3 System provides the function module `TRFC_GET_QIN_ INFO_DETAILS` for this. The interface of the function module is as follows:

Parameter	Meaning
QNAME	Name of the inbound queue from which data is to be read
CLIENT	R/3 client
QDEEP	Return value—contains the number of LUWs in the QUEUE
QTABLE	Return table—contains detailed information on each LUW

Table 6.13 Interface of the Function Module TRFC_GET_QIN_INFO_DETAILS

The table `QTABLE` contains detailed information for each LUW in an inbound queue. It refers to the ABAP Dictionary structure `TRFCQIN`. The fields `ARFCIPID`, `ARFCPID`, `ARFCTIME`, and `ARFCTIDCNT` of the structure together form the TID of the R/3 System, while the TID of the external client is saved in field `ORGTID`. Therefore, an external client that wants to cooperate with the qRFC Manager must call the function module `TRFC_GET_QIN_INFO_DETAILS`, at the latest at the end of the send operation, to determine with which SAP TID its TID is linked. This is only practical, however, if the LUW has not yet been processed. If it has already been processed, the management data for the TID will have been deleted from the table so there is no way of determining the SAP TID for the external client. In our program `QRFCClient`, we deliberately waive use of this function because we do not have any administration of the TIDs in a database.

The consequences of internal TID assignment will be examined with two further tests. Let us first take a look at what happens when an external client sends an LUW that has already been successfully executed in the R/3 System but has not yet been confirmed. Given that the program `QRFCClient` is a copy of program `TRFCClient`, we can simulate the scenario. The program already stores the TID generated by the function `RfcCreateTransID` in a file. The contents of this file will be used if we do not determine a new TID using the function `RfcCreate-TransID`. In addition, `TESTINCHANNEL1` and an RFC trace are activated in the R/3 System. We now activate the function module `Z_RFC_ADD` in the R/3 System twice in succession with the same external TID. Before taking a look at the RFC trace, we recall that in a tRFC call, LUWs are not executed with the same TID if the TID already has the status FINISHED in the SAP system.

If we look now at the RFC trace, we see that the function module Z_RFC_ADD is executed with every call. This is due to the internal allocation of TIDs by qRFC administration in the R/3 System. It automatically assigns a TID for each qRFC call. The status of an LUW is thus no longer checked automatically before it is executed. The concept of status checking is based on the fact that the R/3 System wants to execute the LUW with the TID that the external client sends and not with a self-generated TID. With qRFC calls, the external client is thus solely responsible for ensuring that an LUW is not executed twice. It is no longer assisted by the R/3 System.

Finally we will look at the consequences of internal TID assignment by the R/3 System for two successive qRFC calls. For this, the following addition is made in the program QRFCClient:

```
if((rc = RfcQueueInsert(
              hConnection, "Z_RFC_ADD",
              ExpParam, NULL,
              "TESTINCHANNEL1", 0, TID)) ==
      RFC_OK){
        rc = RfcQueueInsert(
              hConnection, "Z_RFC_SUB",
              ExpParam, NULL,
              "TESTINCHANNEL1", 0, TID)
```

After the first qRFC call comes another with the same TID as the first. We remember that this was not allowed for a tRFC call. We deactivate the TESTINCHANNEL1 in the QIN Scheduler and execute the program QRFCClient. If you look at the content of the inbound queue TESTINCHANNEL1 after execution of the program, you will notice that it contains both the call for the function module Z_RFC_ADD and the call for the function module Z_RFC_SUB, and two different SAP internal TIDs have been assigned to the external TID (see Figure 6.17).

If the inbound queue TESTINCHANNEL1 is activated again, both LUWs are executed. Another consequence of the fact that two SAP internal TIDs are assigned to the external TID is that an external customer, which must align its TID management with that of the SAP system, must also analyze the field QRFCNAM in the return table QTABLE of function module TRFC_GET_QIN_INFO_DETAILS. The function module to be executed is stored in this field.

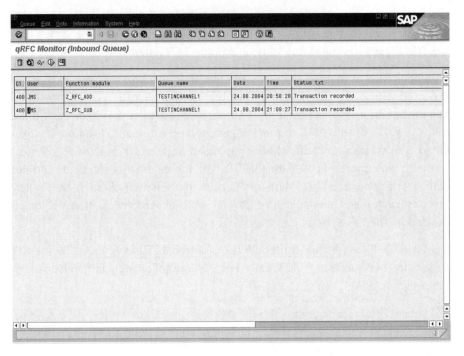

Figure 6.17 Inbound Queue TESTINCHANNEL1 for Two Transactions Sent One after the Other

6.4.4 tRFC and qRFC Calls—Conclusion

To conclude, the concept for transactional and queue RFC calls is very successful in both cases. The qRFC model offers numerous new possibilities for distribution, which cannot be fully described within the scope of this book. For further information we advise you to check out SAP documentation at *http://help.sap.com*.

The implementation is also successful in both tRFC and qRFC—provided, that is, that the R/3 System is the client. For external clients, it would be nice

▶ If an external client could also activate several function modules in an LUW

▶ If—for qRFC calls—the R/3 System used the TID of the external client and not a new SAP-internal TID for the LUW. This would reestablish the unique nature of the TID.

You are also warned against an indiscriminate distribution of qRFC calls: A—usually accidental—serialization can lead to considerable losses in performance. Experience with this new API is necessary in this case.

6.5 Error Messages from an External Server

Up to now, we have intentionally not discussed how an external server can notify the R/3 client of errors. Now, we'll turn to that subject.

Errors can be divided into two different types:

▶ Logical errors
▶ System errors

Logical errors are caused by the fact that the external server cannot process data because there is something missing from the content. One example would be a production order for pre-cut parts in which the information on the measurements is missing.

System errors, on the other hand, are errors in communication between the R/3 System and the server. For example, data could not be sent to the server, and so on.

The difference between the two types of errors lies in the fact that the logical errors affect communication between only one server and one R/3 client. As soon as the client sends correct data, the error is eliminated. System errors, on the other hand, affect the communication between all R/3 clients and the external server. In the event of a system error, the connection handle is invalidated, so the server cannot receive any more requests from an R/3 system. If, for example, the function RfcWaitForRequest is executed with an invalid connection handle, the function returns with the error message RFC_INVALID_HANDLE. System errors can usually be eliminated only by the intervention of a third party, which then, for example, checks the connection between the servers.

Furthermore, when errors are sent, it is also necessary to distinguish what type of server sent the error.

▶ Synchronous server
▶ Transactional server or qRFC server

These different error situations require different forms of feedback from the server to the client.

6.5.1 Error Messages from a Synchronous Server

A synchronous server can send both logical errors and system errors. Both error types will be presented in this section. We will also show how you can implement your own error handling for logical errors.

Sending Logical Errors

Because a logical error affects only one R/3 client, the following must be assured:

▶ The R/3 client must be informed of the error

▶ The connection handle must stay valid so that other R/3 clients are not affected by the error

There are two alternatives for realizing these requirements:

▶ The standard functions of the RFC API

▶ Self-programmed error handling

These requirements are complied with using the function RfcRaise, among other things. It triggers a short dump in the R/3 system, but leaves the connection intact. The interface of the function is as follows:

Variable	Meaning
handle	Connection handle
exception	String from the exception to be sent

Table 6.14 Interface of the Function RfcRaise

We will now think back to the beginning of the chapter. There we introduced the function RFC_DIV in the pocket calculator. The implementation was done in such a way that the function module Z_RFC_GET_NEW_DIVISOR is called in the R/3 System if the R/3 client sends a divisor with the value zero. Instead of asking the user to enter a new divisor, it would also have been possible to simply send an error message informing the user of the invalid situation. The modified implementation of the function RFC_DIV would then look like this:

```
RFC_RC DLL_CALL_BACK_FUNCTION RFC_DIV(
                        RFC_HANDLE hConnection)
{
   RFC_ERROR_INFO_EX ErrorInfo;
   :
   if(ivalue2 == 0){
/*
 Divisor = 0 => Send exception to the R/3 client
*/
      if((rc = RfcRaise(hConnection,
            "ERROR_DIVISION_BY_ZERO"))
          != RFC_OK){
```

```
              RfcLastErrorEx(&ErrorInfo);
              printf("%s\n", ErrorInfo.message);
              return rc;
          }else
              return rc;
/* Divisor <> 0 => Execute division */
      }else{
          iResult = iValue1 / iValue2;
          if((rc = RfcSendData(hConnection, ExpParam,
                               NULL)) != RFC_OK){
              RfcLastErrorEx(&ErrorInfo);
              printf("%s\n", ErrorInfo.message);
              return rc;
          }else
              return rc;
      }
}
```

Listing 6.12 Alternative Implementation for Function RFC_DIV

In the variant presented above, the exception ERROR_DIVISION_BY_ZERO is sent to the R/3 client. Note that the function RfcRaise returns the value RFC_OK after the exception has been sent successfully so that the message loop that checks whether the return value of the function RfcDispatch is RFC_OK, can continue.

In addition to the function RfcRaise, the functions RfcRaiseTable and RfcRaiseErrorMessage are also available for sending an exception to the R/3 client. The interface of the function RfcRaiseTable is:

Variable	Meaning
handle	Connection handle
exception	String with the exception to be sent
tables	Array of type RFC_TABLE that contains the description of the imported tables

Table 6.15 Interface of the Function RfcRaiseTable

To send an additional explanatory text with an exception, you have to use the function RfcRaiseErrorMessage. A text to explain the exception can also be transferred to the interface of the function. The interface of the function RfcRaiseErrorMessage is:

Variable	Meaning
`handle`	Connection handle
`exception`	String with the exception to be sent
`tables`	Array of type `RFC_TABLE` that contains the description of the imported tables
`szErrorMsg`	String with an explanation for the error The string can be up to 200 characters long.

Table 6.16 Interface of the Function RfcRaiseErrorMessage

The short dumps generated by the functions can be viewed in the ABAP dump analysis (Transaction ST22).

Use of the functions `RfcRaiseTable` and `RfcRaiseErrorMessage` is indicated if the R/3 client sends tables to the external server. In contrast to the function `RfcRaise`, the functions `RfcRaiseTable` and `RfcRaiseErrorMessage` release memory space occupied by a table parameter, thus helping to avoid memory leaks. As it is also possible to transfer the value `NULL` for the interface variable `tables` to the functions `RfcRaiseTable` and `RfcRaiseErrorMessage`, it is usually not necessary to use the function `RfcRaise`.

Self-Programmed Error Handling for Logical Errors

The standard functions of the RFC API have the disadvantage that they are not really adequate for processing mass data. Imagine, for example, that the R/3 client wants to send assorted order header data, of which n data records are incorrect. Using the functions of the RFC API, the server would send an exception as soon as it discovered the first erroneous data record. The user would correct the erroneous data record and send the data again. The server would start the check again and send an exception for the next erroneous data record. This procedure is time-consuming and not very effective.

A handier alternative would be if a complete check were run on all data records sent by the R/3 client and—if errors are found—the user were informed of all erroneous data records, so that they could then be corrected. Unfortunately, SAP does not offer any functions for implementing this workaround. The developer has to implement it alone. It is very easy though: It is often sufficient if the server also sends a table with status information back to the R/3 client. The server first checks all data records sent from the R/3 System and writes an entry in the status table for erroneous data records. If errors are found in any of the data records, none will be processed. Instead, the table with the status information is transferred to the client. The report analyzes the table and presents its content.

Sending System Errors

An external server does not usually signal system errors itself. In such an event, the return value of the functions `RfcGetData` or `RfcSendData` would inform an external server that an error occurred in the communication with the R/3 System. The return value of the functions mentioned would be `RFC_SYS_EXCEPTION`. The callback function in the server returns the value to the function `RfcDispatch`, and the latter closes the connection. If the message loop is structured in such a way that it checks the return value of the function `RfcDispatch`, if the value is `RFC_OK` and the loop continues, the running program will also be terminated. You should therefore ensure that a message loop is structured in accordance with the suggestions in Chapters 3 and 4.

6.5.2 Error Messages from the tRFC and qRFC Servers

At the beginning of this section, we differentiated between logic and system errors and saw that a synchronous server can send both types of error. Transactional servers have one limitation in this respect: They can send only system errors. If a function is executed to send logical errors in a transactional server, the logical error is reinterpreted as a system error and the connection handle is deemed to be invalid.

This behavior, rare at first glance, is only rational. In Section 6.3.2 we explained that the callback function of a transactional server cannot return a value to the R/3 client because the program context in which the RFC call was initiated no longer exists. This concept can be extended to logical errors. They can also be realistically evaluated only by the initiator of an RFC call. Given that the context of the initiator of the tRFC call can no longer exist after the execution, callback functions in a tRFC server cannot send any logical exceptions.

This behavior is consistent, but it presents a problem: How can logical errors be sent to the R/3 client using a tRFC server? Finally, in the case of logical errors it is not very helpful to send a system error so that other tRFC calls are not executed either. The idea of callback functions in the client would also be of help here. One solution is based on the idea that when logical errors occur, the server activates a function module in the R/3 client system and transfers the erroneous data records to it. Within the function module, the data records are updated in a database table. To implement this solution, the following components are added to tRFC servers:

- ▶ A function module in the R/3 System that is controlled by the server and to which all erroneous data records are transferred if the R/3 client sends erroneous data
- ▶ A function to execute a separate logon to the R/3 System
- ▶ A database table for recording the error information
- ▶ An interactive report for evaluating the content of the error table

The development of a function module in the R/3 System to which the error information is sent is plausible. But why is it necessary to log on to the R/3 System a second time? Within a tRFC call, only data can be sent to the server. The R/3 System realizes that the current connection is used for executing a tRFC call and does not allow for the fact that the connection handle is used to send data to the client. Calling the functions `RfcCallReceiveEx` and `RfcCallEx` therefore has no effect. Particularly annoying is the fact that when the connection handle of a tRFC is transferred to the function `RfcCallEx`, the return value of this function is `RFC_OK`. This normally indicates that the SAP function module was activated successfully, but in this instance that is not the case: The function module could not be executed.

When implementing the solution, you should note that we can no longer activate the updating of data—for example, on the database—using the function `RfcOnCommitEx`. Remember that execution of the function takes place once the callback function in the server returns the value `RFC_OK`. Because the concept of tRFC and qRFC calls does not provide for logical errors, the callback function must always return the value `RFC_OK` for logical errors, too; otherwise, the connection with the R/3 System will be terminated. As a result, a global variable is also defined in the server. Its value is set in the callback function and is checked in the function. If its value is `RFC_OK`, this means that no logical error occurred and the data can be updated to the database. Otherwise, the data is not updated. The concept also requires that a user check the error table in the R/3 System regularly and try to process erroneous data records again.

Figure 6.18 shows the main principle of the suggestion presented above for implementing logical errors in a transactional RFC.

The function module that is activated by the external server should do the following:

- ▶ Save the data records in the error table
- ▶ Send a message to the SAP Office inbox of the person who sent the data. This step is necessary to inform the user of errors.

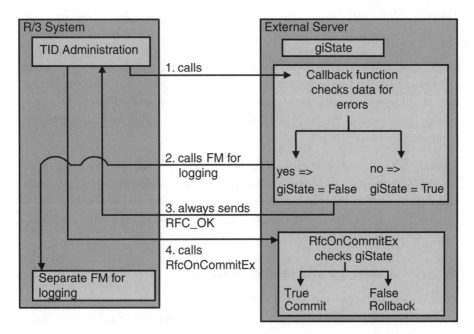

Figure 6.18 Principle of Customer-Developed Handling of Logical Errors in tRFC Servers

To send a message to the user's SAP office inbox, you use the function module SO_DOCUMENT_SEND_API1. There is very good documentation on this in the R/3 System, so we shall not explain it further here.

The interactive report for evaluating the status table is not really necessary (it is still possible to view the content of the table in the Data Browser), but not every user is familiar with the Data Browser or is authorized to use it. Moreover, an interactive report offers the option of implementing additional functions so that erroneous data records can be corrected directly from the report.

These descriptions show you that extending a tRFC server with respect to the sending of logical errors is very laborious, so before implementation you should examine the possibility of using a synchronous server instead, since it can handle logical errors. The direct use of the IDoc/ALE interface from SAP could also be considered, as it offers workflow functions in addition to error handling.

6.6 Parallel Processing

Almost all modern server applications today are—mainly for reasons of performance—faced with the question of possible parallel processing. This is also the case with RFC programming. Parallel processing in the server allows for queries from several SAP clients to be handled simultaneously. This helps to avoid the situation where a query with a particularly high processing time blocks all other queries. Parallel processing is thus one option for eliminating bottlenecks.

In this chapter, we will describe parallel processing only for the Windows operating systems 98, NT4.0, and 2000. The use of threads and other tools for parallelization is system-specific, so a detailed treatment of other systems would go beyond the scope of this book. We will provide some additional information for Linux only.

In dealing with parallel processing, we will look only at the functions of the WIN32 API. The MFC classes are not presented because they primarily encapsulate only the functions of the WIN32 API. For complete documentation on the functions used, see, for example, the MSDN library distributed with the various Microsoft Development Studios.

6.6.1　Multitasking and Multithreading

Most developers will have encountered the terms "multitasking," "multithreading," or "parallel processing" at some stage—and perhaps forgotten them just as quickly, if they don't have much contact with the topic. For the next section, it is important to understand these concepts, so we shall explain them briefly.

When we start a program, we generate an *instance* of the program. The running instance of a program is also called a *process*. Multitasking is an operating system's ability to process or handle several processes (also called *tasks* in some operating systems) at the same time. Multitasking is therefore a prerequisite for parallel processing.

Here, we must differentiate between true parallel processing and "concurrent" processing. As each processor can only handle one process at a given moment, true parallel processing is possible only on machines with multiple processors. On a multiprocessor machine, two processes can run at the same time on different processors. One requirement for using multiprocessor systems, however, is that the operating system support this. All large Unix systems fall into this category. In the case of Microsoft operating systems, Windows NT 4.0, 2000, or XP are suitable, for example.

On single-processor machines, however, we speak of concurrent processing. In this case, each process—in the majority of modern operating systems—is allocated a particular length of time on the processor. As soon as its time is up, it is deactivated and another process is allotted time. This ensures that all processes are allocated some server time. Changing from one process to another is referred to as *process* or *context change*. When a process is blocked, we also sometimes say that the process is *suspended*.

In relation to multitasking, a distinction is also sometimes made between *cooperative* and *preemptive* operating systems.

With a cooperative operating system, the running process must release the processor itself. The process is not interrupted by the operating system. In some cases, this means that a program that requires a high processor effort can hold up an entire server because no other processes can get any processing time.

Preemptive operating systems, on the other hand, block the running process themselves, so that the server will not be brought to a standstill because of one program.

Multithreading is the extension of parallel processing to the sub-process level. One classic example of this is the printing of texts in Word. While the text is being printed, the user can work on another text. Multithreading is thus the ability of a program to execute several sub-tasks at the same time. An important prerequisite for the efficient use of multithreading is that sub-tasks can actually be executed in parallel and will not be serialized.

With multithreading we also differentiate between real and concurrent parallel processing. Multithreading can offer great advantages of time with true parallel processing. With concurrent processing, on the other hand, intensive multi-threading may have a negative effect on runtime if the administration of multiple threads takes up a lot of processor capacity itself.

Usually, multithreading is an advantage on single-processor machines only if individual threads have very long wait times. In such cases, parallel processing allows for better use of system resources.

6.6.2 Creating and Exiting Threads

With Windows, threads are created using the function `CreateThread`. The interface of the function is as follows:

Variable	Meaning
lpThreadAttributes	Determines security attributes and inheritance characteristics. As a rule, it is sufficient to transfer the value NULL here because in that case Windows initializes the thread with default settings.
dwStackSize	Initial size of the stack for the thread
LpStartAddress	Address of the function that should execute the thread
lpParameter	Pointer to a variable that can read and change the thread

Table 6.17 Interface of the Function CreateThread

Variable	Meaning
dwCreationFlags	Properties with which the thread is created. This usually controls whether the thread is executed immediately or first blocked (see flag CREATE_SUSPENDED).
lpThreadID	Identifier for the thread
HANDLE	Return type of the function CreateThread; handle of the thread created

Table 6.17 Interface of the Function CreateThread (cont.)

The most important variable of the function CreateThread is lpStartAddress, because the address of the function that should be executed by the thread is transferred to this variable. The thread function must be of the following type:

```
DWORD WINAPI ThreadProc( LPVOID lpParameter )
```

The variable lpParameter contains the pointer to the data that is transferred to the thread via the variable lpParameter of the function CreateThread.

As a rule, threads are suspended when creating (the CREATE_SUSPENDED flag is set). The internal counter, called the *suspend count*, controls whether a thread is blocked or can be executed. If the suspend count has the value zero, the thread is no longer blocked and can be executed. If the suspend count has a value greater than zero, the thread is blocked and is not executed. Using this concept, it is possible to control a thread dependent on several conditions. The following functions increase or decrease the suspend count of a thread by one:

```
DWORD ResumeThread( HANDLE hThread )
DWORD SuspendThread( HANDLE hThread )
```

Both functions receive the handle to the thread for which the suspend count is to be changed as an argument. If execution is successful, both return the previous value of the suspend count.

The execution of a thread can be terminated by the following functions:

```
VOID ExitThread( DWORD dwExitCode )
BOOL TerminateThread( HANDLE  hThread, DWORD  dwExitCode )
```

It is recommended that you should end a thread with the function ExitThread. It is either called explicitly within the thread function or implicitly as soon as the thread function is terminated with the statement return. A value is transferred to the variable dwExitCode, via which the thread can return status information.

A thread can be terminated from outside using the function `TerminateThread`. This function should only be used in exceptional cases, however, if there is no other way of terminating the execution of a thread. Its execution can be somewhat problematic. You will find further information on this in Microsoft documentation.

With Linux, the analogous functions of the so-called *POSIX Threads* are usually used for creating and managing threads. A thread is then created using the `pthread_create()` function. Among other things, the function to be executed and its arguments are also transferred to this function. A thread can be exited using `pthread_exit()`. You can cancel another thread using `pthread_cancel()`.

6.6.3 The Basics of Synchronization

In every system where several players run in "parallel," the players must be coordinated. This is true for processes, to a certain extent, but even more so for threads. One reason for this is that threads frequently use a lot of shared data, to which access must be synchronized.

We will demonstrate how to do this using a very simple example. Let us assume that we have three threads. The task of thread A is to display data records that are selected by threads B and C. So, thread A can work properly only if threads B and C have selected their data records. It would seem appropriate to solve the problem in accordance with the following listing:

```
bool bThreadBReady = false,
     bThreadCReady = false;
DWORD WINAPI BReadRS( LPVOID lpParameter )
{
/* Select data records */
   :
/* When the data records have been selected, set global variable
   for the completion message to true */
   bThreadBReady = true;
}
DWORD WINAPI CReadRS ( LPVOID lpParameter )
{
/* Select data records */
   :
/* When data records have been selected, set global variable
   for the completion message to true */
```

```
    bThreadCReady = true;
}
int main (int argc, char** argv)
{
    RFC_RC rc = RFC_OK;
    :
/* Check if thread B and C have finished their
   data selection */
    while(!bThreadBReady || !bThreadCReady){};
/* display selected data records */
    :
    return rc;
},
```

Listing 6.13 Example of Explicit Serialization

In the solution outlined above, in the main() function the output of the data records is delayed until the variables bThreadBReady and bThreadCReady have the value true. This solution generally works faultlessly, though it does have disadvantages. Of all the possible solutions, for example, it is the one that creates the greatest processing load and thus has a negative effect on the system response performance. This is because thread A permanently checks the value of two global variables, which means that the operating system has to switch frequently between threads.

A better solution would be one that could act as a gate-keeper. In this mode of operation, a gate-keeper guards a gate. Elements try to get through the gate. If the gate-keeper closes the gate, the elements must wait. If the gate is opened, they can get through. This concept offers the advantage that the elements are automatically informed by the gate-keeper when they can go through the gate, and do not have to constantly ask if they may get through. While the gate is closed, the elements are passive.

Synchronization follows this concept: The gate-keeper is replaced by a synchronization object and our threads take the place of the elements. The synchronization object controls how threads can access a program section by regulating the number of threads that can reside in the program section. To inform a thread that it can enter a section, the synchronization object changes to "signaled" state, and to deny the thread access, the state changes to "non-signaled."

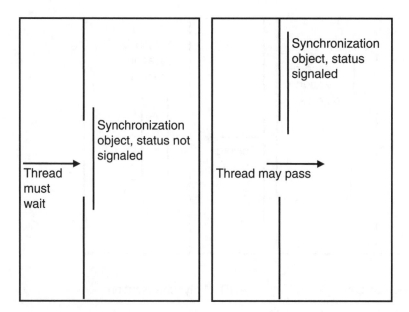

Figure 6.19 1:1 Synchronization

The following synchronization types are differentiated according to the number or threads and synchronization objects involved:

▶ **1:1 synchronization**
A thread waits until one synchronization object switches to the status "signaled" (see Figure 6.19).

▶ **m:1 synchronization**
The thread is blocked until one of m synchronization objects switches to the status "signaled."

▶ **AND$_m$:1 synchronization**
The thread waits until all m synchronization objects have switched to the status "signaled."

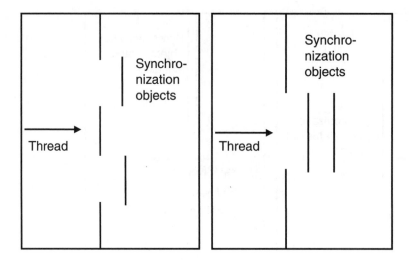

m:1 Synchronization   ANDm:1 Synchronization

Figure 6.20 m:1 and ANDm:1 Synchronization

Figure 6.20 shows that m:1 synchronization can be compared to parallel switching and ANDm:1 synchronization can be compared with series switching.

With 1:n synchronization, n threads wait until one synchronization object switches to the status "signaled." When this happens, all threads are unlocked.

Finally, we are left with just m:n, and ANDm:n synchronization. With these types, n threads are blocked until one of or all m synchronization objects switch to the status "signaled."

Figuratively, you can imagine that 1:n, m:n, and ANDm:n synchronization are like 1:1, m:1, and ANDm:1 synchronization, except that the number of threads involved is greater than one.

A thread must inform the operating system which objects it wants to synchronize with. It can do this in a Windows operating system by calling the following two functions:

▶ `WaitForSingleObject`
▶ `WaitForMultipleObjects`

The function `WaitForSingleObject` is used if the thread wants to be synchronized with one object. The interface of the function is as follows:

Variable	Meaning
hHandle	Handle for the synchronization object
dwMilliseconds	Time interval that determines the maximum time a thread should wait for the synchronization object to switch to the status "signaled." The value INFINITE has the effect that the thread will wait as long as necessary for the object to switch to the "signaled" state.

Table 6.18 Interface of the Function WaitForSingleObject

The return value indicates the status of the object. The following values are possible, among others: WAIT_OBJECT_0, WAIT_TIMEOUT, and WAIT_FAILED. The first value indicates that the object already had the status "signaled." The second value is returned if the object did not switch to the state "signaled" in the allowed time interval. The third value indicates an error; for example, the object no longer exists.

For synchronization with multiple objects, the function WaitForMultipleObjects is required. The interface of the function is as follows:

Variable	Meaning
nCount	Number of synchronization objects
lpHandles	Array with the handles of the synchronization objects
fWaitAll	Determine whether it is necessary to wait until all synchronization objects switch to "signaled" state or not ($AND_{m:1}$ or m:1 synchronization)
dwMilliseconds	Time interval that determines the maximum time the thread should wait for the event. The value INFINITE has the effect that the thread waits as long as necessary for the objects to switch to the "signaled" state.

Table 6.19 Interface of the Function WaitForMultipleObjects

From the return value of the function we can see, among other things, whether any synchronization object has switched to "signaled" state and if so, which. If the variable fWaitAll is set to TRUE, for example, the return value WAIT_OBJECT_0 indicates that all synchronization objects have been found with state "signaled." If the value of the variable were FALSE, the index of the first synchronization object to switch to the state "signaled" is returned.

6.6.4 Synchronization Objects

You have just read that synchronization objects are usually used for the synchronization of threads. We will now take a closer look at two synchronization objects:

▶ Events

▶ Critical sections

Events

Events are the simplest type of synchronization. An event has the two states "signaled" and "non-signaled." Threads synchronize with events in such a way that they always wait until the event switches to the "signaled" state.

We can differentiate between manual reset events and auto reset events. The difference between the two is that an auto reset event is automatically switched to "non-signaled" state as soon as it has released a thread. A manual reset event, on the other hand, waits in "signaled" state until the state is explicitly set to "non-signaled" by a call of the function `ResetEvent`. An auto reset event can thus always unlock only one thread, and a manual reset event can unlock any number of threads.

The following functions are required for managing events:

▶ `CreateEvent`

▶ `SetEvent`

▶ `ResetEvent`

▶ `CloseHandle`

The `CreateEvent` function creates an event. The interface of the function is as follows:

Variable	Meaning
`lpEventAttributes`	Attributes of the event: If the value `NULL` is transferred, Windows sets the default properties
`bManualReset`	Determines whether the reset event is manual or automatic
`bInitialState`	Controls whether the event is in the "signaled" or "non-signaled" state The value `TRUE` sets the "signaled" state
`lpName`	Name of the event If `NULL` is given, an event with no name is created

Table 6.20 Interface of the Function CreateEvent

If execution is successful, the function returns the handle for the event.

The functions `SetEvent`, `ResetEvent`, and `PulseEvent` change the state of an event. All three functions need the handle for the event of which the state is to be changed.

The state of an event is set at "signaled" by the `SetEvent` function.

The `ResetEvent` function sets the state of an event to "non-signaled." The function is needed only for manual reset events because they are not automatically set to the state "non-signaled."

The `CloseHandle` function closes the event. After this function has been called, the event is invalid and can no longer be used. To avoid "starvation" of threads or deadlocks, all threads waiting for an event should be unlocked before the event is closed.

Critical Sections

By critical section, we mean a program section in which there should be only one thread at a given point in time. The synchronization object of the same name under Windows ensures that this condition for a program section is adhered to. Other threads that also want to enter the critical section will be blocked until the section is free again. Critical sections are usually set if threads have read or write access to shared variables, as this guarantees that only *one* thread gets read or write access to the shared variable at any one time.

The following functions are available for managing critical sections

▶ `InitializeCriticalSection`
▶ `DeleteCriticalSection`

A critical section is a structure variable of type `CRITICAL_SECTION`. The structure variable must be initialized before it can be used. For this we use the function `InitializeCriticalSection`. It contains the reference to the structure that should be initialized.

The function `DeleteCriticalSection` releases all resources that were occupied by a critical section. Once it has been deleted, the critical section can no longer be used.

A thread occupies a critical section with the functions `EnterCriticalSection` and `TryEnterCriticalSection` and releases it again using the function `LeaveCriticalSection`.

Each function contains the critical section to be occupied or released as its argument.

The difference between the functions `EnterCriticalSection` and `TryEnter-CriticalSection` is that the first one blocks the thread until the critical section is free, whereas the `TryEnterCriticalSection` function only checks whether the critical section is free. If it is not free, the thread is not blocked and can execute other tasks until the critical section is free.

A thread exits a critical section with the function `LeaveCriticalSection`.[2]

With this background information on parallel processing, we can effectively use threads in RFC programming.

6.6.5 Advantages of Parallel Processing in RFC Programming

One reason parallel processing could be used in RFC programming is that it makes it possible to process multiple requests from R/3 clients in an external server at the same time.

To illustrate this, we will change the callback function RFC_ADD of the pocket calculator from Chapter 3. The result is the program `RFCCalculatorWDelay` (you will find it on the Web site for this book at *www.sap-press.com*). The `Sleep` function is called between the calculation and the return of the result. Under Windows, this function delays the execution of a thread for n milliseconds. Moreover, the import parameter `IP_DELAY` is included in the description of the interface to the R/3 System. Thanks to the parameter `IP_DELAY`, it is possible to control the length of the delay from the SAP system. The implementation of these enhancements in the server looks like this:

```
int iDelay = 0;
:
ImpParam[2] = BuildSimpleParam("IP_DELAY", TYPINT,
                              sizeof(RFC_INT), &iDelay);
:
RfcGetData(hConnection, ImpParam, NULL);
:
/* Stop the execution of the thread for n milliseconds */
Sleep(iDelay);
```

To transfer the time interval to the external server, we add the variable PA_DELAY to the report ZCALLRFCCALCULATOR. The variable is declared using the PARAME-

---

2 The corresponding constructions in a Linux-based system are the `Mutexe` and what are known as *Condition variables*.

TERS statement so that it is displayed on the selection screen. In addition, the variable PA_DELAY must be added to the call for the function RFC_ADD. This can be programmed as shown below:

```
PARAMETERS:  pa_delay TYPE i DEFAULT 30.
:
START-OF-SELECTION.
:
*Convert seconds to milliseconds, because the function
*Sleep expects milliseconds
pa_delay = pa_delay * 1000.
* Call the function RFC_ADD
CALL FUNCTION 'RFC_ADD' DESTINATION 'ZJMSTEST'
       EXPORTING ip_value1 = pa_value1
                 ip_value2 = pa_value2
                 ip_delay  = pa_delay
       IMPORTING ep_result = lp_result.
```

Before executing the modified programs, we once again recall how a request is processed in an external server. The function RfcDispatch receives the message and calls the callback function. Only after the current request has been processed by this function can the external server process another request. We will now delay execution of the callback function by n milliseconds. We will then observe what happens if we use first one, then two SAP clients.

We start the server and then request it to add two values using—at first—one SAP client. A value of 30 seconds is given for the time delay. As expected, the return of the result to the SAP system is now delayed by 30 seconds.

Next, we repeat this call with two SAP clients: A second session can be used in the SAP system for this. In the first session we once again set a value of 30 seconds for the delay in the program ZCALLRFCCALCULATOR. In the second session, however, we set a value of zero seconds for the delay. We start the call with the delay of 30 seconds first, then the call with the zero-second delay.

The program run shows that the first SAP client once again blocks itself for 30 seconds. But it also simultaneously blocks the second client for 30 seconds. The reason the second client is blocked is that because of the delayed execution of the callback function in the first SAP client, the message loop is also blocked so no new requests from SAP clients can be processed until the first client has finished.

This behavior complies with our expectations. Nevertheless, the result is not satisfactory because an SAP client with high processing time blocks the server for all other clients. You can defuse this problem by asking users to spread their requests evenly. However, in practice this rarely works. It is therefore better if the server can process several requests at the same time. Below, we explain how to do this for an external server.

6.6.6 Implementing Parallel Processing in External Servers

For an external server that is to be started with parallel processing, two questions arise:

1. What should the work function of the threads look like?

2. How are the threads to be synchronized?

The purpose of our thread function should be to eliminate a bottleneck. The bottleneck would be a situation in which the server can process only one message at a time, with all other requests blocked until the processing of the current request is complete. If we now swap the message loop out to a thread function, it will be available multiple times. In this way, several requests can be processed at the same time. Thus, for our purposes, the message loop should be in the thread function. The thread function is implemented as follows:

```
DWORD __stdcall MessageLoop(void *phEvent)
{
    RFC_RC rc = RFC_OK;
    RFC_ERROR_INFO_EX ErrorInfo;
    RFC_HANDLE hConnection = RFC_HANDLE_NULL;
    HANDLE hEvent = *(HANDLE*)phEvent;
    if((hConnection = RfcAccept(argv1)) ==
                    RFC_HANDLE_NULL){
        RfcLastErrorEx(&ErrorInfo);
        printf("%s\n", ErrorInfo.message);
        SetEvent(hEvent);
        return DWORD(rc);
    };
    do{
/* Before listen for message from SAP, check if an error occurred:
    yes => Exit thread */
        EnterCriticalSection(&ErrorSection);
        if(gError ==  iTrue){
           LeaveCriticalSection(&ErrorSection);
           rc = RFC_FAILURE;
           break;
        }
```

```
    LeaveCriticalSection(&ErrorSection);
    rc = RfcListen(hConnection);
    switch(rc){
        case RFC_RETRY:{
            Sleep(300);
            rc = RFC_OK;
            break;
        }
        case RFC_OK:{
            if((rc = RfcDispatch(hConnection))
                    != RFC_OK){
                memset(&ErrorInfo, NULL,
                    sizeof(RFC_ERROR_INFO_EX));
                RfcLastErrorEx(&ErrorInfo);
                printf("%s\n", ErrorInfo.message);
/* If an error occurred, set global error variable to
   True and schedule thread */
                EnterCriticalSection(&ErrorSection);
                gError = iTrue;
                LeaveCriticalSection(&ErrorSection);
            }
            break;
        }
        case RFC_FAILURE:{
            EnterCriticalSection(&ErrorSection);
            gError = iTrue;
            LeaveCriticalSection(&ErrorSection);
            break;
        }
    }
    }while(rc == RFC_OK);
    RfcClose(hConnection);
/* Set event for exiting the message
   loop */
    SetEvent(hEvent);
    return DWORD(rc);
};
```

Listing 6.14 Implementing the Message Loop Executed by Threads

The entire message loop was swapped out to the thread function, as was done previously in the main() function. A check for a control variable gError was also inserted, the meaning of which will be explained later. The fact that each thread function creates its own connection to the R/3 system also stands out. This is necessary because data can be exchanged only if the connection is free. A connection remains busy as long as a callback function is still being executed. As parallel processing means that it will be possible for n clients to exchange data with the server at the same time, we now also need n connections.

With the thread function configured, we have another problem: How do we prevent the main() function, and thus the program, from terminating? In our previous servers the termination of the main() function was prevented by the message loop itself. This is no longer the case, however, because the message loop has been swapped out to a separate function, which is executed parallel to the main() function. By swapping out the message loop to the thread function, the element that prevents the main() function from terminating is lost. The fatal consequence is that the server can no longer run because the main() function no longer waits for any messages from the R/3 System. We must, therefore, interrupt the execution of the main() function for the message loop to receive and process messages. This is achieved by synchronization.

If you take a closer look at how a single thread server works, you will see that the message loop is executed until an error occurs in it. The error usually results in the message loop being terminated and the program exited. It is therefore a good idea to interrupt the main() function in a multithreaded server until an error occurs in a message loop. When an error occurs, the main() function unlocks again and the program, including all message loops, should be exited.

Alternatively, it is also possible for only the message loop with the error to be terminated. If all message loops are exited, the server will also be exited. This variant has the disadvantage that the number of exited message loops has a negative effect on runtime performance.

Once we know how synchronization is to be configured, we can think about the most appropriate means of implementing it. We need:

▶ A global control variable for indicating an error
▶ A critical section
▶ Events

The task of the global control variable is to make an error in one thread visible to all other threads, so that each thread can then end its message loop. Before running the message loop, each thread first checks the value of the control variables.

If it is True, the message loop is exited immediately. The programming for the solution is also used in the thread function presented above.

As the control variable is of such central importance, it must be ensured that only one thread can have write or read access to the variable at any one time. That is why we have to introduce a critical section, that controls this. Incidentally, this is another form of synchronization. That is to say, the message loops synchronize with each other, too. Each message loop has to wait for access to the global control variable until no other message loop has access to the control variable.

For the main() function to be exited first, if all message loops have previously been terminated, we use AND_m:1 synchronization, with events as synchronization objects. Thanks to AND_m:1 synchronization, the main() function has to wait until all m events have the state "signaled." If every terminated message loop now sets its state to "signaled" for one event, this means that the main() function has to wait until all message loops have been exited.

When you program the events, two requirements must be considered. All events must be known to the main() function. At the same time, one event from the overall total must be assigned to each thread because each thread should set the state to "signaled" for only one event in the set. The following listing shows how to implement the requirements:

```
/* Constant */
const int ciAnzMessageLoops = 2;
:
int main (int argc, char** argv)
{
    ...
/* Array with events to signal the
   end of each message loop */
   HANDLE hEvents[ciAnzMessageLoops];
:
/* Transfer an event to every message loop,
   the state of which you should set to "signaled" */
   for(int iCounter = 0; iCounter < ciAnzMessageLoops;
       iCounter++){
     hEvents[iCounter] = CreateEvent(NULL, TRUE,
                                     FALSE, NULL);
     CreateThread(NULL, 0, MessageLoop,
                  &(hEvents[iCounter]), 0, NULL);
   }
```

```
/* Wait until all message loops have terminated */
   WaitForMultipleObjects(ciAnzMessageLoops, hEvents,
                          TRUE, INFINITE);
:
```

Listing 6.15 Main Program for Parallel Processing

The array hEvents contains all events that have to switch to the state "signaled" before the main() function can be terminated. The events are also created in the loop in which the threads were created. Each thread is transferred to the previously created event. In this way, each thread is assigned just one event from the total amount of events. After the events have been created, the WaitForMulti-pleObjects function is called in the main() function. The array with the events is transferred to this function, and this step ensures that the main() function will be exited only when all events have the state "signaled."

Before testing the parallel processing, we still have to make one more small adjustment to the callback function. Up to now the arrays for describing the import and export parameters were always configured at the beginning of the callback function and declared as static. That is no longer allowed. You should now use local variables only for the interface parameters.

We have implemented parallel processing in our server and should now produce proof that it is actually better than a server with just one message loop. For our test, we set the number of message loops in the server to two. We start the server and open two sessions in the SAP system. In both sessions, we start the program ZCALLRFCCALCULATOR. In the first session we set the value of the variable PA_DELAY at 45 seconds, and in the second session at zero seconds. Now, if we start the call with the delay of 45 seconds first, just like befor, it will be 45 seconds before the result is returned. If, however, we start the call with the delay of zero seconds at the same time, this call returns a result immediately. This is a significant difference to our server with only one message loop. In it, the second client had to wait until the first client was finished. This shows that the processing of the second client is carried out independently of the processing status of the first call and that processing messages in parallel has real advantages over multiprocessor machines.

Now that we have successfully implemented parallel processing, we must check whether the server really is exited if an error occurs in a message loop. For this test, we insert the variable iError of type Integer in the callback function RFC_ADD. If the variable has the value one, a test error should be simulated so that the function RFC_ADD is left with the value RFC_FAILURE. Implementation is shown in the following listing:

```
RFC_RC DLL_CALL_BACK_FUNCTION RFC_ADD(RFC_HANDLE
                                      hConnection)
{
   :
   iBool iError = iFalse;
   :
   ImpParam[3] = BuildSimpleParam("IP_ERROR", TYPINT,
                          sizeof(RFC_INT), &iError);
   :
   if((rc = RfcGetData(hConnection, ImpParam, NULL))
         != RFC_OK){
      RfcLastErrorEx(&ErrorInfo);
      printf("%s\n", ErrorInfo.message);
      return rc;
   }
   if(iError == iTrue)
      return RFC_FAILURE;
   :
};
```

Listing 6.16 Enhanced Callback Function to Test Parallel Operation

The value of the variables is set in the report ZCALLRFCCALCULATOR. For this, the PA_ERROR variable, which is declared using a PARAMETERS statement, must be added to the report. As a result, the variable PA_ERROR is also displayed on the selection screen.

```
* Structure of the selection screen
PARAMETERS: pa_value1 TYPE i DEFAULT 5
   :
         , pa_error TYPE i DEFAULT 0
   :
START-OF-SELECTION.
   :
CALL FUNCTION 'RFC_ADD' DESTINATION 'ZJMSTEST'
    EXPORTING ip_value1 = pa_value1
              ip_value2 = pa_value2
              ip_delay  = pa_delay
* Set value for simulating a test error.
```

```
        ip_error  = pa_error
IMPORTING ep_result = lp_result.
```

Listing 6.17 ABAP Client Code for the Test from Listing 6.16

If we assign the value one to the variable PA_ERROR, the following happens in the external server: The function RFC_ADD returns the value RFC_FAILURE. The value is forwarded to the function RfcDispatch, the return value of which is checked in the message loop. If the return value of the function RfcDispatch is not RFC_OK, the message loop is exited and the value of the global control variable gError is set to True. In accordance with the thread function presented above, each message loop checks the value of the variable gError. If it is True, the thread function terminates, having first set the state of the event assigned to it at "signaled." If all events have the state "signaled," the main() function in the server is unlocked again and the program terminated. If we start report ZCALLRFCCALCU-LATOR and set the value of the variable PA_ERROR to one, the threads and the program are effectively terminated. This also guarantees that, in the event of an error, the server really terminates and does not simply continue running.

Just one more critical closing remark to finish off our example of a server with parallel processing: To demonstrate the advantages of parallel processing, we artificially delayed server execution. For instructive purposes, it was sufficient to use a single-processor machine. You should note, however, that parallel processing usually shows its true strengths only in multiprocessor systems.

This chapter ends our discussion of the RFC API. We will now look at other techniques.

7   The Business Object

When finding other ways to access the SAP system, SAP used the RFC Library as a basis. The RFC Library was progressively extended by SAP (i.e., it was enhanced by new technologies such as COM, ActiveX, and .NET) and now forms a substantial collection of programming models and procedures for interface programming.

One important technique that SAP pursued was to link the original procedural programming model of the RFC Library with object-oriented approaches. A central concept here—from the programmer's point of view—is the *SAP Business Object* (BO). A business object adopts the concepts of *object-oriented programming* (OOP), insofar as it can be addressed by well-defined and relatively stable interfaces.

To put it simply, business objects currently combine logically-related data and operations in a single unit. In OOP-speak, we call this the "encapsulating of data and the related operations." As a result of this encapsulation, you can dispense with the often tedious search for data and appropriate operations (i.e., function modules). Therefore, a SAP BO plays the role of a class in OOP.

Using these methods offers certain advantages, namely, the interfaces of the BO can be structured clearly. For example, the Business Objects can be ordered according to areas of application and provide well-defined options for documentation. This includes specifying interfaces that should not be used, namely, those that are *obsolete*. With Business Objects, the developer—building on the underlying object-orientation—can bring abstraction and description possibilities to another level.[1]

For a more precise description of this new concept, we'll first look at object-oriented programming in general. After a brief summary of OOP's important concepts, we will compare them with SAP Business Objects. For a more in-depth discussion of OO approaches, please see Appendix A.

7.1   Business Object—Close to the Object

For modeling "things" (read: objects), procedural programming uses structures, on the one hand, and functions that work with these structures, on the other. The structures represent the properties or attributes of an object and the functions represent the operations that affect the data structure. Structures and functions

---

1   In any discussion of BO, it should be remembered that when calling the operations of a BO, the underlying technology continues to be the RFC Library.

are separate from each other however. You can envision this distinction by thinking of functions as links to the structures with which they should work.

In object-oriented programming, the perspective is different. Here, data structures and methods form a unit. The operation that works on the data in an object now forms a part of the object. The data structure and the operation merge to form a single unit; in short, they are *encapsulated*.

With OOP, the data for an object is referred to as its *attributes* and the operations that work on this data are *methods*. OOP is frequently characterized by four terms:

▶ Class
▶ Instance (object in the strictest sense)
▶ Inheritance
▶ Polymorphism

Let's assume that we want to describe a customer in an application. For the description, we will probably use the attributes "Name," "Address," "Contact person," and the method "order." The attributes and methods represent an abstract description of what constitutes a customer. The general description of the attributes and methods is stored in a class. The *class* describes the structure and behavior of a group of objects of similar type.

An *instance* (an "object" in the strictest sense) of the class Customer represents one customer as distinguished from many customers. The fact that an instance represents an element from a group also explains why the methods of a class can generally be used for only one instance of the class. Methods act on data and the attributes of a class get their data in the instance (an exception being static methods).

Inheritance is another identifying characteristic of OOP. Inheritance means that a class can be derived from another class, and can take on all methods and attributes of its superior class. With inheritance, you can configure complex class hierarchies. Let's look at the class Customer again. It's easy to imagine how customers can be differentiated at the sales organization level and to create a class system, as shown in Figure 7.1.

In Figure 7.1 you can see that at the top of the class system we have the Customer class, and after that comes specialization with regard to the individual sales organizations. In the context of a class system, we often speak of *specialization* and *generalization*. The deeper down a class hierarchy that the class is located, the more specialized it is and conversely, the higher up the hierarchy, the more general.

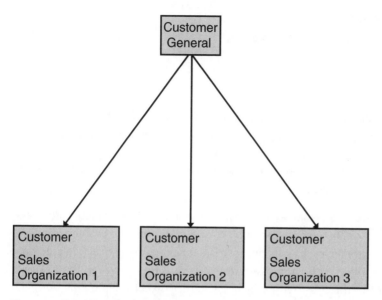

Figure 7.1 Class Hierarchy for a Customer

The final distinguishing characteristic of OOP is *polymorphism*. We could also add Sales to our model (represented by the class CSales). Sales would now like to send product information to customers one and two in the sales organization. To do so, the class CSales should implement the method SendInfo. How should the interface of the method be structured? Differentiation according to sales organization takes place at the second hierarchy level. One approach for the definition of the method would be:

```
CSales::SendInfo
            ( CCustVKORG1 *pCustVKORG1, int iNumbCust1,
              CCustVKORG2 *pCustVKORG2, int iNumbCust2 )
{
    // Logic
}
```

The disadvantage of this solution is that if any changes are made to customer data that contains product information, the interface must be adjusted accordingly. It would be better to have a solution that was not susceptible to changes to the sales organization. This objective is achieved with polymorphism. Polymorphism relies on the fact that a pointer to an object in a derived class is also considered a pointer to the base class, because a derived class is only a more specialized version of its base class. If you consider this information, a new definition of the method SendInfo could be:

```
CSales::SendInfo
         ( CCustomer *pCustomer, int iNumbCustomer )
{
   // Logic
}
```

This form can then be used for all types of customers. Within this method, programming languages that offer polymorphisms can distinguish at runtime which customer group is intended in each case and start an appropriate action accordingly. The different behavior of a method or function depending on type is the core idea of polymorphism.

If in programming, a development method that points to the characteristics class, instance, and so on, is referred to as object-oriented, then the business object is also object-oriented in a sense. Its purpose is to encapsulate logically-related data and operations that can be addressed from the outside. However, the business object differs from a class, with which the term "object-oriented" is normally linked, in the following ways:

▶ The business object recognizes visibility sections for methods. In OOP, you can limit the visibility of methods and attributes using the visibility sections `public`, `protected`, and `private`. The business object recognizes only `public` methods.

▶ The business object is also different from a "normal" (ABAP) class in its implementation. No enhancement is made to the ABAP programming language for a business object. Instead, the familiar language elements such as report and macro are used to implement a BO.

The business object is used in the R/3 System in the following and other areas:

▶ Workflow

▶ Client /server programming

In the last case, multiple external clients interact with the business object.

7.2 Structure of the Business Object

Figure 7.2 shows the structure of a business object in the Business Object Builder (Transaction SW01). We can see that a business object (BO) is made up of several elements:

▶ Key fields

▶ Attributes

► Methods

► Interfaces

► Events

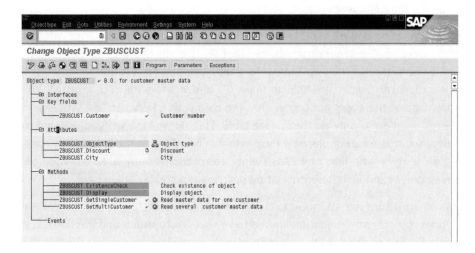

Figure 7.2 Components of the Business Object

As mentioned above, the instance represents an actual example of a business object. The *key fields* determine what information is necessary to create an instance of the business object. Once again, we'll use our customer as an example. To identify it uniquely, we need a customer number. This is one of the key fields for the business object ZBUSCUST.

Attributes are characteristic properties that describe the object in more detail. For a customer, attributes could include name, location, bonus, and so on.

The *methods* are the operations by which the data in the business object can be changed.

An *interface* groups together several methods under a collective name. The interface declares only the methods and does not implement them. The implementation of methods is shifted to the business object that implements the interface. The business object is not obliged to implement the methods of an interface. Therefore, a business object can include an interface in its definition, without implementing the methods of the interface (unlike Java, for example). Standard implementation is also an option.

Events enable communication between different software modules. The following components are involved:

- ▶ Sender

- ▶ Recipient (also called *event receiver*)

- ▶ Linkage table containing information on the software modules to be evaluated by the different events

Communication between the sender and recipient is done in accordance with the ECA principle: The sender triggers an event (E). Details of which software modules want to receive the event (are interested) are stored in the linkage table. The event manager checks the linkage table (C) and notifies the recipient (A). The advantage of the event concept is that the connection between the sender and the recipient exists only via the linkage table. This allows for a swift adjustment to new situations, for example, new recipients can be added to the scenario by making an entry in the linkage table. Events are predominantly used in workflow development and will therefore not be described in greater detail here.

We will now turn our attention to the implementation of the components of the business object, with execution limited to key fields, attributes, and methods. The attributes and methods of the business object are realized by a report. Within the report, each attribute (and each method) is enclosed between macro statements. The following program extract shows an excerpt from the report ZBUSCUST that implements the business object ZBUSCUST (they usually have the same name).

```
BEGIN_DATA_CLASS OBJECTTYPE. " Do not change.
*                              DATA is generated
DATA:
      BONUS LIKE ZKNA1JMS-EXPSALES.
* Do not change. DATA is generated
END_DATA_CLASS OBJECTTYPE.
BEGIN_DATA OBJECT. " Do not change. DATA is generated
DATA:
" begin of private,
"    to declare private attributes remove comments and
"    insert private attributes here ...
" end of private,
  BEGIN OF KEY,
      CUSTNO LIKE ZKNA1JMS-CUSTNO,
  END OF KEY,
      KEY LIKE SWOTOBJID-OBJKEY,
* Declaration of structure _ZKNA1JMS in the original program
* without comments!
      _ZKNA1JMS LIKE ZKNA1JMS.
```

```
END_DATA OBJECT. " Do not change. DATA is generated
GET_PROPERTY BONUS CHANGING CONTAINER.
* Update logic for the realization of the attribute
* Bonus Container
  SWC_SET_ELEMENT CONTAINER 'Bonus' OBJECT-BONUS.
END_PROPERTY.
BEGIN_METHOD GETCITY CHANGING CONTAINER.
* Update logic for the realization of the method GETCITY
* Container
   DATA. lp_city TYPE ort01_gp
  SWC_SET_ELEMENT CONTAINER 'EP_CITY' lp_city.
END_METHOD.
```

Listing 7.1 Implementation of the Business Object ZBUSCUST

The program extract shows that the report consists of the following parts:

▶ Data declaration part for instance-independent attributes, which is framed by the macros BEGIN_DATA_CLASS and END_DATA_CLASS

▶ Data declaration section for instance-dependent attributes, which is framed by the macros BEGIN_DATA and END_DATA

▶ Key definition that exhibits its own area in the data declaration part, which is enclosed by the statements BEGIN OF KEY and END OF KEY

▶ Implementation of the attributes, which appear between the macros GET_PROPERTY and END_PROPERTY

▶ Implementation of methods, which are surrounded by the macros BEGIN_METHOD and END_METHOD

Also remarkable is that within a method or attribute, the macro SWC_SET_ELEMENT is called. This macro belongs to a group of macros that update the internal table Container. This is one of the key internal tables in business objects. All data for the instance of a business object is administered in this table at runtime. The internal table references the Data Dictionary structure SWCONT, which is configured as shown in Figure 7.3.

In the internal table, the data for the instance of a business object is managed according to the following principle:

Name of element = value for the element

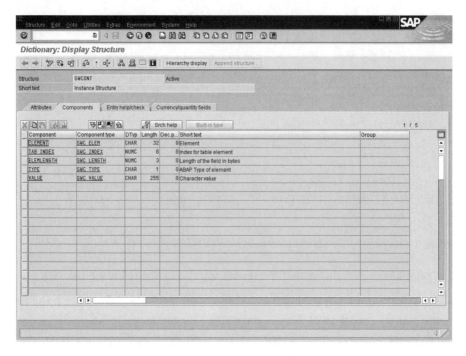

Figure 7.3 Structure of Table SWCONT

The following macros are provided for reading and writing values in the internal table `Container`:

▶ `SWC_GET_ELEMENT` for reading individual values or the content of a structure variable

▶ `SWC_SET_ELEMENT` for setting the value for an individual variable or a structure variable

▶ `SWC_GET_TABLE` for reading the values of an internal table

▶ `SWC_SET_TABLE` for writing values in an internal table

The interface of the macros `SWC_GET_ELEMENT` and `SWC_SET_ELEMENT` is defined in the same way, and is described in the following table:

Variable	Meaning
&1	Transferring the `Container` table that administers the data of the BO instance
&2	Name of the element that should be read or for which a value should be set
&3	Variable that takes on the value read or for which the values must be set

Table 7.1 Interface of the Macros SWC_GET_ELEMENT and SWC_SET_ELEMENT

The call for the macro `SWC_SET_ELEMENT` might look like this:

`SWC_SET_ELEMENT CONTAINER 'EP_STREET' lp_street.`

In the example above, the method can use the exporting interface parameter `EP_STREET`. The value for the export parameter is read from the local variable `LP_STREET`.

The interfaces of the macros `SWC_GET_TABLE` and `SWC_SET_TABLE` are also identical. Their structure is:

Variable	Meaning
&1	Transferring the `Container` table that administers the data of the BO instance
&2	Name of the table from which data is to be read or for which data is to be set
&3	Table from which the data is to be read or to which data is to be written

Table 7.2 Interface of the Macros SWC_GET_TABLE and SWC_SET_TABLE

Next comes the call for the macro `SWC_GET_TABLE`:

```
SWC_GET_TABLE
          CONTAINER 'IT_NEW_CUSTOMER' lt_new_customer.
```

In this example, we assume that the method has the table `IT_NEW_CUSTOMER` in its interface. The data in the `Container` table is transferred to the local table `LT_NEW_CUSTOMER`.

In the following sections, we'll present the development of the individual components of a business object. We'll focus on the implementation of API methods and key fields, because only these BO components can be activated by an external client.

7.3   The Structure of the Business Object Builder

The basics for developing a business object are presented using our customer example. The data basis for the business object is the database table ZKNA1JMS. It should have the following methods, among others:

▶ `GetSingleCustomer` for reading the master data on a customer

▶ `GetMultiCustomer` for reading multiple customer master data records

▶ `CreateNewCustomer` for creating new customers

The *Business Object Builder* is the tool provided in the SAP system to create business objects. It is started using Transaction SWO1. When you call the transaction, the initial screen for maintaining business objects opens.

Here, you enter the names of the business objects to be created and click on **Create**. A dialog box appears in which you must enter the following:

Entry	Meaning
Supertype	The superordinate BO, from which the current BO is derived Entry here is optional
Object type	Name that determines what type of object it is (application-specific)
Object name	Name of the BO in the Business Object Repository (user-selected)
Name	Name of the BO that can be used to search for the business object
Description	Longer, more informative description of the BO
Program	Name of the program that realizes the BO
Application	Allocation of the BO to an application group

Table 7.3 Tasks for Creating a Business Object

When assigning a name, you must adhere to the following naming convention: The name of the object type and the program must be in the customer name range. They must, therefore, start with Z or Y (Z is more commonly used).

It is also common to use the abbreviation BUS in the name of the object type and the program, to make it easier, for example, to locate those programs that execute on a business object.

Furthermore, the object type and the program are frequently given the same name, so if you know the name of the object type, you can immediately identify the corresponding program. The object name and the name—as well as the short description—are usually documentary in nature and are frequently identical. The entries for our business object can be seen in Figure 7.4.

Once we have entered and confirmed details for the business object ZBUSCUST, we branch to the overview for the elements in a business object. Two possibilities are available in the overview:

▶ Create new elements for a business object
▶ Branch to the detail view for existing elements

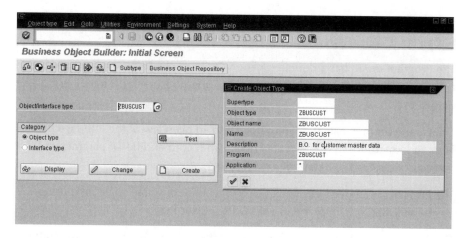

Figure 7.4 Initial Dialog for Creating an Object Type

The overview is made up of a hierarchical list that displays the possible elements for a business object. If you double-click on a node, the elements that belong to that node are displayed.

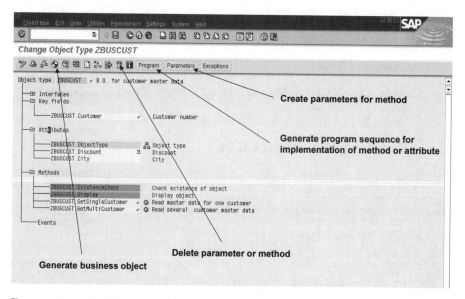

Figure 7.5 Important Functions of the Business Object Builder

The menu bar is located above the hierarchical list (see Figure 7.5). The following menus are of particular significance:

▶ Program

▶ Parameter

▶ Error list

▶ Change release status

The **Program** menu has a double function. You can create the program sequence for the implementation of an attribute or a method or—if it already exists—to branch to it.

The **Parameter** menu allows you to branch to an overview of the interface parameters for a method. In this overview, you can record additional parameters for a method or display the details of existing parameters.

The **Error list** is an overview of all the errors in the business object in question. It can be accessed using the menu path **Goto · Error list**.

The business object and its elements can be set to different release statuses using the function **Change release status**. The menu can be accessed via the path **Edit · Change release status**. From here, you can change the release status for the object or for its components. For more information, see Section 7.6.

To create a new element for a business object, position the cursor on the hierarchy node that will administer the element in question. Next, click on **Create**. The maintenance dialog for creating the element is displayed. The procedure is similar for **Change** and **Display**. Position the cursor over the existing element and then click on **Change** or **Display**.

The maintenance of the key fields and methods for the object ZBUSCUST are presented in the next sections.

7.4   Creating the Object Key

The object key determines what information is necessary to create the instance of a business object. The object key consists of one or more key fields. If you want to create a key field for a business object, you must enter the following details:

▶ The name of the key field

▶ Description

▶ Data type reference, which determines the technical properties of the key field

Figure 7.6 shows the details for the key field Customer of business object ZBUS-CUST.

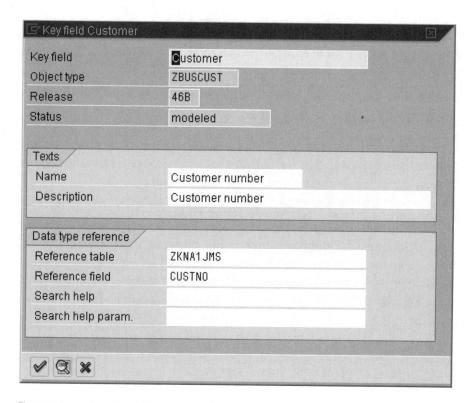

Figure 7.6 Create a Key Field

As mentioned earlier, key fields are enclosed by the macro statements `BEGIN OF KEY` and `END OF KEY`. Implementation for the key field `Customer` in the program ZBUSCUST would look like this:

```
begin_data object.
:
   data:
:
   begin of key.
      Customer like zknaljms-custno.
   end of key.
:
end_data object.
```

Listing 7.2 Implementation of the Key Field Customer in the Program ZBUSCUST

7.5   Methods of the Business Object

After the key fields have been implemented for the object ZBUSCUST, we create the methods. Methods can be divided into:

▶ Instance-dependent and instance-independent methods

▶ Synchronous and asynchronous methods

Instance-dependent methods can, as a rule, be executed correctly only if the key fields of the business object are provided with values. We'll look at instance-dependent methods in greater detail in the next section.

Synchronous methods are executed directly. They can return the result of the processing to the calling program. *Asynchronous methods* are executed by a separate process. Consequently, they cannot return the result to the client directly. Asynchronous methods are not used in the development of external clients often because the external client does not receive any information regarding the status of the execution. Therefore, we won't discuss asynchronous methods in greater detail here.

The implementation of a method is enclosed by the following macro statements:

▶ BEGIN_METHOD <Name> CHANGING CONTAINER

▶ END_METHOD

A BO method always has the following structure:

```
BEGIN_METHOD <Name> CHANGING CONTAINER.
* local data
DATA: lp_custno type kunnr
        , lt_customer_data type standard table of zknaljms
                        with header line
                        initial size 0.
* Read the importing parameter of the interface
  SWC_GET_ELEMENT CONTAINER 'IP_CUSTNO' lp_custno
* Logic
  DoSomething
* Set data for the exporting parameter of the
* interface
  SWC_SET_TABLE
        CONTAINER 'ET_CUSTOMER_DATA' lt_customer_data.
END_METHOD.
```

Listing 7.3 General Structure of a BO Method

You can see that the actual logic of the method is enclosed by the macros for reading and setting the values for the interface parameter. You should apply the structure presented above for all methods.

7.5.1 Instance-Dependent Methods

As mentioned, instance-dependent methods can be executed reasonably only if the key fields of the business object are provided with values. Instance-dependent methods should not be equated with those methods in conventional OOP. In conventional OOP, an instance-dependent method can be executed only if an instance of the class has been created. For the business object, the term "instance-dependent" refers to the setting of values for the key fields of the business object. To use the business object, the runtime object must be created in any case. This is done using the function module SWO_CREATE of the function group SWOR in the R/3 System, which, for example, is called internally using the macro SWC_CREATE_OBJECT. Subsequently, both instance-dependent and instance-independent methods of the business object can be executed—regardless of whether the key fields have received values. An instance-dependent method can also return a meaningful result if it has the appropriate import parameter in its interface. If the implementation for a method looks like the following example, its result will be independent of the object key, whether or not the instance-independent indicator is set in the attributes for the method.

```
BEGIN_METHOD GETSINGLECUSTOMER CHANGING CONTAINER.
DATA:
* local variable, in which the BO data from the
* internal table CONTAINER is saved
        IP_CUSTNO LIKE ZKNA1JMS-CUSTNO,
        ES_CUSTOMER_DATA LIKE ZKNA1JMS.
* Read the transferred customer number from the internal
* table CONTAINER
  SWC_GET_ELEMENT CONTAINER 'IP_CUSTNO' IP_CUSTNO.
* Function module call
  CALL FUNCTION 'Z_RFC_GET_SINGLE_CUSTOMER'
    EXPORTING
      IP_CUSTNO = IP_CUSTNO
    IMPORTING
      ES_CUSTOMER_DATA = ES_CUSTOMER_DATA
    EXCEPTIONS
      OTHERS = 01.
  CASE SY-SUBRC.
```

```
   WHEN 0.              " OK
   WHEN OTHERS.         " to be implemented
 ENDCASE.
* Set the data for the exporting parameter
* ES_CUSTOMER_DATA
  SWC_SET_ELEMENT
     CONTAINER 'ES_CUSTOMER_DATA' ES_CUSTOMER_DATA.
END_METHOD.
```

Listing 7.4 Implementation of an Instance-Independent Method

The customer number is transferred to the method GETSINGLECUSTOMER using the interface parameter IP_CUSTNO and as a result this method can be executed independently of the object key.

If the implementation for the method GETSINGLECUSTOMER looks like the following one, however, it is in fact instance-dependent. The key fields must then be assigned values.

```
BEGIN_METHOD GETSINGLECUSTOMER CHANGING CONTAINER.
DATA: ES_CUSTOMER_DATA LIKE ZKNA1JMS.
* Function module call
   CALL FUNCTION 'Z_RFC_GET_SINGLE_CUSTOMER'
     EXPORTING
       IP_CUSTNO = OBJECT-KEY-CUSTNO
     IMPORTING
       ES_CUSTOMER_DATA = ES_CUSTOMER_DATA
     EXCEPTIONS
       OTHERS = 01.
   CASE SY-SUBRC.
     WHEN 0.              " OK
     WHEN OTHERS.         " to be implemented
   ENDCASE.
* Set the data for the exporting parameter
* ES_CUSTOMER_DATA
  SWC_SET_ELEMENT
     CONTAINER 'ES_CUSTOMER_DATA' ES_CUSTOMER_DATA.
END_METHOD.
```

Listing 7.5 Implementation of an Instance-Dependent Method

Now the value of the key field `CUSTNO` is transferred to the function module `Z_RFC_GET_SINGLE_CUSTOMER`. It can therefore select the customer master data record only if a value has been set for the key field `CUSTNO`.

The term *instance-dependent* is therefore somewhat weaker for the business object than it is for other object-oriented programming. We recommend that you only develop instance-dependent methods in such a way that you use the data from the key fields. This recommendation should be adhered to, if only for reasons of transparency to third parties.

Furthermore, you should note that an external client that uses the ActiveX controls described below to activate the methods of a business object can only reasonably execute instance-independent methods. This is due to the fact that the ActiveX controls activate the function module in the R/3 System directly and in the proxy object for the business object there is no allocation between the key fields of an object and the importing parameters of the function module.

7.5.2 Implementation of Methods Using ABAP Program Forms

The actual logic of the methods occurs in the ABAP programming language. The statements are located between the macros `BEGIN_METHOD` and `END_METHOD`, which enclose a method.

The following options are available for programming the logic:

▶ Function module
▶ API function
▶ Transaction
▶ Dialog module
▶ Report
▶ Other

If the method is to be activated by an external client, you should select the **API function**. An API function is implemented internally by an RFC-enabled function module. API functions are also referred to as BAPIs (*Business Application Programming Interface*) and are now perhaps better known by this name. The following example shows the implementation of the function module `Z_RFC_GET_SINGLE_CUSTOMER`, for which direct activation using the functions of the RFC API was presented in Chapter 4.

```
BEGIN_METHOD GETSINGLECUSTOMER CHANGING CONTAINER.
DATA:
* local variable, in which the BO data from the
```

```
* internal table CONTAINER is saved
        IP_CUSTNO LIKE ZKNA1JMS-CUSTNO,
        ES_CUSTOMER_DATA LIKE ZKNA1JMS.
* Read the transferred customer number from the internal
* table CONTAINER
    SWC_GET_ELEMENT CONTAINER 'IP_CUSTNO' IP_CUSTNO.
* Function module call
    CALL FUNCTION 'Z_RFC_GET_SINGLE_CUSTOMER'
      EXPORTING
        IP_CUSTNO = IP_CUSTNO
      IMPORTING
        ES_CUSTOMER_DATA = ES_CUSTOMER_DATA
      EXCEPTIONS
        OTHERS = 01.
    CASE SY-SUBRC.
      WHEN 0.              " OK
      WHEN OTHERS.         " to be implemented
    ENDCASE.
* Set the data for the exporting parameter
* ES_CUSTOMER_DATA
    SWC_SET_ELEMENT
        CONTAINER 'ES_CUSTOMER_DATA' ES_CUSTOMER_DATA.
END_METHOD.
```

Listing 7.6 Implementation of the BO Method Using the Function Module Z_RFC_GET_SINGLE_CUSTOMER

7.5.3 Creating a Method

There are two possible ways to create a method:

▶ Semi-automatic creation

▶ Fully automatic creation

With the *semi-automatic* procedure, the attributes of the method and the interface parameters are created manually and the implementation is generated. With the *automatic* procedure, the attributes of the method, the interface parameter, and the implementation of the method are all generated by SAP. The latter method can only be used by function modules however.

Next, we'll describe the steps that must be executed in order for a function module to implement a method. You can transfer these steps to other analogous ABAP program forms. Again, note that the fully automatic procedure can be used only by function modules.

The Semi-Automatic Creation of a Business Object Method

With the semi-automatic procedure, the user records the attributes and interface parameters of the method in the appropriate maintenance dialog. The data maintenance is carried out in two steps: The attributes of the method are maintained, and then, the interface parameters.

We'll show the maintenance of the attributes and interface parameters for the method `GetSingleCustomer`. It should be carried out using the function module `Z_RFC_GET_SINGLE_CUSTOMER` of the function group `Z_RFC_SERVICES`. Furthermore, the method should have the same interface as the function module.

To go to the maintenance of the method attributes, position the cursor on the **Method** entry and click on **Create**. Answer "no" to the question *Create with function module as template?* Once you have done this, the dialog box for manually recording the attributes of a method is displayed. The method attributes are divided into the following groups:

▶ General attributes

▶ Result type

▶ The type of ABAP program form for implementing the method logic

You can use the tabs to go to the maintenance dialog for each of the groups. Figure 7.7 shows the maintenance dialog for creating a method.

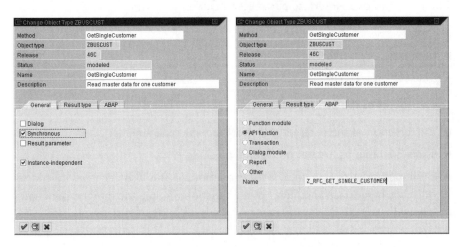

Figure 7.7 Detail Views of the Maintenance Dialog for the Attributes of a Method

The general attributes are used to specify whether this is a synchronous method, whether it returns its result in the form of a result parameter, and whether it is an instance-independent method. The customer number is transferred to the inter-

face of the function module Z_RFC_GET_SINGLE_CUSTOMER. Given that the interface of the method should be the same as the interface of the function module,
the method GetSingleCustomer will also have access to the importing parameter IP_CUSTNO in the interface. Therefore the attributes have to be activated
instance-independently for the method, because its execution is not linked to a
specific customer. In Chapter 8, we'll look at how an external client calls the
method, so the method must be executed synchronously. Consequently, you
must also set the **Synchronous** attribute.

Finally, you must specify the ABAP program form that will contain the logic of the
method. The options mentioned are available here. The method GetSingleCustomer is contained by the function module Z_RFC_GET_SINGLE_CUSTOMER. Furthermore, the method is to be activated by an external client. So we select **API
function**. The name of the function module Z_RFC_GET_SINGLE_CUSTOMER must
also be entered. This entry concludes the maintenance of the attributes of a
method, so we can now move on to the maintenance of the interface parameters.

To maintain the interface parameters for a method, position the cursor on
Method. Then, in the Business Object Builder, select the **Parameter** function and
you will branch to the overview of the interface parameters for a method. In the
overview, click on **Create** and a dialog box will appear in which you can maintain
the properties for an interface parameter (see Figure 7.8).

The properties of an interface parameter include:

▶ Texts
▶ Parameter attributes
▶ Data type reference

The attributes of the parameter determine:

▶ The direction of the parameter (import or export parameter)
▶ If this is a table parameter (**multiline** indicator)
▶ If the method is contained by a function module, it is also necessary to specify
  with which interface parameter of the function module the method parameter
  is linked.

  Note that in order to address the method via an external client, it is not sufficient to link the method parameter with the corresponding function module
  parameter in the implementation of the method. This is because the proxy
  object for the business object, which is used in the external client, draws its
  information on the link between interface and function module parameters

from tables in the Data Dictionary and not through the direct execution of the business object method.

| Object Type ZBUSCUST: Edit Parameters for Method DOSOMETHING | ☒ |

Parameter	IP_CUSTOMER_NO
Object type	ZBUSCUST
Release	46B

Texts
| Name | IP_CUSTOMER_NO |
| Description | Customer number |

Parameter attributes
- ☑ Import   ☐ Mandatory
- ☐ Export
- ☐ Multiline
- Name in function module   IP_CUSTNO

Data type reference
- ◉ ABAP Dictionary
  - Reference table   ZKNA1JMS█
  - Reference field   CUSTNO
- ○ Object type

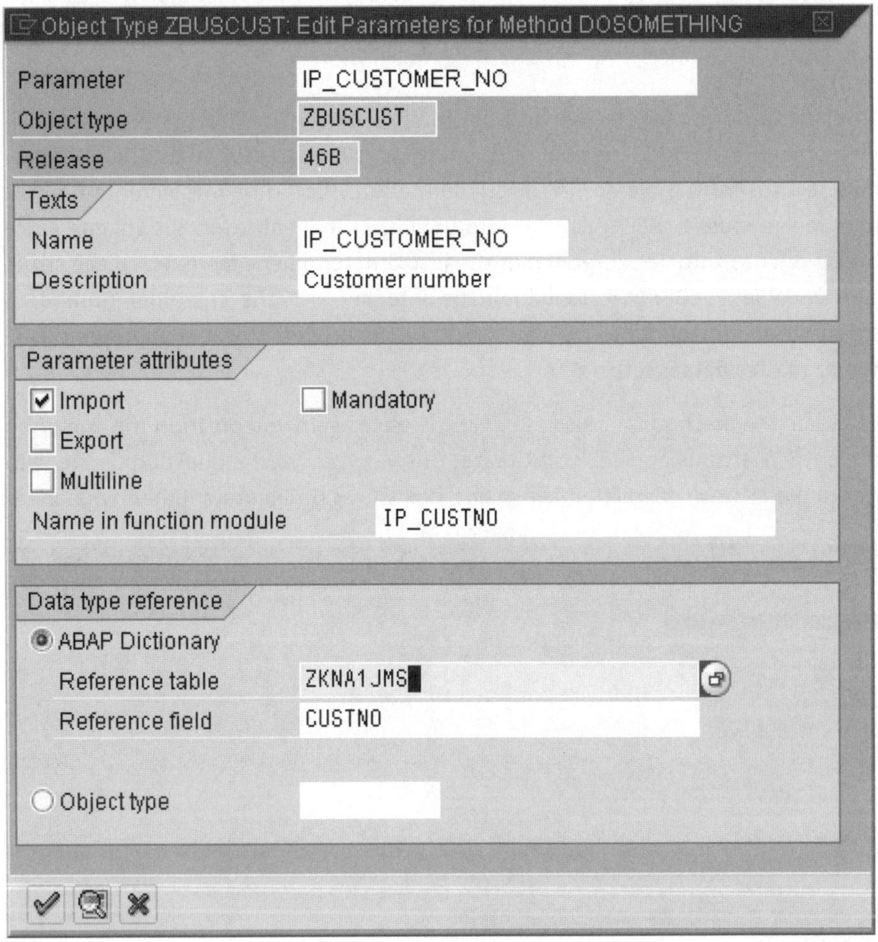

Figure 7.8 Creating the Interface Parameters for a Method

Under data type preference, you specify either an element of the Data Dictionary that describes the technical attributes of the interface parameter, or a business object if the interface parameter is an object.

After the method has been described in full, the method GetSingleCustomer is implemented in the report ZBUSCUST using the function **Program**.

The Fully Automatic Creation of a Business Object Method

To be able to apply the fully automatic procedure, you must define the interface of the function module that will be used to create the BO method. Furthermore, if an API method is being created, the attribute **Remote-enabled module** must be set for the processing type of the function module. In addition, it is an advantage if the interface of the function module has been released; otherwise, the BO method itself cannot be released. This also applies to the semi-automatic procedure.

To present the procedure, we add the method `GetMultiCustomer` to the business object ZBUSCUST. The goal of the method is to read several customer master data records from table ZKNA1JMS. The method should be implemented by the function module Z_RFC_GET_MULTI_CUSTOMER. The entries in the maintenance dialog refer to this. The interface of the function module is made up of the structure variable `IS_CUSTNO`, to which the interval with the customer number is transferred, and the table `ET_CUSTOMER_DATA` to which the corresponding customer master data is returned.

To create the method `GetMultiCustomer`, once again you position the cursor on the entry **Methods** and click on **Create**. Answer "yes" to the question *Create with function module as template?* The dialog box shown in Figure 7.9 then appears.

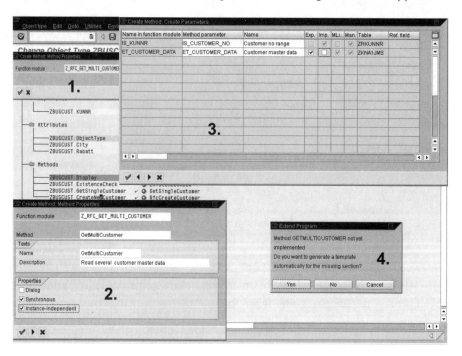

Figure 7.9 Creating the BO Method with Function Module as Template

You can see the following windows:

1. The dialog box for entering the function module.

2. The dialog box for entering the general properties for the method. Here we notice that the number of properties is limited to **Dialog**, **Synchronous**, and **Instance-independent**. In the dialog box, the Result flag is missing (it appears when methods are created manually, see Figure 7.7.) For a function this is correct because function modules usually return data aggregates or several values to the customer. The leading Z in the suggested method name should also be removed.

3. A dialog box with a default for naming the interface parameter in the BO method. The suggested name is based on the names of the interface parameters of the function module. The proposed names can be overwritten.

4. A dialog box that asks if you want to generate a template for the new method. Answer "yes."

After confirming the last question, code is inserted into the program ZBUSCUST, thus completing the implementation of the method:

```
BEGIN_METHOD GETMULTICUSTOMER CHANGING CONTAINER.
DATA: ls_custno type zrg_custno
      lt_new_customer TYPE STANDARD TABLE
                      OF zknaljms
                      INITIAL SIZE 0.
* Read the interval from the table container
  SWC_GET_ELEMENT
      CONTAINER 'IS_CUSTNO' ls_custno.
* Function module call
  CALL FUNCTION 'Z_RFC_GET_MULTI_CUSTOMER'
      EXPORTING
          IS_CUSTNO = ls_custno
      TABLES
          ET_CUSTOMER_DATA = lt_customer_data
    EXCEPTIONS
          OTHERS = 01.
  CASE SY-SUBRC.
    WHEN 0.          " OK
    WHEN OTHERS.     " to be implemented
  ENDCASE.
```

```
* Set the data for the export parameter
  SWC_SET_TABLE
     CONTAINER 'ET_CUSTOMER_DATA' lt_cutomer_data.
END_METHOD.
```

Listing 7.7 Implementation of the Method GETMULTICUSTOMER

The implementation presented above is not the standard implementation: it has been slightly modified manually. This modification has been made to use the new options of the ABAP programming language for the declaration of the internal table, whereas the original implementation still works with the specification

```
data: et_customer_data like zknaljms occurs 0.
```

This form of the declaration should not really have been used since Release 4.0B and exists only for reasons of downward compatibility for older releases. Furthermore, the names of the local variables in the original implementation corresponded to the names of the interface parameters. They should, however, comply with the naming conventions presented in Chapter 2, so that IS_CUSTNO becomes LS_CUSTNO and ET_CUSTOMER_DATA is changed to LT_CUSTOMER_DATA. After implementation, the program form in the attributes of the method must still be changed to **API function**.

In this chapter, we've seen that the description of a method, including its implementation, is carried out by the Business Object Builder, without your having to write even a few lines of code. Unfortunately, changing the interface of a method is not as simple. If changes are made to the interface parameter of a method or the program form for realizing the logic, the Business Object Builder does not perform any automatic adjustments to the implementation. Adjustments have to be made manually. Modification of the implementation should be carried out only then if the method is executed by external clients.

7.6 Object Release and the Business Object Repository

For a business object and its components to be used, they must be released. For an object type and object component, we can differentiate among the following release states:

▶ Modeled

▶ Implemented

▶ Released

▶ Obsolete

The developer must set the release state for an object type or object component manually using the menu **Edit · Change release state**. There is no automatic adjustment.

An object component gets the status "modeled" once its attributes have been described. The status changes to "implemented" once the statements for implementing the components have been created in the report. The status is changed to "released" when the component has been developed so that it no longer changes to clients. For example, this is the case for methods when the description of the interface is stable, and no other parameters will be deleted or redefined.

You should note that the status of an object component is limited by the object type. If the object type is not released, the object components cannot be released. It is therefore recommended that you first release the object type, and then the object components.

The API methods of our business object ZBUSCUST are displayed in the *Business Object Repository* (BOR) after they have been released. The BOR is the central location in the R/3 System in which all information on business objects and their API methods are stored. It is started either in the Business Object Builder using the **Business Object Repository** function, or directly using Transaction BAPI. The BOR presents the API methods of the business objects according to the following aspects:

▶ The logical allocation of the business object to a component in the component hierarchy. This will make it possible to determine interfaces for modules quickly.

▶ Alphabetical sorting of business objects

The business object ZBUSCUST is shown in Figure 7.10 in the alphabetical view of the BOR.

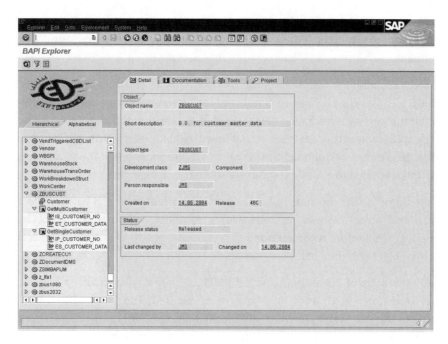

Figure 7.10 The Business Object Repository

7.7 Guidelines for Developing API Methods

Frequently, the aim of external clients is to write data in the R/3 System, after the data has first been processed by one or more API methods. All the processing steps—up until the data is updated to the database—are referred to as a *Logical Unit of Work* (LUW) or *Transaction*. For transactions, the ACID principle from the database world applies:

▶ **Transactions are atomic (A).**
The term *atomic* refers to the updating of data in the database. Either all or no data is updated.

▶ **Transactions are consistent (C).**
If a transaction is executed more than once, it must always produce the same result; and if the underlying data model is consistent, this consistency must be maintained.

▶ **Transactions are isolated (I).**
Each transaction is completely self-contained. There are no dependencies on other transactions that could affect the result in any way.

▶ **Changes made using a transaction are durable (D).**
Once the data has been written to the database, changes can no longer be made.

An API method executes one processing step and is therefore a transaction—or part of a transaction. It must therefore satisfy the aforementioned requirements as a single action. In practice, it also arises that several BAPIs must frequently be grouped in an LUW. Therefore, SAP recommends that BAPIs can also be bundled without violating the ACID principles.

One consequence of this grouping or bundling is that typically the *client* should end the transaction with a COMMIT WORK or a ROLLBACK WORK. This can be done by calling the special BAPIs BapiService.TransactionCommit() or BapiService.TransactionRollback(). A BAPI itself should not use the COMMIT and ROLLBACK commands. Unfortunately, this rule does not apply to some BAPIs, particularly older ones. As a developer of BAPI clients, you should therefore know whether your target BAPI behaves according to this recommendation. SAP requires that this information is disclosed in the BAPI documentation.

The bundling of several BAPIs in a single LUW requires further consideration. Because one of the demands made on BAPIs is that they can be used independently—in compliance with ACID—certain operation sequences are not allowed:

▶ If an instance of a business object is changed—generated or deleted—this new status can be read only after a COMMIT WORK.

▶ It is also not possible for an instance within the same LUW to make changes to the same data twice. Every change must be carried out in a separate LUW and updated with a COMMIT WORK. Figure 7.11 shows the transaction model once more.

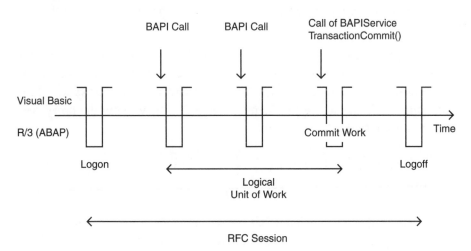

Figure 7.11 The SAP Transaction Model

These limits are not set for a combination of operations on different instances however.

SAP provides an official BAPI programming guide for the development of business objects. It covers both technical and conceptual aspects for the development of business objects. The guide is regularly updated by SAP, so it is a very useful source of information for all developers who want to work in the area of business object development. You will find it in the SAP Help Portal under

http://help.sap.com/sapdocu/core/47x200/HELP-
DATA/DE/a5/3ec8074ac011d1894e0000e829fbbd/frameset.htm.

The SAP Help Portal also offers many other tips on all areas of development for R/3.

7.8 Possibilities for Activation

A BAPI is therefore just a method of a business object that is implemented by an RFC-enabled function module.

Because the business object itself follows an object-oriented approach, SAP distinguishes two alternatives for accessing BAPIs.

- ▶ Function-oriented
- ▶ Object-oriented

With the function-oriented approach, the function module that realizes the method is activated directly. The call can be made using the functions of the RFC API for example.

The idea behind the object-oriented concept is that there is a proxy class for the business object in the external client. The proxy class offers the client all the API functions of the business object and, for its part, undertakes the activation of the appropriate methods in the R/3 System. Figure 7.12 shows how the proxy class fits into the concept.

The following alternatives are available for object-oriented access:

- ▶ ActiveX controls (developed by SAP)
- ▶ DCOM Connector
- ▶ Java Connector

The first two options can be used only on Windows platforms, whereas you can use the Java Connector on any platform.

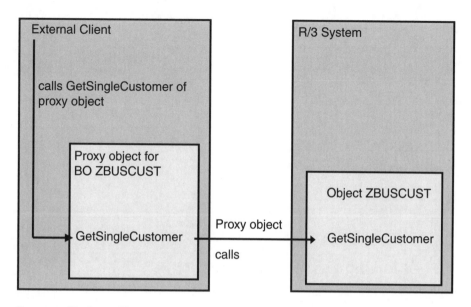

Figure 7.12 The Proxy Object

ActiveX controls include several control elements that can be used to control both the API methods of a business object and also typical RFC-enabled function modules. The control elements are presented in Chapter 8.

Another option that we should also mention is the DCOM Connector that was developed jointly by SAP and Microsoft. It enables the simple integration of any COM objects with the ActiveX controls described above and thus also with BAPIs. One important function of the DCOM Connector is to generate the proxy classes and make them available in the form of a DCOM component. The DCOM Connector is not being further developed by SAP however. Its successor at SAP is the .NET Connector, which fulfills similar tasks for the .NET languages and will certainly play an increasing role in the development of the .NET framework. We will not explain it further in this book.

The third popular option is the Java Connector. It also allows access to the API methods of a business object and is described in Chapter 9. It is particularly worth mentioning that the Java Connector can be used across different platforms.

You can get more information on the latest developments in the area of controlling API methods on the SAP Service Marketplace, alias /connectors.

8   Calling BAPIs from Clients

In the last chapter, you saw how a business object in the R/3 System is created. You also learned how methods of a business object can be called through ActiveX controls. How these calls are performed and which ActiveX controls SAP has developed for calling BAPIs is the topic of this chapter.

8.1   What Are COM and ActiveX?

According to Murphy, ActiveX is:

> "A successful attempt to draw off the arrogance of computer programs into modules and to make it mobile."

It often seems that Murphy was correct in his assessment. The modularization of software components through COM and ActiveX technologies has already been sufficiently described; therefore, the following sections are intended only to provide a glance at the concepts of COM and ActiveX.

COM stands for *Component Object Model*. The idea behind COM is the separation of the definition and implementation of an interface. The interface provides a description of data and methods. It is a kind of contract that stipulates the form and manner of communication between a client and a server. One advantage of a COM interface is that it is binary. This is what makes it possible for a client and a server that were developed in different programming languages to communicate with each other.

The following COM simulation should help you better understand the concept of an interface. Our simulation will use C++ structures and classes to illustrate the principle of COM. The starting point for our simulation is a vehicle. A vehicle has the property, or *attribute*, of speed. The methods "Increase" and "Decrease" applied to the speed affect the speed of the vehicle. Thus the interface for the vehicle could look like this:

```
struct IVehicle
{
    virtual long GetSpeed(void) = 0;
    virtual void IncreaseSpeed(long lSpeed) = 0;
    virtual void DecreaseSpeed(long lSpeed) = 0;
}
```

Listing 8.1 Interface of the Vehicle

The interface IVehicle forms the basis for communication between client and server. The server implements the methods of the interface, and the client calls them.

For the methods of the interface to be reasonably useful, they must first be implemented by a class. The implementation of the interface is performed in our COM simulation in this way:

```
class CVehicle : public IVehicle
{
public:
// Constructors and Destructor
    CVehicle(){m_lSpeed = 0;};
    ~CVehicle(){};
public:
// Methods
    long GetSpeed(void){return m_lSpeed;};
    void IncreaseSpeed(long lSpeed);
    void DecreaseSpeed(long lSpeed);
private:
// Member
    long m_lSpeed;
};
void CVehicle::IncreaseSpeed(long lSpeed)
{
    m_lSpeed += lSpeed;
}
void CVehicle::DecreaseSpeed(long lSpeed)
{
    m_lSpeed -= lSpeed;
}
```

Listing 8.2 Implementation of the Interface

You see that the CVehicle class inherits from the IVehicle interface and implements the IncreaseSpeed, DecreaseSpeed, and GetSpeed methods of the interface. In COM, a class that implements the methods of an interface is also referred to as a *CoClass, COM class,* or *Co-class*.

A client who wants to use the methods of the IVehicle interface must complete the following steps:

- Declare a pointer variable to the interface whose methods he or she wishes to use.

- Create an instance of the class that supports the interface.

In our simulation, the client could obtain an instance of the `CVehicle` class as shown below:

```
// Declare a pointer to the interface
IVehicle *pVehicle = NULL;
// Call an auxiliary function to obtain an
// instance of the CVehicle class
GetCoClass(CLSID_Vehicle, IID_IVehicle, &pVehicle);
```

The client declares a pointer variable of type `IVehicle*`. Via the `GetCoClass` function, it requests an instance of the `CVehicle` class and assigns the instance to the `pVehicle` pointer variable. Using polymorphism, the pointer variable can also administer classes that are derived from the `IVehicle` interface. The client obtains an instance of the `CVehicle` class, but can execute only the methods that the `IVehicle` interface provides because it has declared only one pointer variable of the type of this interface.

The `GetCoClass` function creates an instance of the `CVehicle` class. To achieve this, the function transfers the values `CLSID_Vehicle` and `IID_IVehicle` at its interface. Using the information, the server can determine the class from which an instance is to be created, and using the identifier for the interface, it is possible to check whether the class supports the interface at all. In the COM reality, the instance of a CoClass is not created via the `GetCoClass` function. One option in COM for creating a CoClass is the `CoCreateInstance` function. Figure 8.1 shows the relationships once again.

ActiveX is an expansion of the COM concept to control elements. ActiveX controls also provide an interface via which the client can communicate with the control element; in some circumstances, several COM classes are issued with one ActiveX control. The technology is comparable to Java applets or Java beans.

The development of ActiveX controls has its origin in VBX components. These are software modules that can be integrated into Visual Basic. At the transition from 16- to 32-bit operating systems, these old *control elements* became unusable, and Microsoft defined the OCX components (OLE control extensions) as the new standard. They are based on the OLE 2 standard. In this context, the terms COM and OLE 2.0 are often used synonymously.[1]

---

1 The OLE 2.0 standard must not be confused with the OLE 1.0 standard, which is a technique for combined documents.

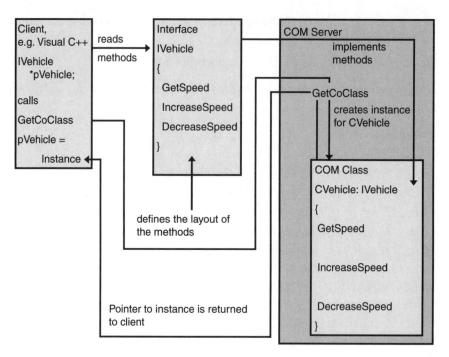

Figure 8.1 Communication Paths in COM

Before dealing with these SAP ActiveX controls for calling the methods of a business class, we will comment on a behavior that gives ActiveX beginners a headache. Particularly in the field of SAP ActiveX controls, some classes that are included with ActiveX controls cannot be instantiated directly by the client.

This behavior results from the fact that the classes of an ActiveX control do not a priori support OLE automation. Rather, every class of an ActiveX control that was developed on the basis of the *Microsoft Foundation Class* must call the `EnableAutomation` method of the class `CCmdTarget`, which supports automation. Calling the `EnableAutomation` method is usually performed in the constructor of the respective class.

If the call is not present, the class does not support automation at first, and the client cannot create an instance of the class directly. For a client to come into possession of a valid instance of such a class, a second auxiliary class must exist that supports automation and provides a method for creating the first class.

The method of the auxiliary class creates an instance of the first class and calls the method EnableAutomation for the instance of the first class. The new instance of the first class is passed to the client. Now the client owns a valid instance of the first class and can execute the methods of the first class

8.2 "What Is Your Name?" or an Introduction to the Use of ActiveX Controls

The sections that follow describe the ActiveX controls provided by SAP for calling the methods of a business object. This entry into the use of ActiveX controls also involves a change in programming language. SAP developed the ActiveX controls primarily to be able to develop external clients for the R/3 System more quickly in Visual Basic (VB). This is why all examples in this chapter are written in VB. In the following, we assume that the reader has experience with VB and with a VB development environment, for example the Visual Basic Version 6 used here. For a detailed discussion of this topic, we refer to the extensive technical literature (see Appendix A).

Our object, `ZBUSCUST`, has the `GetCustomerName` method. In our first project, an external client is to call up the methods and display the name of the customer.

Our first program must therefore fulfill three tasks:

1. It must log itself onto the R/3 System.
2. It must log itself off of the R/3 System.
3. In the meantime, it must call up the `GetCustomerName` method of the `ZBUS-CUST` business object (BO) via the proxy object.

For the first example, we first create the `ShowCustomerName` project in Visual Basic. We choose the **standard EXE** as the project type. We will successively expand the project by the elements for calling the `GetCustomerName` method.

8.2.1 The SAP BAPI Control

For the development of an external client that calls a BAPI method, it is sufficient to integrate a single ActiveX control from SAP. In this case, it is the *BAPI control*.

The following classes are included with the BAPI control:

▶ `SAPBAPIControl`
▶ `SAPBusinessObject`

The `SAPBAPIControl` class is the central class of the ActiveX controls delivered by SAP for calling the methods of a business object. It is the only class able to create the BO proxy object. This BO proxy object is, as mentioned in Chapter 7, the object via which the client calls the methods of the business object in the R/3 System. The `SAPBAPIControl` class can create all classes for data exchange. In addition, the `Connection` attribute represents a valid instance of the `Connection` class of the still unmentioned SAP Logon control. This allows the `SAPBAPICont-`

`rol` class to set up a connection to the R/3 System. It is sufficient to integrate the BAPI control in one client alone in order to call the methods of a business object in R/3.

The following tables show the most frequently used methods and attributes of the `SAPBAPIControl` class:

Method	Meaning
AboutBox	Display a dialog box with version information
CreateTransactionID	Create a transaction number for asynchronous data transmission
DimAs	Method for creating structure and table objects
GetSAPObject	Method for creating the BO proxy object

Table 8.1 Overview of the Most Frequently Used Methods of the SAPBAPIControl Class

Attribute	Meaning
BAPIExceptionCodes	Specifies whether the text or the exception ID is returned to the BO proxy object for an exception in the function module that implements a BAPI method. If the value for the attribute is set to True, only the ID of the error as it was stored in the interface of the function module is returned. If the value is False, a text that contains the name of the BO method in which the error occurred is output, in addition to the ID of the error.
Connection	Attribute for administering an R/3 connection. The Connection attribute is a valid instance of the Connection class.
LogFileName	Specify the file for the trace recordings, by default: *dev_bapi.trc*
LogLevel	Specify extent of the recording: value range from 0–9.
TransactionID	For transactional clients; ID under which the data is sent to an SAP system.

Table 8.2 Overview of the Most Frequently Used Attributes of the SAPBAPIControl Class

Among the methods listed above, the methods `DimAs` and `GetSAPObject` as well as the `Connection` attribute must be especially stressed. When you look at their descriptions, you note that the attributes and methods mentioned alone, in combination with classes that can instantiate themselves, are sufficient to call the methods of business objects in the R/3 System. In our first example, we will use only the methods and attributes mentioned above.

The second class of the `BAPIControl`, `SAPBusinessObject`, is for administering several BO proxy objects. The class provides the following methods for administering BO proxy objects:

Method	Attribute
Add	Add BO proxy object to the collection
Item	Access to a BO proxy object in the collection via the index
Remove	Remove BO proxy object from the collection

Table 8.3 Methods of the SAPBusinessObject Class

The `Count` attribute of the `SAPBusinessObject` class indicates how many BO proxy objects are currently in the collection.

To integrate the BAPI control into the project, we can select the **Project · Components** menu in the Visual Basic 6 development environment, for example. A list of all registered ActiveX controls is displayed. The controls that are to be integrated into the project are selected here.

8.2.2 Opening a Connection with the R/3 System

Logging on to and off of the R/3 System is performed using the `Connection` attribute of the `SAPBAPIControl` class. The `Connection` attribute represents a valid instance of the `Connection` class. The `Connection` class is a class that is delivered with the logon control. Therefore, it is also discussed in Section 8.5.2. At the moment, all we need is the information that a connection to the R/3 System was opened using the methods `Logon` and `Logoff`. The `Logon` method offers the option of using the `bSilent` variable to specify whether the logon is to be performed without a logon dialog (i.e., silent) or with a logon dialog. If the `False` value is transferred in the `bSilent` variable, the logon is performed using a logon dialog.

Armed with this information, you can begin with the development of the logon to the R/3 System. On the form in our project, we first place three buttons with the following functions:

▶ Logging on to the R/3 System
▶ Logging off of the R/3 System
▶ Calling the BO method

For logging on and off, it is sufficient to place the call-up of the `Logon` and `Logoff` methods for the buttons. It is a sign of good programming style when:

▶ The user can log himself or herself onto the R/3 System only once.

▶ The BO method can be called up only after successfully logging on.

These requirements are met by alternately activating and deactivating the functions for logging on, logging off, and calling up. This means that the functions for logging off and calling the BO methods are inactive until a successful logon to the R/3 System takes place. The logon function is deactivated then. In reverse, after logging off, the logon function is reactivated and the functions for calling the BO methods and the functions for logging off are deactivated. Logging on to the R/3 System can be implemented as follows:

```
Private Sub CBSAPLogon_Click()
On Error GoTo Errorhandler
' Make connection with SAPsystem
    If m_oSAPBAPICtrl.Connection.Logon(0, False) <> _
        True Then
        Exit Sub
    End If
' Deactive Logon.function => multiple logon
' is prevented
    CBSAPLogon.Enabled = False
    CBSAPLogoff.Enabled = True
' Create BAPI proxy object
    Set m_oBUSCust = _
        m_oSAPBAPICtrl.GetSAPObject("ZBUSCUST")
' Function for callup of method GetCustomerName
' activate
    CBCallMethod.Enabled = True
    Exit Sub
Errorhandler:
    MsgBox Err.Description, vbOKOnly
End Sub
```

Listing 8.3 Implementing the Logon to the R/3 System

You can see that after a successful logon, the function for logging on is deactivated so that multiple logons are prevented. At the same time, the functions for logging off and calling up the BO methods are activated. In addition, after a successful logon, the BO proxy object is also created. Logging off itself could be programmed as follows:

```
Private Sub CBSAPLogoff_Click()
    m_oSAPBAPICtrl.Connection.Logoff
```

```
    CBSAPLogoff.Enabled = False
    CBSAPLogon.Enabled = True
    CBCallMethod.Enabled = False
End Sub
```

Listing 8.4 Implementing Closing of the R/3 Connection

When logging on to the R/3 System, no test takes place for whether a connection to the R/3 System exists at all. This is not necessary for the `Logoff` method because it checks internally whether a connection exists. If this is not the case, it is terminated without doing anything.

Finally let us look at the initialization of the form:

```
Private Sub Form_Load()
    CBCallMethod.Enabled = False
    CBSAPLogoff.Enabled = False
End Sub
```

Listing 8.5 Initialization of the Form

The initialization consists only of a deactivation of the functions for logging off and calling the BO methods, because no connection to the R/3 System exists when the program is started.

The first program has now been developed to the extent that it is possible to log onto the R/3 System. Let us execute the program and see whether a logon occurs. If we select the **Logon** function, a dialog box will be displayed in which the R/3 System can be selected and the user-specific logon data can be entered. After confirmation of the data, our client should log onto the gateway of the appropriate R/3 System. This can be checked, for example, through a separate logon to the appropriate R/3 System. If you open the SAP Gateway Monitor in the respective R/3 System, the list of external clients should include your own program.

8.2.3 Calling the Business Object Method

After showing how to make a connection with the R/3 system, we turn to the most important aspect of programming with ActiveX controls: calling the methods of a business object.

For the first test, we require a simple method. It should have an importing and an exporting parameter. Therefore, we add the `GetCustomerName` method to the ZBUSCUST BO. The interface of the method is:

Parameter	Type	Meaning
IP_CUSTOMER_NO	CUSTNO	Customer number
EP_CUSTOMERNAME	NAME1	Name of the customer

Table 8.4 Interface of the GetCustomerName Method

In the R/3 System, the GetCustomerName method is supported by the Z_RFC_GET_CUSTOMER_NAME function module. The interface of the function module is identical with the GetCustomerName method of the ZBUSCUST BO. The logic of the function module is:

```
*"-----------------------------------------------
*"*"Local Interface:
*"  IMPORTING
*"     VALUE(IP_CUSTOMER_NO) TYPE  CUSTNO
*"  EXPORTING
*"     VALUE(EP_CUSTOMERNAME) TYPE  NAME1
*"  EXCEPTIONS
*"     ERROR_CUSTOMER_DOES_NOT_EXIST
*"-----------------------------------------------
SELECT SINGLE name1
  FROM zknaljms
  INTO (ep_customername)
 WHERE CUSTNO = ip_customer_no.
* If the customer does not exist, trigger
* exception
IF sy-subrc <> 0.
   RAISE error_customer_does_not_exist.
ENDIF.
```

Listing 8.6 Implementation of the Z_RFC_GET_CUSTOMER_NAME Function Module

After expanding the ZBUSCUST BO by the GetCustomerName method, we can discuss calling it from an external client. For this call we must perform the following steps in the client.

▶ Declaring the proxy object of the ZBUSCUST BO

▶ Instantiating the proxy object BO

▶ Inserting a dialog for entering the customer number

▶ Calling up the GetCustomerName method

To call the ZBUSCUST BO in the R/3 System, we require a proxy object in the client that forwards the calls. When creating the proxy object, the question arises which class this proxy object has. No class exists in Visual Basic that has the methods of the ZBUSCUST BO. Without the correct data type, the callup of the GetCustomerName would be rejected as faulty during execution of the program.

The dilemma is solved by *late binding*. The type of the class is left open during late binding. Instead a generic placeholder is inserted, for example the Object type in Visual Basic. When executing the program, no method call for the Object type is checked for correctness. The developer must himself ensure that the instance of a class that has the called-up methods and attributes is assigned to the object. Late binding allows us to call up methods of an object whose appearance is not known until program runtime. We can therefore declare the proxy object as Object as long as we ensure that an instance of a class that recognizes the GetCustomerName method is assigned to the object during runtime. We therefore declare in our form:

```
Dim m_oBUSCust As Object
```

To create an instance of the proxy object BO, call up the GetSAPObject method of the SAPBAPIControl class. The interface of the method is:

Variable	Meaning
ObjType	Name of the object type. As an alternative, the name of the business object can be specified.
Objkey1 to 10	Values for the key fields of the object. Specifying them is optional. It is absolutely necessary for instance-dependent methods to correctly initialize the instance in the R/3 System.

Table 8.5 Interface of the GetSAPObject Method

Assignment of the variables Objkey1 to 10 to the key fields of the business object in the R/3 System is performed based on the sequence of the declaration of the key fields in the business object. The Objkey1 variable in the client is linked with the first key field in the business object. It continues to the Objkey10 variable.

The GetCustomerName method of the ZBUSCUST BO is an instance-independent method, so we do not have to make any specifications for the key fields.

When calling up the GetSAPObject method, note that it can be successful only when a connection to the R/3 System was opened previously. The reason for this is that the GetSAPObject method calls a series of function modules in the R/3 System to determine information on the structure of the business object. Because in our example the setup of the connection to the R/3 System is implemented in the "Logon" function, the creation of the BO proxy object is also implemented there, as can be seen in the listing above.

The GetCustomerName method is called up by the BO proxy object as soon as the user executes the CustomerName function. The GetCustomerName method is transferred in the IP_CUSTOMER_NO parameter. The name of the customer is returned in the EP_CUSTOMERNAME parameter. The call of the method might look like this:

```
Private Sub CBCustName_Click()
Dim CustomerNo As String, _
    CustomerName As String
On Error GoTo Errorhandler
' Dialog for determining the customer number
    FDLGGetCustNo.Show vbModal
    CustomerNo = FDLGGetCustNo.GetCustNo
' Call BO method
    m_oBUSCust.GetCustomerName _
                        IP_CUSTOMER_NO:=CustomerNo, _
                        EP_CUSTOMERNAME:=CustomerName
    MsgBox CustomerName, vbOKOnly
    Exit Sub
Errorhandler:
    MsgBox Err.Description, vbOKOnly
End Sub
```

Listing 8.7 Call of the BO Method by the BO Proxy Object

First the customer number is entered via a modal dialog box. Then the GetCustomerName method is called up by the proxy object to determine the name of the customer. Finally, the name of the customer is displayed.

Now you must ensure that the BO proxy object is removed from the working memory as soon as the program is ended. To do so, add the following rows to the Unload event of our form:

```
If Not m_oBUSCust Is Nothing Then
   Set m_oBUSCust = Nothing
End If
```

You will find the full ShowCustomerName program on the Web page for this book.

8.2.4   What Is a BAPI Proxy Object Anyway?

In our first example, we left the class type for the BO proxy object generic, i.e., open, and used the `GetSAPObject` method to assign to the `SAPBAPIControl` class the instance of a class, using which we called up the `GetCustomerName` method of the `ZBUSCUST` BO in the R/3 System. Here it is possible to get the wrong impression that the `GetSAPObject` method is a kind of "class factory" that can generate and instantiate new, specific class descriptions. This is not the case, however.

The data type of our proxy object is still the generic `Object` data type. However how can this generic object access the methods of a special class? Without going too deeply into the details of COM, we want to show roughly what the proxy object is about.

If a COM client wants to execute the methods of a COM class, two alternatives are available:

▶ Direct callup of the method of the COM class

▶ Indirect callup of the method using an auxiliary method

The first alternative was described at the beginning of the chapter. The idea of the indirect call is that the name of the method that is actually to be executed is transferred to the auxiliary method. This auxiliary method checks for the existence of the target method. If the target method exists in the class, it is executed; otherwise, the auxiliary method returns an error. This procedure, which seems a little inconvenient at first, has the advantage of being open. The "open" concept goes in two directions:

▶ On the one hand, it allows the use of programming languages that cannot directly call the methods of a COM class (for example Visual Basic) for the development of COM clients. In this way, Visual Basic could be integrated into the COM concept, although it cannot directly call the methods of a COM class.

▶ The concept also allows non-COM software modules to be used as COM servers. Finally, the auxiliary method can be implemented in such a way that it internally calls a non-COM software module.

An auxiliary interface that offers a method for calling the target method is required to implement the concept. In the COM world, the auxiliary interface is referred to as the `IDispatch` and the method as `Invoke`. The name of the target method to be run is transferred to the `Invoke` method.[2] It then calls the target methods internally. In a VB program, the sequence is hidden in the following row,

```
m_oBUSCust.GetCustomerName _
                IP_CUSTOMER_NO:=CustomerNo, _
                EP_CUSTOMERNAME:=CustomerName
```

which internally commands the `Invoke` method of the `IDispatch` interface to run the `GetCustomerName` method in the class of the server (remember that the `GetCustomerName` method belongs to an R/3 business object). For further runs, an agreement is made that the class in the server that implements the methods of the `IDispatch` interface is to be called `CDispImpl`.

The fact that the business object in the R/3 System does not display any COM class leads us to think that it is also possible to use non-COM software modules as COM servers. To be able to run business object methods, the `Invoke` method in the `CDispImpl` class is implemented in such a way that it sends RFC calls to the R/3 System and executes the corresponding SAP function module. In this regard, the SAP implementation differs from the standard implementation, which makes no RFC calls. The `CDispImpl` class administers the assignment of the name of the BO method to the SAP function module that implements the method. The table is referred to from here on as the *dispatch table*.

The question arises of how the dispatch table is supplied with data on the structure of the BO and its implementation. To obtain the necessary information, the `GetSAPObject` method of the `SAPBAPIControl` class internally calls the `SWO_TYPE_INFO_GET` function module of the `SWOR` function group in the R/3 System. Via the function module, all information on the structure of the `ZBUSCUST` BO is transferred to the instance of the `CDispImpl` class. In particular, it is informed in the form of a table that SAP function modules are used to implement the individual BO methods. Armed with this information, the `Invoke` method can determine the function modules corresponding to the `GetCustomerName` method and execute them. Figure 8.2 shows the relationships once again.

---

2 In reality, an identifier—a number—is transferred, with an assignment existing between the method name and the identifier.

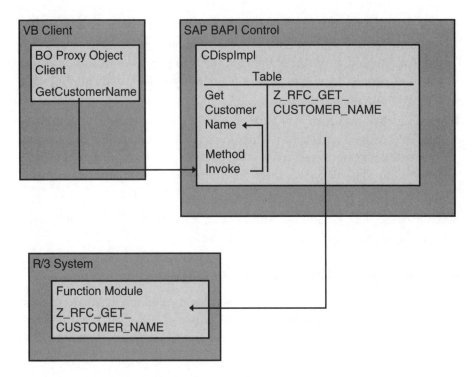

Figure 8.2 Calling the BO Method with a Proxy Class

In conclusion, we stress again that the description above is a simplification of the reality. For details, we refer to the appropriate special literature.

We now have successfully developed an external client that calls the GetCustomerName method of the ZBUSCUST BO using BAPI controls. Before looking at advanced programming techniques, we should look at questions relating to how to better structure complex programs. These include:

▶ Naming conventions
▶ Wrapping the proxy object in its own class

8.3 Naming Conventions During Programming

Naming conventions make it possible to recognize the properties of a variable from the name. In this way, the developer is informed at all times of the properties of the variables he is using. Frequent moving to the location of the declaration becomes unnecessary. The following naming conventions have been agreed on for our example, and can also be found in daily practice.

- Attributes of a class begin with m_

- The data type of a variable is always at the beginning of its name in small letters. For example, a variable of the `Boolean` type begins with a small b and an object variable with an o. If the variable of Boolean type is the attribute of a class, it always begins with m_b.

- If the variables are structure or table objects for data exchange with an R/3 System, an `I` or an `E` designates whether the parameter is imported or exported. An `S` or `T` designates whether it is a structure or a table. A table object that is exported to the SAP system therefore has the `oET` prefix. If the table is the member of a class, the prefix is expanded to `m_oET(Name)`.

These conventions are quite practical because it can be seen immediately from the prefix what data type is behind the variable.

8.4 Wrapping the BAPI Proxy Object

In our first example, the BO proxy object was the member of our windows class. This procedure is acceptable for simple test programs. However, it is a different story when the BO proxy object is to call up several methods whose interfaces have many parameters.

In the R/3 System, the business object and its methods form a unit. Therefore, the BO proxy object should also reflect the uniformity of methods, attributes, and exchange parameters. To achieve this, wrapper classes are often used. They offer the following advantages:

- Higher program transparency

- Better reusability of the program components

Higher program transparency results from the fact that it is clearly visible for a wrapper class which table and structure objects are required for which BO proxy object. In addition, certain tasks can be administered centrally, such as creating the interface parameters or removal of the object from working memory. The higher transparency reduces the development effort substantially for later adaptations in the program logic.

The reusability of program components is achieved because, for a wrapper class, the logic for calling up BO methods is separated from the window class. It can be saved in a separate file and integrated into other projects.

The following class suggestion for our first example shows how a wrapper class can, in general, be structured.

```
Dim m_oBUSCust As Object, _
    m_oConnection As SAPLogonCtrl.Connection

Private Sub InitialMembers()
    Set m_oBUSCust = Nothing
    Set m_oConnection = Nothing
End Sub

Private Sub Class_Initialize()
    InitialMembers
End Sub

Private Sub Class_Terminate()
    InitialMembers
End Sub

Public Function CreateBOObject(oBAPICtrl As SAPBAPIControl, _
                        oConnection As _
                        SAPLogonCtrl.Connection) As Boolean
    On Error GoTo Errorhandler
    Set m_oConnection = oConnection
    Set m_oBUSCust = oBAPICtrl.GetSAPObject("ZBUSCUST")
Errorhandler:
    MsgBox Err.Description, vbOKOnly
End Function

Public Function GetCustomerName(ByVal CUSTNO As String)
                                                As String
On Error GoTo Errorhandler
' Convert customer number into an internal format
    CUSTNO = String(10 - Len(CUSTNO), "0") + CUSTNO
    If Not m_oBUSCust Is Nothing Then
        m_oBUSCust.GetCustomerName IP_CUSTOMER_NO:=CUSTNO, _
                        EP_CUSTOMERNAME:= _
                        GetCustomerName
    Else
        MsgBox "No proxy object created", vbOKOnly
        GetCustomerName = ""
    End If
Errorhandler:
```

```
      MsgBox Err.Description, vbOKOnly
      GetCustomerName = ""
End Function
```

Listing 8.8 Setup of the CBUSCust Wrapper Class

The class draft shows that the wrapper class has the following variables and methods:

▶ **Object variable m_oBUSCust**
This represents the BO proxy object. It is used to call all methods of the business object in the R/3 System.

▶ **Central method CreateBOObject**
Serves for creating the BO proxy object and adopting the connection data. At its interface, the method receives valid instances of the Connection class of the SAPLogonCtrl and the SAPBAPIControl class. It sets up its own object variable, m_oConnection, of the Connection class type according to the data of the transferred connection and calls up the GetSAPObject method of the oBAPICtrl object variable in order to create the BO proxy object.

▶ **Method GetCustomerName**
This method internally calls the GetCustomerName method of the BO proxy object. Performing additional checks of the transferred data is worth considering for more complex methods.

▶ **Method InitialMembers**
Object variables are initialized in this method.

In addition, a wrapper class requires a method for creating the interface parameters if tables or structures are exchanged. This is usually a private method of the class. There are two possible alternatives for calling up the method, depending on which way of creating the interface parameters is selected:

▶ **Callup in the constructor**
This variant is advisable if the TableFactory control is used.

▶ **Callup in the CreateBOObject method**
If the DimAs method of the SAPBAPIControl is used for creating the interface parameters in the client.

Because the interface of the GetCustomerName method has been kept very simple, the CBUSCust wrapper class still does not have an appropriate method. It will be added later when data aggregates are to be exchanged between the R/3 System and the external client.

8.5 A Better Method for Setting Up a Connection to the R/3 System

In our first example program, the connection to the R/3 System was implemented via the `Connection` attribute of the `SAPBAPIControl` class. We have also learned that the attribute represents a valid instance of the `Connection` class of the logon control. Now the program is to be expanded so that the connection is no longer set up via the `Connection` attribute of the `SAPBAPIControl` class, but rather directly via the logon control.

The procedure offers the following advantages:

▶ Higher program transparency, because it can be seen which class administers the connection

▶ Option of administering several R/3 connections, because additional connections can be opened using the `NewConnection` method introduced below

▶ Development of an event handler for events of the `SAPLogonControl` class

The logon control is delivered in the *wdtlog.ocx* file. The file is located in the directory *C:\Program files\SAP\FrontEnd\Controls*.

The control is again integrated into the `ShowCustomerName` project via the **Projects · Components** menu. The following classes are delivered with it:

▶ `SAPLogonControl`
▶ `Connection`

This control also provides the following two enumeration types:

▶ `CRfcConnnectionStatus`
▶ `CSAPLogonControlEvents`

The central tasks of the `SAPLogonControl` class are:

▶ Instantiating the `Connection` class
▶ Providing event handlers for events of the dialog for selecting the R/3 System. We have already used the selection dialog in our first example. The implementation of event handlers is presented further below.

The `SAPLogonControl` class provides the `NewConnection` method to create an instance of the `Connection` class. This is a parameter-free method. It returns an instance of the `Connection` class when it has been run successfully. The `NewConnection` method is very important because it is the only method able to create an instance of the `Connection` class. The other methods of the logon control are of lesser significance and are not presented here.

In addition to creating an instance of the `Connection` class, the `SAPLogonControl` class offers the option of specifying the data for the logon to the R/3 System in attributes designed for this purpose. However, in practice, this data is specified directly in the instance of the `Connection` class. Therefore, the attributes are also presented there.

The `Connection` class administers the connection to the R/3 System itself. The class provides the methods listed below to perform administration:

Method	Meaning
LastError	Displays a dialog box with information on the last error to occur in a way similar to the `RfcLastError` function of the RFC API
Logoff	Logs off of the R/3 System
Logon	Logs on to the R/3 System
Reconnect	Attempts to restore a cut connection
SystemInformation	Outputs a dialog box with information on the R/3 System
SystemMessage	Outputs system messages in a dialog box

Table 8.6 Methods of the Connection Class

Of the methods listed above, `Logon`, `Logoff`, `Reconnect`, and `LastError` are used very frequently.

Attributes for the specification of connection data can be divided into four groups:

▶ User data

▶ Data for logging on to a particular application server

▶ Data for load balancing

▶ Other logon information

To specify user data, the following attributes of the `Connection` class are used:

Attribute	Meaning
User	User
Password	User's password

Table 8.7 Attributes for Specifying the User Data

Attribute	Meaning
Client	Client
Language	Logon language

Table 8.7 Attributes for Specifying the User Data (cont.)

To log on to a particular application server, values must be set for the following attributes:

Attribute	Meaning
ApplicationServer	IP address of the computer on which the application server is located
SystemNumber	System number according to which the port is determined
GatewayHost	As an alternative, the IP address of the computer on which the gateway is located can also be specified
GatewayService	Specifies the port to which the gateway listens

Table 8.8 Attribute for Specifying the R/3 System

If load balancing is to be used, the following attributes must be used instead:

Attributes	Meaning
MessageServer	IP address of the computer on which the message server is installed
GroupName	Name of the logon group

Table 8.9 Attributes for Defining Load Balancing

In addition to the attributes for specifying the user and system data, further attributes with which the properties of a connection can be set also play a role. These include:

Attribute	Meaning
ABAPDebug	Activates the ABAP debugger
IsConnnected	Connection status: The return value is of the CRfcConnectionStatus enumeration type

Table 8.10 Attributes for Specifying the Properties of the R/3 Connection

Attribute	Meaning
RfcWithDialog	Activates the dialog capability; R/3 Dynpros can be displayed in the client. Only useful if an SAP GUI is running on the client
TraceLevel	Sets extent of the trace recording; value range from 0–9

Table 8.10 Attributes for Specifying the Properties of the R/3 Connection (cont.)

The list above shows that the status of a connection to the R/3 System can be determined from the IsConnected attribute. However, when using it, note that the attribute has a valid value only after callup of the Logon or Logoff method of the Connection class. If the IsConnected attribute is requested before this, the result can be false (see also Section 8.5.3). The return type of the attribute is CRfcConnectionStatus. It is an enumeration type for determining the connection status. It can have the following values:

Value	Meaning
tloRfcConnectCancel	Connection has been terminated
tloRfcConnected	Connection exists
tloRfcConnectFailed	Logon to the R/3 System failed
tloRfcConnectParameterMissing	Logon to the R/3 System not possible due to missing data
tloRfcConnectNotConnected	No connection currently exists

Table 8.11 Values of the CRfcConnectionStatus Counting Status

8.5.1 Integrating the Logon Control into the Client

After presenting the properties of the SAP logon control, we now want to use it in our project. This means that the connection to the R/3 System is now to be administered by an instance of the Connection class. To do so, we insert the m_oConnection object variable of the Connection type in our project, ShowCustomerName. Logging on to the R/3 System and closing the connection to the system are controlled via this m_oConnection object variable. To achieve this, the methods of the Connection class mentioned above are called up in the functions for logging on and off. The new implementation of the function for logging on would look like this:

```
Private Sub CBSAPLogon_Click()
On Error GoTo Errorhandler
' Make connection via an object of the connection-
```

```
' class
    If m_oConnection.Logon(0, False) <> _
        True Then
        Exit Sub
    End If
:

Error handler:
    MsgBox Err.Description, vbOKOnly
End Sub
```

Listing 8.9 Using the Connection Class to Log On to the R/3 System

This listing shows the difference from the first example of the logon method: The logon is now performed by the `m_oConnection` object variable, which is an instance of the `Connection` class, and no longer by the `Connection` attribute of the `m_oSAPBAPICtrl` class.

Because the `Connection` class also offers the option of specifying the values for connection to the R/3 System directly in the corresponding attributes, the following alternative for logging on is also conceivable:

```
With m_oConnection
    .ApplicationServer = "10.10.34.131"
    .SystemNumber = 1
    .System = "- D46 (Demo - 4.6b)"
' User Data
    .User = "valid user"
    .Password = "valid password"
    .Client = "099"
    .Language = "EN"
End With
```

Listing 8.10 Specifying the Connection Arguments in the Attributes of the Connection Class

Chapter 4 showed that when RFC API is used, it is possible for an external client to log onto the R/3 System using a configuration file. The SAP logon control also offers this option. It provides the `UseSAPRFCIni` attribute for working with a configuration file. If the value `True` is stored here, the system data is read from the configuration file. It must be noted that the attribute does not work for early versions of the SAP logon control.

8.5.2 Events of the SAPLogonControl Class

Now that the logon control has been successfully integrated into our project, we want to briefly discuss the events of the `Connection` class.

In general, events of ActiveX controls are used to inform the client of the occurrence of events to which he can react. "Reacting" is performed by the client providing a method which is called by the ActiveX control as soon as an event occurs. The concept of a callback function is used again. The methods that are called by the ActiveX control as soon as the event occurs are often referred to as *event handlers*.

The `Connection` class sends the following events:

Event	Meaning
Cancel	Triggered when the logon dialog of the `Connection` class is ended using a cancel function
Click	Triggered when the button of the logon control is clicked
Logon	Triggered when an R/3 connection is opened via the `Logon` method of the `Connection` class
Logoff	Triggered when an R/3 connection is closed via the `Logoff` method of the `Connection` class
Error	Should be triggered in an error situation. Unfortunately it is not specified what type of error it is. The event is not triggered if an exception is triggered in a function module or if the logon to the R/3 System fails.

Table 8.12 Events of the SAPLogonControl Class

We will now present the development of an event handler for the `Logon` event in our project. To provide an event handler for events, complete the following steps:

▶ Create the event handler

▶ Specify the events that the control is to send to the client

Creating an event handler is very simple. In our form, we first switch to the program view. In the dropdown list with the elements of the form, we select the `m_oSAPLogonCtrl` object variable, which is an instance of the `SAPLogonControl` class. The events for the control element are then displayed in the right dropdown list. Clicking the `Logon` event selects it and creates a body for the method at the same time. Body means that only the interface of the method is created. The logic to be executed for the `Logon` event must be implemented in the body by the developer himself:

```
Private Sub m_oSAPLogonCtrl_Logon _
                        (ByVal Connection As Object)
    MsgBox "Event Logon passed", vbOKOnly
End Sub
```

Listing 8.11 Event Handler for the Event Logon

The event handler alone is not sufficient for the client to be able to react to events. You must also specify in the `Events` attribute of the `SAPLogonControl` class which events the logon control should send to the client. A combination of the values of the `CSAPLogonControlEvents` enumeration type is stored in the `Events` attribute to make the specification. The `CSAPLogonControlEvents` enumeration type specifies the maximum number of events that can be reacted to.

Value	Meaning
tloDisableAllLogonEvents	Deactivates all Logon events
tloEnableAllLogonEvents	Activates all Logon events
tloEnableOnCancel	Activates the Cancel event
tloEnableOnClick	Activates the Click event
tloEnableOnError	Activates the Error event
tloEnableOnLogon	Activates the Logon event
tloEnableOnLogoff	Activates the Logoff event

Table 8.13 Value Range of the CSAPLogonControlEvents Counting Type

To be able to react to the `Logon` event, the `tloEnableOnLogon` value must be specified in the `Events` attribute of the `SAPLogonControl` class in the following way:

```
m_oSAPLogonCtrl.Events = tloEnableOnLogon
```

The combination of several values is also permitted. This makes it possible for the client to react to several events. An example of a combination is:

```
m_oSAPLogonCtrl.Events = tloEnableOnLogon + _
                         tloEnableOnLogoff
```

In this listing, the client signals that it provides event handlers for the events `Logon` and `Logoff`. It is useful to specify which events the program is to react to using its own event handlers when loading the form.

8.5.3 Recognizing a Disconnection

Developers of an external application are often confronted with the problem that they would like to be able to react to a disconnection to the R/3 System. Therefore, they search for an event that signals the disconnection. In particular, the Cancel event seems a clear choice. However it soon becomes disappointingly apparent that it does not help to solve the problem. We saw above that the Cancel event applies only to the logon dialog.

When we look at the problem in more depth, it becomes clear that no event can exist through which the SAP system can signal the disconnection to an external program. An application opens a connection to the R/3 System. The client's connection to the SAP system is cut, for example, for technical reasons. Now the system is to signal the client by an event that the connection no longer exists; that is, it is expected that the SAP system informs the client via a no longer existent connection that the connection was cut. This, of course, does not work. If the connection between the SAP system and an external client is cut, data can no longer be sent via this connection.

Unfortunately, the IsConnected attribute of the Connection class does not solve the problem either because it does not test the current connection. The status of the IsConnected attribute changes only by calling up the Logon and Logoff methods of the Connection class.

One approach to solving the problem is for the external client to constantly call a method in the R/3 System. This transfers the polling to a thread. We now want to look at the implementation of this solution. The following steps are performed to achieve this:

▶ Loading over the ExistenceCheck method of the IFEXIST interface in the ZBUSCUST BO in the R/3 System

▶ Creating a timer control element in the FShowCustomer form of the ShowCustomerName program

▶ Expanding the CBUSCust wrapper class in the client program by the ExistenceCheck method

▶ Calling up the ExistenceCheck method in the Event timer

The ExistenceCheck method of the ZBUSCUST BO is loaded over in the SAP system as shown in the following (see also Chapter 7):

▶ The Synchronous flag is set in the general attributes of the method.

▶ In the ABAP/4 attributes, **API function** is selected as the type, and the SAP function module RFCPING is entered. Because RFCPING is a parameter-free function module, no importing or exporting parameters must be created for the method.

▶ Then the method call is generated.

▶ Finally, the status of the method is set to "released," and the ZBUSCUST BO is generated.

In the client program, the CBUSCust class is also expanded by the Existence-Check method. The return value of the attribute is of the type CRfcConnec-tionStatus. Within the function, the ExistenceCheck method of the ZBUS-CUST BO in the R/3 System is called up via the proxy object. If the method can be called up, the function returns the value tloRfcConnected, otherwise tloRfc-NotConnected.

```
Public Function ExistenceCheck() As _
                            CRfcConnectionStatus
On Error GoTo Errorhandler
    m_oBUSCust.ExistenceCheck
    ExistenceCheck = tloRfcConnected
    Exit Function
Errorhandler:
    ExistenceCheck = tloRfcNotConnected
    Exit Function
End Function
```

Listing 8.12 Implementing the ExistenceCheck Function in the CBUSCust Class

Finally, in the Timer event, the ExistenceCheck method is called up and the return value checked. If the return value does not equal tloRfcConnected, the user can be informed of the situation via a dialog. In our example, the MsgBox function is used for this task. vbYesNo was selected as the message box type so the user can try to set up the connection to the R/3 System again. The following listing is a programming suggestion.

```
Private Sub m_oTimer_Timer()
' Check whether the connection to the R/3 system still exists
 If m_oCustomer.ExistenceCheck() <> tloRfcConnected _
    Then
    If MsgBox("Connection broken ! Try to Reconnect?" _
            , vbYesNo) = vbYes _
        Then
' Try to restore connection
        If m_oConnection.Reconnect() = False Then
            MsgBox "No connection!", vbOKOnly
```

```
' Deactivate timer
         m_oTimer.Enabled = False
      End If
   Else
' Deactivate timer
      m_oTimer.Enabled = False
   End If
 End If
End Sub
```

Listing 8.13 Testing the Connection Status in the Timer Event

8.6 Concepts for Creating Data Aggregates

Chapter 4 showed which steps are to be performed to exchange structures and tables using the RFC API with the R/3 System. This topic will now be expanded to cover the ActiveX controls from SAP.

In external clients that were developed using the RFC API, a manual description of the field structure for the data aggregate was created in such a way that it corresponds to the structure in the Data Dictionary of the R/3 System. For external clients that were developed with the SAP ActiveX controls, manual creation of the structures in the client is not necessary. Instead, structures and tables are represented by instances of the Structure and Table classes. The classes are delivered with the SAP TableFactory control. To define the object variables and create instances, you can use these alternatives:

▶ SAP BAPI control

▶ SAP TableFactory control

The use of BAPI controls for creating tables and structure objects is often linked with late binding so that integration of TableFactory controls is not necessary. The tables and structures are first defined as object variables of the Object type, and an instance of the Structure or Table class is generated using the DimAs method of the SAPBAPIControl class. The interface of the method DimAs is:

Variable	Meaning
Object	Reference to a valid BO proxy object
Method	Name of the method
Parameter	Name of the parameter in the method

Table 8.14 Interface of the DimAs Method of the SAPBAPIControl Class

The program extract shows how the structure object is to be created in the client program, namely for the ES_CUSTOMER_DATA structure in the GetSingleCustomer method of the ZBUSCUST BO in the R/3 System:

```
Dim m_oISCustomerData As Object
Set m_oISCustomerData = m_oBAPICtrl.DimAs(m_oBUSCust, _
            "GetSingleCustomer", "ES_CUSTOMER_DATA")
```

The DimAs method internally creates the description of the structure by calling function modules in the R/3 System and obtaining data from them on the arrangement of the structure. This includes the following information:

▶ Number of columns in the structure

▶ Layout of columns in the structure

▶ Technical properties and name of each column

The technical properties of a column include information on:

▶ Data type

▶ Permissible number of characters in a column

▶ Number of decimal places

▶ Position of column in the structure

In addition, the structure or table object in the client administers the storage area in which the data sent to or from the SAP system is stored.

In the second method via the TableFactory control, the TableFactory control is at first also integrated into the project. Object variables of the class types Structure and Table are then declared in the program. Then a structure or table object is created using the NewStructure or NewTable methods of the TableFactory. After the CreateFromR3Repository method of the Structure or Table class is called up, the description of the field structure is determined automatically from the Data Dictionary.

This two-step procedure is necessary because the parameter-free methods NewStructure and NewTable do not create a description of the field structure. For exactly this reason, the CreateFromR3Repository method, which exists both for the Structure and Table classes, must be called up next.

Calling up the CreateFromR3Repository method automatically creates the structure. To do this, the method calls function modules in the R/3 system that send back a description of the arrangement of the structure. The interface of the method is defined in the same way for both classes and has the following structure:

Variable	Meaning
R3Connection	Instance of the Connection class of the SAPLogonControl The instance must have an open R/3 connection.
RepositoryEntry	Name of the Data Dictionary structure or table whose field structure is to be used for the creation of the field description
ParameterName	Name of the parameter in the method

Table 8.15 Interface of the CreateFromR3Repository Method

If the ES_CUSTOMER_DATA structure of the ZBUSCUST BO was created in the client program using the TableFactory control, the programming would be as follows:

```
Dim m_oISCustomerData As SAPTableFactoryCtrl.Structure
' Create structure object
Set m_oISCustomerData = m_oSAPTabCtrl.NewStructure
' Create description of field structure
m_oISCustomerData.CreateFromR3Repository _
        m_oConnection, "ZKNA1JMS", "ES_CUSTOMER_DATA"
```

The two procedures described share the trait that a connection to the appropriate R/3 System is required for creating the description of the field structure. They differ in the number of steps that must be performed to create a complete data aggregate object. When the SAPBAPIControl class is used, only one step is necessary (call of the DimAs method). When the SAP TableFactory controls are used, two steps must be performed (creation of the object, then creation of the field structure description).

In addition to the basic procedures mentioned, there is also the option of combining the two alternatives. In the combination, the TableFactory control is also integrated into the project. The object variables are defined by the Structure or Table type. However, the instances of the classes are created using the DimAs method of the SAPBAPIControl class. The procedure just described is, however, of limited suitability, as is shown below. A table would be created using the method described above in the following way:

```
Dim m_oITCustomerData As SAPTableFactoryCtrl.Table
' Create table object including structure
Set m_oITCustomerData = m_oBAPICtrl.DimAs(m_oBUSCust, _
            "GetCustomerData", "ET_CUSTOMER_DATA")
```

In contrast to the RFC API, all variants have the advantage that the manual creation of a structure in the client is not necessary. This shortens development times substantially.

8.7 The SAP TableFactory Control in Detail

As mentioned, the TableFactory control can be used to create instances of the `Structure` and `Table` classes. It is included in the *wdtaocx.ocx* file. The file is located in the directory *C:\Program files\SAP\FrontEnd\Controls*.

The TableFactory control has the hierarchical structure shown in Figure 8.3.

At the top of the hierarchy is the `SAPTableFactory` class. On the second level of the hierarchy follow the classes `Tables`, `Table`, and `Structure`. The `Table` class administers exactly one internal table. `Structure` correspondingly administers exactly one structure. The class `Tables` can administer several objects of `Table`. The `Table` class is listed again on the third level of the hierarchy. This is because both `SAPTableFactory` and `Tables` can create instances of the `Table` class.

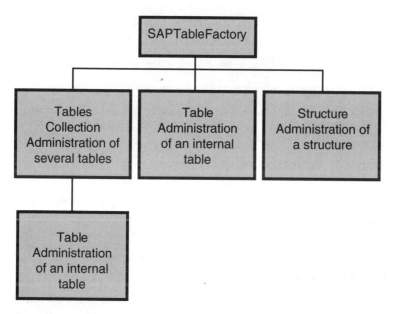

Figure 8.3 Hierarchy of the TableFactory Control

The hierarchy makes clear which instances can be created by which class. The rule applies that an instance of a class lower down in the hierarchy can be created only by the method of a class above it. The superior class is usually the direct predecessor. Classes that are not at the top of the hierarchy can never be directly instantiated.

It is also notable that, in the hierarchy there is a `Collection` class for table objects—the `Tables` class—but no analogous class for administering several structure objects.

The `SAPTableFactory` class has the following methods:

Methods	Meaning
AboutBox	Dialog box with version information on the TableFactory control
NewStructure	Creates an instance of the `Structure` class
NewTable	Creates an instance of the `Table` class
NewTable	Creates an instance of the `Tables` class

Table 8.16 Methods of the SAPTableFactory Class

The attributes of the `SAPTableFactory` class are:

Attribute	Meaning
Index	Index for identifying the instance of the class in the array
Name	Name for identification of the instance of the control in a program
Object	Returns the container object - usually a window class (e.g., form)
Parent	Returns the superior container object - usually a window class (e.g., form)
Tag	Attribute for storing additional values

Table 8.17 Attributes of the SAPTableFactory Class

With the exception of the `Name` attribute, the attributes are of subordinate importance during daily use.

8.8 Administering Structures with the SAP TableFactory Control

The creation of structure objects has already been dealt with in Section 8.6, so the focus in the immediately following sections will be on the topics:

▶ Reading and setting values in structure objects

▶ Determining structure properties

▶ Special features of creating structure objects with the BAPI and the TableFactory control

8.8.1 Accessing Data in Structures

Reading and setting values for the fields of a structure is performed using the `Value` attribute of the `Structure` class. When doing this, the column whose content is to be accessed is identified using the `Index` variable. The index can be both the position of the column in the structure and the name of the column itself. Access using the column name is the usual way, because the name is expressive. Access via the customer number would be programmed as follows:

```
Dim CustNo As String
CustNo = m_oISCustomerData.Value("CUSTNO")
```

To determine the technical properties of a column in a structure, the `Structure` class provides the attributes listed below:

Attribute	Meaning
`ColumnDecimals`	Number of decimal places of the data type the column is based on
	The method delivers a valid value only if the field in the Data Dictionary is of the type `P`, `Curr`, or `Quan`.
`ColumnLength`	Maximum number of characters in the column
`ColumnName`	Column name
`ColumnOffset`	Position of column in the structure
`ColumnSAPType`	Data type of the column
`Value`	Value of the field

Table 8.18 Methods for Determining the Properties of a Field

The data type of a field is stored in the `ColumnSAPType` attribute. The attribute has the return type `CRFCType`. This is a counting type. It can take the following values:

Value	Meaning
`RfcTypeBCD`	Packed number
`RfcTypeByte`	Field is of type `Byte`
`RfcTypeChar`	`Character` field
`RfcTypeDate`	Date field
`RfcTypeFloat`	Float

Table 8.19 Values of the Type CRFCType

Value	Meaning
`RfcTypeHex`	Hexadecimal data type
`RfcTypeLong`	Four-byte integer
`RfcTypeNum`	Numeric field
`RfcTypeShort`	Two-byte integer
`RfcTypeTime`	Field is of type `Time`

Table 8.19 Values of the Type CRFCType (cont.)

8.8.2 Note When Working with Structures!

In Section 8.6, we indicated that a little care must be taken when creating structure objects. This statement is to be refined here.

If the structure is an exporting parameter in the method of the business object in the R/3 System, it does not matter whether the structure object was created by the BAPI control or the TableFactory control.

It is a different story if the structure was defined as an importing parameter. In that case, it is crucially important whether the structure object was created using the BAPI or the TableFactory control. If the structure object was created using the `DimAs` method of the BAPI control, transmission of data to the SAP system works perfectly. If the structure object was created using the `NewStructure` and `CreateFromR3Repository` methods, its data cannot be transmitted to the R/3 System. What is astounding about this behavior is that it does not lead to an error. The data is simply not transmitted.

Another phenomenon arises in this context. We have seen that to achieve comprehensible programming, it is desirable to specify the class of an object variable when it is declared. Declarations according to the pattern

```
Dim xy As Object
```

should be avoided if possible.

Therefore it is useful to declare object variables that represent instances of the class `Table` and `Structure` as

```
Dim m_oIT_Table As SAPTableFactoryCtrl.Table
```

or

```
Dim m_oIS_Structure As SAPTableFactoryCtrl.Structure
```

If the `m_oIT_Table` object variable is assigned an instance of the `Table` class using the `DimAs` method of the `SAPBAPIControl` class, the declaration above is unproblematic. The instance will be assigned correctly.

The situation for structures looks a little different here as well. If an instance of the `Structure` class is to be created using the `DimAs` method of the `SAPBAPIControl` class, and the object variable was declared as described above, the error message *Type mismatch* will appear during runtime. A program that contains the following sequence generates the error mentioned:

```
Dim m_oIS_Structure As SAPTableFactoryCtrl.Structure
' Create instance of the Structure class
Set m_oIS_Structure = m_oBAPICtrl.DimAs(m_oBUSCust, _
            "GetSingleCustomer", "ES_CUSTOMER_DATA")
```

The conclusion drawn from the error message would be that no instance of the `Structure` class can be created using the `DimAs` method. However, this cannot be correct. If you use late binding, which is described below, to declare the structure object, and you use the `DimAs` method for creating the instance, the object may call up methods of the `Structure` class. This is an indication that the object is an instance of the `Structure` class. Otherwise, calling up methods of the `Structure` class would fail during runtime.

```
Dim m_oIS_Structure As Object, _
    CustNo As String
' Create instance of the Structure class
Set m_oIS_Structure = m_oBAPICtrl.DimAs( m_oBUSCust, _
            "GetSingleCustomer", "ES_CUSTOMER_DATA")
' Call up method of the Structure class. No runtime
' error !!!
CustNo  = m_oIS_Structure.Value("CUSTNO")
```

The `TypeName` function could be used to determine the correct class. It contains the object for which the class is being sought as a transfer variable and returns the name of the class as string. The type of the class is determined during runtime. This is why the object variable can also be declared as `Object`. This has no influence on the result.

Unfortunately, this idea for determining the class also fails. The `TypeName` function returns only the `Object` value. This means that the class cannot be determined.

The options for creating an instance of the `Structure` class can be summarized in the following overview:

Direction	Create by		
	Class	Method	Special Features
Send to SAP system	`SAPBAPIControl`	`DimAs`	Object variable must be of `Object`type
Receive from SAP system	`SAPBAPIControl`	`DimAs`	Object variable must be of `Object`type
Receive from SAP system	`SAPTableFactory`	`NewStructure` `CreateFrom-` `R3Repository`	

Table 8.20 Overview of the Options for Creating a Structure

8.9 Working with Tables

Tables are represented in a client by an instance of the `Table` class of the Table-Factory control. The options listed above are available to create an instance of the `Table` class. The `Table` class has a special place in the TableFactory control, because it is itself at the top of a hierarchy of classes that was developed especially for dealing with tables. The following sections deal with the classes for working with tables and the options for data access.

8.9.1 The Class Hierarchy for Working with Tables

The classes shown in Figure 8.4 have been provided for working with tables.

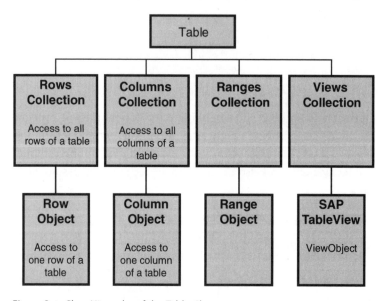

Figure 8.4 Class Hierarchy of the Table Class

At the top of the hierarchy is the `Table` class. On the two subsequent levels of the hierarchy follow the classes `Rows`, `Columns`, `Ranges`, and `Views`.

The classes `Rows` and `Columns` allow access to all rows or columns of a table. The `Views` class administers the views linked to a table object. Views represent the contents of the tables in various ways. They are represented by instances of the `SAPTableView` class. The `SAPTableView` class and its links to a table object are described further below. The classes `Ranges` and `Range` are not described in this book because they are rarely used in practice.

On the third level of the hierarchy, we find the classes `Column`, `Row`, `Range`, and `SAP Table ViewObject` . They allow access to exactly one element of the collection classes that come before them. For example, the `Column` class allows access to a column from the group of all columns of the `Columns` class. The principle of specialization can be clearly recognized here. The successor classes in the hierarchy are limited in content to an aspect of their predecessor and offer their own methods and attributes for it.

It is also true of the `Table` class and its successor that an instance of a subordinate class can be created only by a method of its predecessor class. Direct creation of an instance is usually not possible.

8.9.2 Important Attributes of the Table Class

The `Table` class has many useful attributes that provide information on the structure of the table:

Attribute	Meaning
Cell	Read or write access to the value of a table field
ColumnCount	Number of columns
ColumnName	Name of a column
Columns	Access to the `Columns` object
Name	Name of the table
RowCount	Number of rows
Rows	Access to the `Rows` object
Value	Read or write access to the value of a table field
Views	Access to the views linked to the table.

Table 8.21 Attributes of the Table Class

Many more attributes exist in addition to the ones listed. However they are of lesser importance in daily use and are therefore not listed here.

8.9.3 Structure of the Example Programs

The following sections deal with handling internal tables and their subordinate classes. The listings shown throughout this chapter originate for the most part from the programs ShowMultiCustomer, for displaying several customer master data records, and CreateCustomer, for creating new customer master data records. Both programs are on the Web site for this book at *www.sap-press.com*. In addition to showing the user the methods for creating data records, the CreateCustomer program also shows how the structure description of a table can be laid out manually.

The development of the programs will not be presented because a complete description would be excessively long and would therefore not be practical to include in this chapter. Because we are focusing on the handling of SAP ActiveX controls, listings have only a supporting role by illustrating relationships. Therefore, only the structure of the programs is explained.

In both programs, the business proxy object is administered by the CBUSCust class. The structure was presented at the beginning of this chapter and successively expanded.

In addition to the functions for logging on and off, the following new functions are integrated into the form class of the programs ShowMultiCustomer and CreateCustomer:

▶ GetCustomerData

▶ Back

▶ Next

▶ GetCustByID

The GetCustomerData function is used to read customer master data from the R/3 System. To do so, the function internally calls the GetCustomerData method of the CBUSCust class and transfers the interval for the customer master data to be read.

The functions Back, Next, and GetCustByID were implemented so that the user can navigate between the individual customer master data records. The functions Back and Next indicate the predecessor or successor of the current data record, and the GetCustByID function allows the display of a data record via specification of the data record index.

In addition to the functions mentioned, the `CreateCustomer` program also offers functions for adding and deleting data records. These include the following:

▶ Adding a row to a table

▶ Inserting a row in a table

▶ Deleting a row from a table

▶ Deleting all rows from a table

8.9.4 Reading Data Records in a Table

Reading and writing data are central aspects of working with internal tables. These are the topics of this and the following section.

Three types of data access exist for tables:

▶ Direct

▶ Via the row

▶ Via the column

Direct access is the most intuitive and the most frequently used. It is performed by specifying the column and row index. The following attributes of the `Table` class can be used for direct access:

▶ `Cell`

▶ `Value`

The interfaces of the two attributes are identical. They both have the following structure:

Variable	Meaning
Row	Index of the row
Column	Column index
	Both the index of the column and the column name can be specified, with the latter being the one most frequently used

Table 8.22 Interface of the Attributes Cell and Value of the Table Class

If, for example, you want to determine the customer number of the second data record, the appropriate call for the `Value` attribute would be:

```
m_oITCustomerData.Value(2, "CUSTNO")
```

For this call, it should be noted that the column name is capitalized. The readout of all values in a table, for example in order to load the visualization in a grid control, could be implemented using two loops. The first loop runs via all rows of a table, and the second via all columns. It would look like this:

```
Dim iCurrRow As Integer, _
    iCurrCol As Integer, _
    Value As String
' Loop via the rows
For iCurrRow = 1 To m_oITCustomerData.RowCount
' Loop via the columns
   For iCurrCol = 1 To m_oITCustomerData.ColumnCount
' Access to the value of the field
      Value = m_oITCustomerData.Cell(iCurrRow, iCurrCol)
   Next iCurrCol
Next iCurrRow
```

Listing 8.14 Readout of Table Values Using Two Loops

In this listing, instead of the `Value` attribute, the `Cell` attribute is used for accessing the content of a field.

In the second option, row-oriented access, first the entire row of a table is accessed and then each individual field in the row.

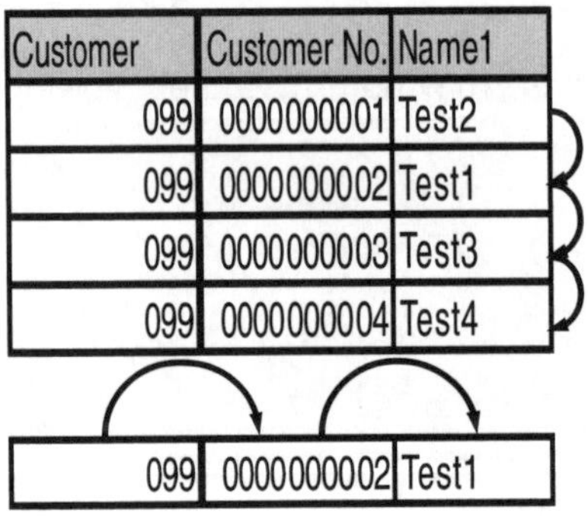

Figure 8.5 Row-Oriented Access

Row-oriented access is performed by the classes:

▶ Rows

▶ Row

The classes `Table`, `Rows`, and `Row` work together closely (see also Figure 8.4). From the `Rows` attribute of the `Table` class, you obtain access to the `Rows` object belonging to the table. The Rows object administers all rows of the table. Each individual row of the table is accessed via the Item attribute of the Rows object, where the row is incorporated by an instance of the class Row. In doing so, the index of the row to be accessed is transferred to the Item attribute of the Rows. The value of the field of the row can then be accessed using the Value attribute of the Row class. The identification of the field is performed either via the field name or its position in the structure. The following listing shows how accessing a value via the Row object is performed:

```
Dim oRow As Row, _
    CUSTNO As String
' Access to the second row
Set oRow = m_oITCustomerData.Rows.Item(2)
' Access to the customer number in the second data record
CUSTNO = oRow.Value("CUSTNO")
```

Listing 8.15 Accessing a Value via the Row Object

In addition to direct and row-oriented access, there is also column-oriented access, which is used less frequently. Column-oriented access means that access is performed first on the columns of a table and then on the rows within a selected column. This allows access to all selected values for exactly one field of the table.

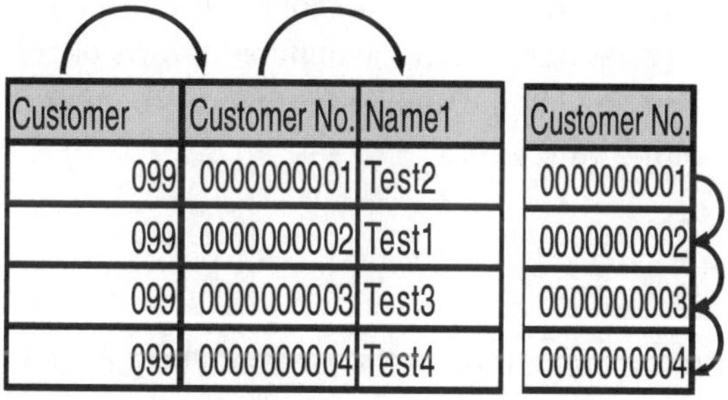

Figure 8.6 Column-Oriented Access

Figure 8.6 shows how via column-oriented access, for example, all selected customers can be determined.

The following classes are used for column-oriented access:

▶ Columns

▶ Column

Here, all columns of a table are represented by the Columns class, and an individual column of the entire group by the Column class. Using the Columns attribute of the `Table` class, you obtain a valid instance of the `Columns` class, and via the `Item` attribute of the `Columns` class it is possible to access an instance of the `Column` class. To do this, either the column name or the column index is specified in the `Item` attribute. Access to the contents of a row is finally achieved via the `Value` attribute of the `Column` class. The `Value` attribute of the row index is transferred for the access. For column-oriented access, access to the customer number of the second data record would be programmed as follows:

```
Dim oColumn As Column, _
    CUSTNO As String
' Access to the customer number column
Set oColumn = m_oITCustomerData.Columns.Item("CUSTNO")
' Access to the customer number in the second row
CUSTNO = oColumn.Value(2)
```

In the listings, the attributes `Rows` and `Columns` of the `Table` class are used to obtain `Row` and `Column` objects. These attributes are write-protected attributes. They allow read access only. Write access is forbidden. Instructions such as the following lead to runtime errors:

```
Set m_oITCustomerData.Rows = oTable2.Rows
```

When performing index-oriented access, note that the row and column index must always have a valid value to avoid program terminations. An index has a valid value if it begins with a one and does not exceed the number of rows or columns of the table. One option for determining the number of rows or columns in a table is using the two attributes of the `Table` class:

▶ `RowCount`

▶ `ColumnCount`

The `RowCount` attribute returns the number of rows in the table and the `Column-Count` attribute returns the number of columns. The following listing shows how the test of a row index for a permissible value—together with a simultaneous correction—could look:

```
Dim iRowCount As Integer
' Check if the table object contains data records
iRowCount  = m_oITCustomerData.RowCount
If iRowCount < 1 Then
   MsgBox "No Data selected", vbOKOnly
   Exit Sub
End If
' If the index is less than one, set it
```

```
' to the lower limit - one
If iRowIndex < 1 Then
    iRowIndex = 1
' If the index is greater than the number of read
' data records, set it to the upper limit
ElseIf iRowIndex > iRowCount  Then
    iRowIndex = iRowCount
End If
```

Listing 8.16 Testing the Row Index for a Permissible Value

8.9.5 Changing Data Records

After presenting read access to the data of a table, we will now look at write access. Writing is not limited to changing existing data, but also includes insertion and attachment of new data records, as well as the deletion of existing data records.

The same methods as for reading can be used for changing received data. They are just as effective.

The following methods exist for attaching rows:

▶ AppendRow of the `Table` class
▶ Add of the `Rows` class

Both methods have no parameters and attach a row onto the table. The fields of the new rows are filled with their type-conform initial values.

The following methods exist for inserting rows:

▶ InsertRow of the `Table` class
▶ Insert of the `Rows` class

Both methods expect the index for the insertion position at their interfaces. The fields of the new rows are filled with their type-conform initial values here as well.

If the methods for attaching and inserting new data records are performed successfully, the instance of the newly created `Row` object is returned. The values for the new row can then be entered. This is similar to attaching or inserting new rows in a table using the RFC API, only now an object instead of a pointer is returned.

These two methods are provided for deleting a table row:

▶ DeleteRow of the Table class
▶ RemoveRow of the Rows class

Both methods receive the index of the row to be deleted.

Using the RemoveAll method of the Rows class, all rows of the respective table can be deleted.

Manually changing the column number of tables is unusual. It is usually used when the structure description in the client program is laid out manually. The following methods of the Columns class are provided for operations on columns:

▶ Add—for attaching a column
▶ Insert—for inserting a column
▶ Remove—for deleting a column
▶ RemoveAll—for deleting all columns

The Add and Insert methods return the newly created Column object if the operation is successful. The Insert and Remove methods receive the index for the insertion position of the column or the column to be deleted at their interfaces.

8.9.6 Alternatives for Creating the Field Description

In addition to the techniques shown above for creating the description of the field structure of a table, other more rarely used options also exist:

▶ Copying the description of the field structure from another table object
▶ Manual creation of the description of the field structure

Copying the Structure Description

To copy the description of the field structure, the Table class provides the CreateFromTable method. It receives the instance of the table object whose structure description is to be copied at its interface. A prerequisite for copying is that the source object for the copying procedure has a valid structure description. If the copying procedure has been performed successfully, the method returns the value True, otherwise False. The method is only useful if two tables are required with identical field structures.

Manual Creation of the Structure Description

Manual creation of the structure description is occasionally used in the development phase of a client because it provides the option of testing functions of the client without an R/3 System being available.

The manual creation of the structure description is performed in three steps:

▶ Creating an instance of the `Table` class
▶ Specifying the byte size of the individual data records
▶ Entering the technical properties for each individual table column

The instantiation of the `Table` class is performed in this case using the `NewTable` method of the `SAPTableFactory` class, because the `NewTable` method creates a table object without field description.

The size of the data record in bytes is determined by the `Create` method of the `Table` class. The interface of the method is:

Variable	Meaning
TableName	Name of the table
TableLength	Byte size of a data record

Table 8.23 Interface of the Create Method of the Table Class

The byte size of the structure can be determined according to the same procedure described in Section 4.2. Because our table object refers to the database table ZKNA1JMS, the byte size of a data record is 188 bytes.

After the number of characters has been specified for a table object, it possesses a valid instance of the `Columns` class. The `Add` method of the `Columns` class mentioned above allows attaching new columns to a table, with the instance of the `Column` class being returned.

The technical properties of a column are specified by the attribute (see Table 8.24) of the `Column` class.

Attribute	Meaning
Decimals	Number of decimal places
Index	Position of column in the structure
IntLength	Max. number of characters in a field

Table 8.24 Attributes for the Technical Properties of a Table Column

Attribute	Meaning
Name	Column name
Offset	Offset of the field in the structure
Type	Data type of the field The value entered here has the counting type CRFCType as the data type (the type is described in the sections on structures).

Table 8.24 Attributes for the Technical Properties of a Table Column (cont.)

If values are specified for attributes, the structure of the table can be defined manually. For the definition it is usually sufficient if only the properties Name, Type, and IntLength are assigned values. The following suggestion shows how a method for the manual creation of the technical properties of a column could look:

```
Private Sub AppendColumn(oColumns As Columns, _
                         Name As String, _
                         Typ As CRFCType, _
                         iLength As Integer)
Dim oColumn As Object
' Attach column
    Set oColumn = oColumns.Add(Name)
' Specify properties of column
    With oColumn
        .Name = Name
        .Type = Typ
        .IntLength = iLength
    End With
End Sub
```

Listing 8.17 Methods for Attaching a Column to a Table Object

The call for the MANDT field of the ZKNA1JMS table would look like this:

```
AppendColumn m_oITCustomerData.Columns,
                "MANDT",RfcTypeChar, 3
```

8.10 Visualization of the Table Contents

The TableFactory control was discussed in the previous section. However, the method for displaying the selected data records was quite primitive. These days, several data records are no longer displayed individually, but rather in an overview. The control elements that allow the simultaneous display of several data records are often referred to as a *data grid* (see Figure 8.7). SAP has also developed a data grid control for displaying data records. Its components are delivered with the TableView control. The control is delivered in the *wdtvocx.ocx* file, which is located in the *C:\Program files\SAP\FrontEnd\Controls* directory.

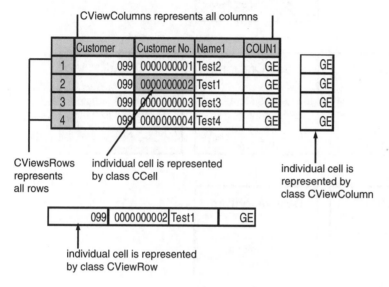

Figure 8.7 Elements of the Data Grid

Like internal tables, the data grid consists of rows and columns. The rows and columns are represented by classes in the program. The layout for the grid control can be specified via the attributes of the classes. The concept is so far reaching that it is possible to define the visual appearance for an individual cell. This is useful for the display of totals, for example.

In the next sections, we will consider the following aspects of dealing with the SAP TableView control:

▶ Hierarchy of the classes of the TableView control

▶ Options for designing the layout of the data grid

▶ Access to the cells

▶ Specifying the data source for the SAPTableView class

▶ Concepts for the insertion and deletion of rows

▶ Working with the clipboard

8.10.1 Hierarchy of the Classes of the TableView Control

The classes delivered with the TableView control also have a hierarchical structure as shown in Figure 8.8.

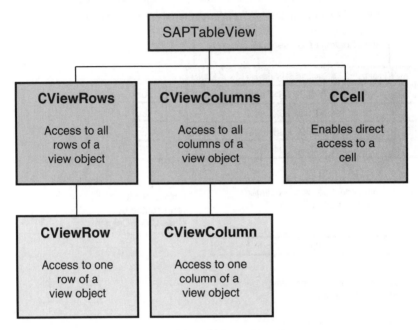

Figure 8.8 Hierarchical Structure of the TableView Control

At the top of the hierarchy is the SAPTableView class. It represents the data grid itself.

On the second level of the hierarchy we find the classes CViewRows, CViewColumns, and CCell. The classes allow access to aspects of the data grid. For example, the CViewRows class allows access to rows of the data grid.

The classes CViewRows and CViewColumns are collections. Access to an element of the group is obtained via classes specialized for this purpose. They are found at the third level of the hierarchy. The CViewRow class represents the individual row of the data grid and the CViewColumn class the individual column.

When you compare the hierarchical structure of the TableView control with that of the classes for the Table object, similarities between the two become apparent. Classes that are custom-made for accessing a table area exist in both hierarchies. For example, the SAPTableView, CViewRows, and CViewRow levels can be compared with the Table, Rows, and Row levels.

The TableView control expands the concept for accessing the cell data by an object-oriented component. The individual cell of a data grid is represented in the program by an instance of the CCell class. The instance encapsulates all properties of the cell that can be influenced by the corresponding methods and attributes of the CCell class. The properties include the layout as well as the value in the cell itself.

For the creation of instances of the classes included with the TableView control, classes on a subordinate hierarchy level can also usually be created only by the method of a superior hierarchy level.

8.10.2 Specifying the Layout of the Data Grid

The layout of the data grid can be defined in two ways:

▶ Statically

▶ Dynamically

In static definition of the layout, the properties are set using the corresponding dialog box of the data grid. It has the structure shown in Figure 8.9.

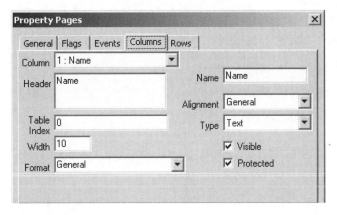

Figure 8.9 Dialog Box of the Data Grid for Static Setting of the Layout

By clicking the tabs, you can go to the detail views for setting the properties for the particular element of the data grid.

In dynamic definition, the values for the attributes in the program are set in the instance of the corresponding class. The dynamism concept has more far-reaching effects, however. As shown below, an option exists for linking the data grid with a table object. In this case, the column and row properties are transferred from the table object. These include the column name, the index, and the display format. Default values are used for the rest of the values. Then only the general properties for the data grid must be set. When setting the properties, observe the rule that dynamically set properties overwrite statically set properties.

The properties of the layout can be divided into three groups:

▶ General properties of the data grid

▶ Properties of a row

▶ Properties of a column (the largest group)

The general properties are stored as attributes of the `SAPTableView` class; they include:

Attribute	Meaning
ColumnCount	Number of columns
RowCount	Number of rows
FixedColumns	Number of fixed columns
FixedRows	Number of fixed rows
ShowGridLines	Display horizontal and vertical separation lines
ShowHScrollBar	Activate horizontal scroll function
ShowVScrollBar	Activate vertical scroll function
ShowColHeaders	Marking line for column selection
ShowRowHeaders	Marking line for row selection

Table 8.25 General Properties of the Data Grid

Statically setting the values for the properties can be performed in the **General** and **Flags** detail views of the maintenance dialog.

The properties of a row are set via the attributes of the `CViewRow` class. They include:

Attribute	Meaning
Font	Font
Height	Height of the row
Protection	Write protection for the row

Table 8.26 Properties of a Row

The following attributes belong to the properties of a row:

Attribute	Meaning
Alignment	Alignment of the data in the column
Font	Font
Format	Way in which the data is displayed, e.g., date format
Header	Column heading
Index	Position of the column
Name	Column name
Protection	Write protection
Type	Data type of the values to be displayed
Visible	Visibility of the column
Width	Column width

Table 8.27 Properties of a Column

The attributes are stored in the CViewColumn class.

If the properties for columns and rows are to be created statically, go to the Columns and Rows detail views of the maintenance dialog.

As seen above, columns and rows can be write protected. The write protection itself is activated in two steps:

1. First it is specified that the data grid can always offer write protection. To do so, the EnableProtection attribute of the SAPTableView class is set to the value True.

2. Subsequently, the write protection is activated for the individual row and column. To do this, the Protection attribute is set to the value True for the particular row or column.

After both options for specifying the layout of the data grid have been presented, the question arises when which variant is used. The static specification of properties is often used when working with any data source because the data grid can determine information on the column and row layout only from a table object. Dynamic setting, on the other hand, is used when linking the data grid with a table, because the rows and columns of the data grid should have the same properties as the corresponding rows and columns of the table object.

Finally, we will show how the properties can be set for the individual cell in the data grid. It was mentioned above that each cell of a data grid is represented by an instance of the `CCell` class. It has the following attributes for influencing the appearance of a cell:

Attribute	Meaning
Font	Font
Protection	Write protection for the row

Table 8.28 Attributes of the CCell Class for Influencing the Layout of a Cell

To influence the properties of the corresponding cell, you only have to obtain the instance of the `CCell` class, which represents the respective cell in the program and sets the value for the corresponding attribute in the instance. How to obtain this object is described in the following section.

8.10.3 Accessing the Cells in a Data Grid

Access to a cell in a data grid—as with a table—can be performed as follows:

▶ Directly

▶ Row-oriented

▶ Column-oriented

Accessing a cell is performed either to determine a value that is in the cell or to change the visual properties of the cell.

The TableView control offers a solution for both possibilities. You can use the `Value` attribute to access the value. The attribute is defined for the classes `SAPTableView`, `CViewRow`, and `CViewColumn`.

However, to change the visual properties of the cell other than the value, you must use the `Cell` attribute, which also has the classes mentioned. The attribute returns an instance of the `CCell` class. As shown above, `CCell` has attributes that influence the layout of a cell. As the value in a cell also represents a property of the cell, the `CCell` class has the `Value` attribute so that it is possible to access the value in a cell via `CCell`.

The interfaces of the `Cell` and `Value` attributes are always defined in the same way for an individual class. For example, the attributes of the `SAPTableView` class have the interface:

Variable	Meaning
Row	Row index
Col	Column index
	In contrast to the Table class, it is not possible to specify a column name.

Table 8.29 Interfaces of the Attributes Cell and Value of the SAPTableView Class

The structure of the interface for the attributes is therefore always displayed in a table.

Direct access to the value in a cell or the cell itself is implemented via the Cell and Value attributes. The structure of the interface for the attributes can be seen in Table 8.29. Direct access to the cell is usually used when the SAPTableView object is not linked with a table in order to manually transfer the data into the data grid.

Row-oriented access to the cell in a data grid is implemented via the CViewRows and CViewRow classes. The CViewRows class allows access to rows of the data grid. The Item attribute of CViewRows allows you to then access the individual rows of the data grid. The row is represented by an instance of the CViewRow class. The Cell and Value attributes make it possible to address an individual cell of the row. In doing so, the attributes of the index of the field to be addressed are transferred.

If the data grid has four lines and 11 columns, row-oriented access to the value in the second row and the fifth column would be programmed like this:

```
Dim oViewRow As Object, _
    Value As Variant
' Access to the second row
Set oViewRow = m_oTVCustomer.Rows.Item(2)
' Access to the fifth row
Value = oViewRow.Value(5)
```

In the listing, late binding is used for the oViewRow object variable. This is necessary because with early binding the creation of instances of the CViewRow class fails with the *Type mismatch* error message. This also applies to the CViewRows class.

Column-oriented access to a cell of the data grid is performed using the CView-Columns and CViewColumn classes. The CViewColumns class allows access to all columns of the data grid. Access to an individual column of the data grid is obtained via the Item property of the CViewColumns class. The column index is transferred in the Item attribute. The CViewColumn class represents an individual column of the data grid. It also has the attributes `Cell` and Value. The index of the row that is addressed within the current column is transferred to them.

Column-oriented access to the value in the second row and fifth column from the previous example would be programmed as follows:

```
Dim oViewColumn As Object, _
    Value As Variant
' Access to the fifth column
Set oViewColumn = m_oTVCustomer.Columns.Item(5)
' Access to the value in the second row
Value = oViewColumn.Cell(2).Value
```

The program sequence this time accesses the value of the cell via the `Cell` attribute, which is also permissible. Here, as well, note that late binding is used for the `oViewColumn` object variable.

Recognizing Access to a Cell

For write access to the value of a cell, it is often necessary to develop a testing routine to be run at a value change. In this way, data can be checked for permissibility before it is transferred into a table, for example.

The data grid, like the SAP logon control, uses events to inform the client program that states have arisen. For the application to be able to react to events, two steps are required:

▶ Developing a routine to be run when events occur

▶ Specifying which events the TableView control is to send to the client

The TableView control can send the following events while accessing a cell:

Event	Triggering Time
AfterInput	Sent after the new value has been inserted into the data grid This is the case when the cell loses the input focus.
BeforeInput	Sent after the new value has been inserted into the data grid
Click	Sent when the cell is clicked
DataChange	Sent after the new value has been transferred into the data grid. This is the case when the cell loses the input focus. It is sent after the AfterInput event. However, it is also sent when the data of a table is transferred into the data grid.
DblClick	Sent when the cell is double-clicked

Table 8.30 Events of the SAPTableView Class When a Cell Is Accessed

Event	Triggering Time
KeyDown	Sent when a cell of the data grid has the focus and a key is pressed
KeyUp	Sent when a cell of the data grid has the focus and a previously pressed key is released
SelChange	Sent when the input focus changes from one cell to another

Table 8.30 Events of the SAPTableView Class When a Cell Is Accessed (cont.)

An event handler for the TableView control is programmed in the same way as an event handler for the events of the SAP logon control:

▶ Selecting the object variable of the SAPTableView type

▶ Selecting the event for which a separate testing routine is to be created

After the event is selected, a body is inserted for the event handler in the window class, which must be supplemented by a separate logic.

To specify the event that the table control is to send to the client, there are two options:

▶ Static specification in the detail view of the maintenance dialog

▶ Dynamic specification

Static specification is performed by simply selecting the events to be sent in the **Events** detail view. Figure 8.10 shows this detail view.

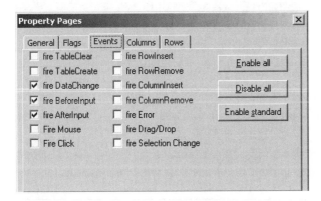

Figure 8.10 Events of the TableView Control

Here, the events DataChange, BeforeInput, and AfterInput are to be sent to the client.

Dynamic specification of the events to be sent to the client is performed in the Events attribute of the SAPTableView class. Here you can specify a combination of the values of the `CViewEvents` enumeration data type. It can have the following values:

Value	Meaning
tavDisableAllEvents	No event is sent to the client
tavEnableAfterInput	Sending of the `AfterInput` event
tavEnableAllEvents	Sending all events of the TableView control to the client
tavEnableBeforeInput	Sending of the `BeforeInput` event
tavEnableClickEvent	Sending the `Click` event, for example, double-clicking an event
tavEnableColumnInsert	Sending the `ColumnInsert` event
tavEnableColumnRemove	Sending the `ColumnRemove` event
tavEnableDataChange	Sending the `DataChange` event
tavEnableDragDropEvents	Sending events during the drag and drop procedure (not addressed in this book)
tavEnableError	Sending error events
tavEnableMouseEvent	Sending mouse events, e.g., `MouseMove`
tavEnableRowInsert	Sending the `RowInsert` event
tavEnableRowRemove	Sending the `RowRemove` event
tavEnableSelection-ChangeEvent	Sending the `SelectionChange` event
tavEnableStandardEvents	Sending standard events
tavEnableTableClear	Sending the `TableClear` event
tavEnableTableCreate	Sending the `TableCreate` event

Table 8.31 Value Range of the CViewEvents Counting Data Type

If the events `tavEnableBeforeInput` and `tavEnableAfterInput` are to be sent to the client, the specification in the `Events` attribute would be made as follows:

```
m_oTVCustomer.Events = tavEnableBeforeInput + _
                  tavEnableAfterInput
```

8.10.4 Specifying the Data Source for the Data Grid

The data source for the grid control can be either a `Table` object of the SAP Table-Factory control or any other data source.

Table Object as a Data Source

First we will look at linking the data grid with an instance of the `Table` class. To do so, perform the following steps:

▶ Linking the `Table` class with the `SAPTableView` class

▶ Transferring the data from the `Table` to the `SAPTableView` class

In the hierarchy of the `Table` class, the `Views` class is subordinate to the `Table` class. As mentioned, the `Views` class administers all instances of the `SAPTableView` class that are assigned to the table. Figure 8.11 illustrates the relationships. It also shows that a `Table` object can easily administer several views of the data contained in it. However, this does not apply in the other direction. An `SAPTableView` object can be linked to only one `Table` object.

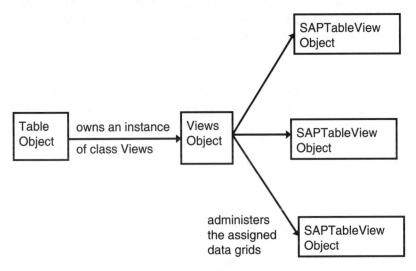

Figure 8.11 Assignment of Data Grids to a Table

The `Views` class has the following methods and properties for administering `SAPTableView` objects:

Method	Meaning
Add	Attach SAPTableView object to the table
Insert	Insert SAPTableView object into the table
Item	Access an assigned instance of the SAPTableView class
Remove	Remove an individual SAPTableView object
RemoveAll	Remove all SAPTableView objects linked with a table

Table 8.32 Methods of the Views Class for Administering Views

Property	Meaning
Count	Number of views linked to the table.

Table 8.33 Properties of the Views Class for Administering Views

An SAPTableView object can be linked with the corresponding Table object by the Add method of the Views class. Transporting the data from the table to the data grid is initiated by the Refresh method of the Table class. No data transmission takes place without this method being called. "Data transport" means that the values of the table and the technical properties of the columns are transferred to the data grid. Therefore, it is not necessary to manually specify the properties of the rows and columns if the data grid is linked to a Table object. When calling up the method, note that the method is defined in the TableView control as SCODE Refresh( ). The return type Long, which is displayed in the object browser of the VB development environment, is the only type into which the original data type is transformed. The original return type of a method can be determined in the OLE Viewer.

The SCODE is a Microsoft-defined data type based on the Long data type. It gives the caller of an ActiveX or COM method information on the status of the execution. The SCODE data type does not meet the regulations of OLE automation, however. This leads to Visual Basic interpreting the SCODE data type as a Long data type during loading of the TableView control; however, calling the Refresh method during execution of the program fails with the error message *Object doesn't support this property or method* if early binding is used. The following example shows a call that causes the error described above during translation.

```
Dim m_oITCustomerData As SAPTableFactoryCtrl.Table
:
' Method for linking of table with view
Public Sub SetView(ByVal oNewView _
```

```
                   As SAPTableView.SAPTableView)
' Linking the table with the data grid
   m_oITCustomerData.Views.Add oNewView.Object
' Direct call of the Refresh method by the table
' object leads to error message during translation of the
' program
   m_oITCustomerData.Refresh
End Sub
```

Listing 8.18 Faulty Call of the Refresh Method

The Refresh method is called directly via the m_oITCustomerData object variable, which has the Table object type. Visual Basic cannot convert the SCODE data type into the long data type during early binding. The problem is solved by using late binding because a check is not performed here until runtime for which data type the Refresh method returns, and the type conversion works correctly at this point in time.

```
Dim m_oITCustomerData As SAPTableFactoryCtrl.Table
:
' Method for linking table with view
Public Sub SetView(ByVal oNewView _
                        As SAPTableView.SAPTableView)
' Declaration of the dummy table
   Dim oDummyTable As Object
' Linking the table with the data grid
   m_oITCustomerData.Views.Add oNewView.Object
' Align dummy table with original table
   Set oDummyTable = m_oITCustomerData
' Call of the Refresh method by the dummy object,
' that is declared as object
   oDummyTable.Refresh
   Set oDummyTable = Nothing
End Sub
```

Listing 8.19 Correct Call of the Refresh Method

In this listing, the Refresh method is no longer called directly by the m_oITCus-tomerData object variable. Instead, the oDummyTable object variable, which has the Object type, is introduced. The oDummyTable variable calls up the Refresh method after first having the m_oITCustomerData object variable assigned to it.

The Refresh method copies the data to the data grid. This becomes clear if the Remove method is called up after the call of the Refresh method. The Remove method deletes the link with the data grid specified via the index. Although the data grid is no longer linked with the Table object after the Remove method of the Views class is no longer linked to the Table object, the data grid still displays the table data. This is why the Refresh method must be called up after each change in the data in the Table object. The data of the Table object is not copied back into the data grid until after the Refresh method is called again.

Transporting the data from the data grid to the assigned Table object is a different story. There the data of the data grid is transmitted immediately back into the linked table without a corresponding method being called up from outside.

Linking the Data Grid with an Unspecified Data Source

If you want to link the data grid with an unspecified data source, use the procedure mentioned above for accessing the individual cell of the data grid. If, for example, you are administering address data in a two-dimensional field, the address data can be transmitted with row-oriented access into the data grid as follows.

```
' Field with address data
Dim Addresses(1, 1) As String
Addresses (0, 0) = "Meiners": Addresses (0, 1) = "Bonn"
Addresses (1, 0) = "Nüßer": Addresses (1, 1) = "Bonn"
Dim iRowCounter As Integer, _
    oRow As Object, _
    bColsCreated As Boolean
For iRowCounter = 0 To UBound(Addresses(), 1)
' For each row in the array, attach row
' to the data grid
    Set oRow = m_oTVCustomer.Rows.Add()
    For iColCounter = 0 To UBound(Addresses(), 2)
' Arrange columns only once
        If bColsCreated = False Then
            m_oTVCustomer.Columns.Add
        End If
' Transfer value in the cell of the data grid;
' Increment column specification by one, because
' the loop via the columns starts with the value
' zero, but the column counting for the data grid
' itself must begin with one
```

```
    oRow.Value(iColCounter + 1) = _
            Adresses(iRowCounter, iColCounter)
  Next iColCounter
  bColsCreated = True
Next iRowCounter
```

Listing 8.20 Example of Row-oriented Data Transmission of Data into the Data Grid

In this listing, rows are attached to the data grid within a loop via the rows of the Addresses field. The columns are attached to the data grid in an embedded loop via the columns, and, at the same time, the data is copied from the field into the corresponding row object. Here, the bColsCreated variable ensures that the columns are attached only once. It should be mentioned again that the object variable is for rows of the Object type and not the CViewRow type, because the CViewRow type leads to the *Type mismatch* error mentioned above.

8.10.5 Concepts for Inserting and Deleting Rows and Columns

The classes CViewRows and CViewColumns also offer methods for changing the number of rows and columns in a data grid. The CViewRows class provides the following methods for administering rows:

Method	Meaning
Add	Attaching a row to the data grid
Insert	Inserting a row into the data grid
Remove	Deleting a row from the data grid, with the index of the row to be deleted being transferred to the method

Table 8.34 Methods for Administering the Rows in a Data Grid

The methods of the CViewColumns class for administering columns are:

Method	Meaning
Add	Attaching a column to the data grid
Insert	Inserting a column into the data grid
Remove	Deleting a column from the data grid, with the index of the column to be deleted being transferred to the method

Table 8.35 Methods for Administering the Columns in a Data Grid

The Add and Insert methods each return the instance of the newly created CViewRow or CViewColumn class. If a new column is inserted into the data grid, the layout of the column must also be specified. This is done using the attribute of the CViewColumn class.

The number of rows and columns in the data grid can be specified using the following attributes:

Attribute	Class	Meaning
ColumnCount	SAPTableView	Number of columns in the grid
RowCount	SAPTableView	Number of rows in the grid
Count	CViewColumns	Number of columns in the grid
Count	CViewRows	Number of rows in the grid

Table 8.36 Attributes for Determining the Number of Rows and Columns in a Data Grid

Sometimes it is necessary to develop testing routines that must be run when the user inserts rows into the data grid or deletes them from it. The TableView control sends events for inserting and deleting rows to inform the client of the occurrence of states. The events are summarized in the following table:

Event	Triggering Time
ColumnInsert	Sent when a column is inserted into the data grid
ColumnRemove	Sent when a column is deleted from the data grid
RowInsert	Sent when a row is inserted into the data grid
RowRemove	Sent when a row is deleted from the data grid

Table 8.37 Events of the SAPTableView Class for Recognizing Operations on Rows and Columns

The development of event handlers for the TableView control was already presented in the discussion of access to cells and will not be explained further here.

If the user of the program is to be offered the option of inserting additional rows into a table, two alternatives are available if the data grid is linked to an instance of the Table class.

▶ Inserting the row into a table
▶ Inserting the row into the data grid

Attaching a row to the table with subsequent visualization of the row in the data grid could be programmed as follows:

```
Public Function AppendRow() As Boolean
Dim oDummyTable As Object
On Error GoTo Errorhandler
' Attach row
   If m_oITCustomerData.AppendRow() Is Nothing Then
' Error message, if no row was attached
      MsgBox "Unable to append Row!", vbOKOnly
      AppendRow = False
      Exit Function
   End If
' Row attached => Update view
   Set oDummyTable = m_oITCustomerData
   oDummyTable.Refresh
   Set oDummyTable = Nothing
   AppendRow = True
   Exit Function
Errorhandler:
   MsgBox Err.Description, vbOKOnly
   AppendRow = False
End Function
```

Listing 8.21 Attaching a Row with Visualization in the Data Grid

The AppendRow function shows that the following steps were performed to implement the requirements:

▶ Attaching the row to a table

▶ Updating all views linked to the table by calling up the Refresh method of the Table class

The development of the second suggestion (insert row into the data grid) will not be presented here, because it is very complex and should be used only in exceptional cases (see below). The disadvantage of the second alternative is that the new row of the data grid is not linked to the table. The table does not know the new row in the data grid at all. This becomes clear when the row counter of the data grid is compared with that of the table after an insertion operation. The row counter of the data grid is one greater. The consequence of this is that changes in the data of the respective row of the data grid do not have an effect back on the table, which leads to a data inconsistency. This is a serious disadvantage. It can be remedied by attaching an additional row to the table object and transferring the data manually from the data grid to the table object.

Which of the options mentioned should be used for inserting a new row? Using methods of the `Table` class is better for the following reasons:

▶ The table is to determine the content of the data grid and not vice versa. This consideration is also supported by the hierarchy of classes for dealing with tables. There the `View` object is subordinate to the table. The method of attaching the new row to the table meets this consideration.

▶ The new row in the data grid is linked with the table row. Changes to the contents of the data grid have an effect on the table. No separate routine must be developed to ensure data consistency between the table and the data grid.

The insertion of new lines into the data grid is advisable if

▶ The data source for the data grid is not a table.

▶ Testing routines are to be run during insertion or deletion of rows.

8.10.6 Working with the Clipboard

The data grid from SAP is used in dialog applications. In these applications, the user works very often with the clipboard; that is, he or she inserts data from one application into another. For the data grid in particular, it is advisable to exchange data with Excel via the clipboard.

Data exchange with the clipboard is implemented via the following parameter-free methods of the `SAPTableView` class:

▶ `PasteFromClipboard`

▶ `CopyToClipboard`

The `PasteFromClipboard` method reads the data from the clipboard, and the `CopyToClipboard` method inserts the data into the clipboard.

The `CreateCustomerTV` program, which can also be found on the Web page for this book, shows a suggestion for integrating the clipboard into an application. In the `CreateCustomerTV` program, the main menu includes a **Clipboard** menu item. The **Clipboard** menu contains the menu items **Paste From Clipboard** and **Copy To Clipboard.** The call of the methods mentioned is integrated into the logic of the functions:

```
Private Sub PastefCB_Click()
    m_oTVCustomer.PasteFromClipboard
End Sub
```

Listing 8.22 Inserting from the Clipboard

```
Private Sub CopyToCB_Click()
    m_oTVCustomer.CopyToClipboard
End Sub
```

Listing 8.23 Copying to the Clipboard

We end our discussion of the ActiveX controls for the development of external clients with these points on the TableView control.

9   SAP and Java

The ways of interface programming for the R/3 System described in the previous chapters are very similar in their basic structure. This is not surprising, as they're all derived from the RFC Library, and in some cases, *only* the programming environment used changes. So, initially, it seems that one could view Java as simply an additional language for SAP interface programming. In truth, Java and the technology based on it is much more. Java is the environment that prompted a radical change in thought on interfaces to the SAP system. Before Java, the theme of integration, however important it was for customers, was more of a peripheral *interface* problem. Since the onset of Java (and later, to some extent, also Microsoft .NET), a different technology has had an effect on the very heart of the SAP system. The SAP Java Connector (JCo), which we'll describe here, is the beginning of a new paradigm for interfaces to R/3.

The Java programming language makes great claims for itself. It asserts to possess the following properties of a development platform—all of the main properties that have been sought after throughout the history of development platforms:

▶ Object-oriented

▶ Platform-independent

▶ Component-based

▶ Integrating

We will briefly consider these aspects and their significance for cooperation with the SAP system:

▶ **Object-oriented**
Java is a true object-oriented language with a one-branch class hierarchy—without an option for multiple inheritance, but with the option of still having a class de facto inherited from several sources, that is, interfaces. The binding between names and values or implementations is generally performed during runtime, that is, Java always uses late binding. Like many languages, Java allows easy code reuse through easy-to-use packages (via import). This option is used intensively for developing extensive expansions, which, besides the obvious elegance of the language, is an important reason for the high acceptance of Java.

▶ **Platform-independent**
Java was originally developed as a language for embedded devices and then positioned as a platform for Web applications. A central property for this application was the ability to run Java programs on all computer platforms having a *Java Virtual Machine* (JVM). To achieve this, the source code of a Java program

can be translated into an intermediate code that is then interpreted by the virtual machine. This form of platform-independence of a Java program is similar to what SAP achieves for ABAP programs via porting the application server. The intermediate code for SAP is the ABAP load.

Like SAP systems, Java in its original implementation was limited to 32-bit platforms. A 64-bit version was not created until Java pushed into the server world.

▶ **Component-based**
The idea of intensively reusing software was first incorporated into Java with the development of *JavaBean* technology. JavaBeans can be viewed as software components, that is, reusable software modules with a well-defined interface. They are comparable with ActiveX Controls, in particular, because they're also used primarily for desktop applications.

The analog components of the server side arose a relatively short time later and form the basis of the *Java Second Edition Enterprise platform* (J2EE). These special Java classes work with application servers in a way that is similar to the SAP Application Server, and can therefore be compared conceptually with BAPIs.

Today, the J2EE-platform with all its expansions is a full-performance development and runtime environment whose specifications are reminiscent of the "old" SAP concepts in many respects.

▶ **Integrating**
In addition to an environment for developing new components, the J2EE platform has numerous expansions with which existing applications can be integrated into the J2EE framework. Among these, we should mention the *Java Connector Architecture* as a more recent development that has a generic interface for linking external systems.

This approach of the J2EE makes clear that the SAP system has at least a dual relationship with the J2EE and Java world:

1. The SAP system is a legacy system that is to be embedded in a Java/J2EE environment.

2. The SAP system is a competing integration platform.

The success of the Java platform and the obvious elegance of many Java solutions has generated a heavy demand for Java in the SAP world. The following points are integral to this demand:

▶ Addressing the SAP system from Java (i.e., the SAP system as legacy system)

▶ Letting the SAP system access its own or foreign Java applications (i.e., the SAP system as a competing integration platform)

▶ Using the elegance of Java applications as a replacement for ABAP

SAP moved to meet demands with a connector intended to act as a Java wrapper for the RFC Library—the SAP Java Connector (JCo).

This approach was developed further to combine the full performance of the J2EE world with the options of SAP solutions. SAP developed its own J2EE engine for this purpose, integrated Java into the original application server, and created a J2EE conform expansion of the JCo, the SAP Connector.

In this book, we limit ourselves to the first aspect, that is, the JCo, because this is a logical continuation of the previous chapters. Furthermore, for us to adequately address the entire J2EE framework would far exceed the scope of this book, since the SAP J2EE Application Server is a completely new development environment and uses a changed programming paradigm. Therefore, we will not delve into it further in this book.

However, with the JCo as the foundation on which J2EE-conform communication with the SAP system is performed, an SAP Connector-based solution can be thought of as an expansion to the topics that we will discuss below.

9.1   The SAP Java Connector

The *SAP Java Connector* (JCo) can be used both for programming Java clients for the SAP system as well as for the development of Java servers. In SAP terminology, the first case is referred to as *inbound* and the second as *outbound*. In both cases, the name refers to the point of view of the SAP system.

The JCo is implemented as a dynamic library and as a Java JAR file. Therefore, it can be used for standalone Java applications and for integrated applications, for example, as part of the J2EE framework.

9.1.1   Basics of the JCo

Direct calls of the RFC Library from Java applications using the *Java Native Interface* (JNI) are possible, but they don't provide a convenient programming environment. Several aspects should make this clear:

▶ The RFC Library is a procedural library: it does not directly know essential language elements of object-oriented programming. A problem occurs when working with exceptions, which is indispensable in large Java applications, but can be implemented only in the C world with great effort, for example, via the setjmp and longjmp library routines.

▶ The data types of the ABAP environment and the Java environment must be adapted, and the multiple language capability of the SAP system must be accounted for using suitable code-page conversion.

- To ensure adequate performance, pronounced caching is necessary, especially for server-side applications. This would also have to be specially implemented for the Java world.

With JCo, SAP has provided its own Java wrapper for the RFC Library, intended to solve the aforementioned and other problems.

The JCo accesses the RFC Library using the JNI Application Programming Interface (API). This layer, which is placed directly over the underlying dynamic libraries, for example `sapjcorfc`, is protected from the outside by additional Java classes. These classes (RFC and middleware) take the aforementioned conversion tasks from the C world over into the Java world. After all, the application code sees only the classes and interfaces that are in the `com.sap.mw.jco` package and its extensions.

9.1.2 Ways of Using the JCo

The JCo plays an important role both in internal SAP development and in programming external Java-based clients and servers. Internally, the JCo is the central connective element for linking the classical SAP Application Server for ABAP and the J2EE engine from SAP. In this context, the JCo can access all forms of RFC communication with the SAP system.

In the external use of the JCo, as we have described it here, the classical forms of RFC calls are possible: synchronous ("normal") RFC, transactional RFC, and queued RFC. For the last two forms, transaction IDs and ,if necessary, queue IDs are also specified in the appropriate methods of the JCo classes. The transaction IDs must be administered by the client using methods of the JCo (such as `crea-teTID` and `confirmTID`) in a way similar to classical RFC. Accordingly, the JCo in the server role must implement the administration of transactions and queues.

However, when looking for the most important uses of JCo, we see that synchronous communication with the JCo acting as a SAP client is dominant. This is not surprising because the integration of the JCo into J2EE environments is of central importance. Therefore, we'll focus on this synchronous communication in the JCo world in the next sections.

But first, a comment on security: Because the JCo is based on the RFC Library, security-relevant forms of communication are also supported. For example, you can use the Secure Network Communication (SNC) library of SAP from the JCo and thereby use single sign-on (SSO).

9.1.3   The JCo Package

The classes of the JCo package are implemented as internal classes of the JCo class. A rough breakdown of the available classes yields the following types:

▶ The JCo package knows classes that provide information on the type of the *RFC connection*. These include the basic Connection class and its derived classes Client and Server, which define whether an application works outbound or inbound. Pool classes, which administer a group of client connection, should also be mentioned here, as well as the Attribute classes, which can provide information on the connection (partner, language, etc.).

▶ The data that can be exchanged with the SAP system are implemented in another group of classes. Here, a distinction can be made between the descriptive data—or metadata—and the *real* data. The metadata has its corresponding MetaData basic class and its derivative Record, which is itself the basis for other data classes. These include the classes Structure (which corresponds to an SAP structure), Table (counterpart to an internal table), and Parameter-List which contains the real import and export arguments of a function. From this last class come two classes that were developed especially for working with requests (Request class) and responses (Response class).

▶ The *fields of a record* or its derivative can be individually addressed generically via the Field and FieldIterator classes. A FieldIterator goes through a group of Fields—for example a Structure or a Table row—and returns the next one each time.

▶ The next type of classes involves the description of the *RFC module* ("function") to be executed. A Repository object is the counterpart of the SAP repository, and can contain the description, that is, the metadata, of many functions. It is cached, as is its SAP-side counterpart. This function is implemented in the BasicRepository parent class.

▶ The metadata of a function can be administered in the FunctionTemplate class. This class also forms a basis for instantiating the real function (Function class). This function object contains argument values (ParameterList) and can be considered *one* call.

▶ Correct reporting of *error situations* is important for programming on the Java side. Adapted exception classes perform this task: the Exception basis class and its derivatives, AbapException and ConversionException, as well as the wrapper J2EEAbapException.

▶ Finally, the package contains two *auxiliary classes* for performance measurement (Throughput class) and for server programming (ServerThread class).

If you worked your way through the book this far, you should be familiar with the basic structure of the JCo package.

9.1.4 JCo Releases

At the publication of this book, JCo is available in Version 2.1.1 and requires an RFC-Library of Version 6.20 or higher. JCo-based applications can be used with R/3 systems of Release 3.1H or higher; however, integration of the JCo into a J2EE-based environment requires SAP Basic Version 6.20 or higher.

The following standalone examples should also run with older versions of the JCo, but, they were tested with Version 2.1.1.

9.2 Using the JCo

9.2.1 Basic Structure of a JCo Application

The JCo is linked to the classic client-server model due to its origin as a wrapper of the RFC Library. The basic structure of a JCo-based client application therefore corresponds to the previously considered RFC clients:

▶ Setting up a connection to the SAP system (directly or pooled)

▶ Generating the necessary internal JCo variables that take the data from the SAP system or to it

▶ Calling the methods of a BAPI

▶ Evaluating the return values

▶ Logoff

These individual steps are each defined in the following sections. Thereafter, a relatively simple complete program that shows these components as an example is presented.

This chapter does not examine how JCo is used as an independent Java-based RFC server. We think this omission is appropriate because Java servers today are primarily located in the J2EE framework due to advancing integration of the classical R/3 System with the J2EE platform.

9.2.2 Connection Setup

Connection setup is implemented using an object, as is almost every other action in an object-oriented environment. In client programming with the JCO, a connection to the SAP system (or to an RFC server in general) is represented by an object of the JCO.Client type (*client* here refers to the connection and not an SAP client):

```
JCO.Client mconnection;
```

However, an object of this type is not generated via a direct constructor call, but rather by calling a static method of the JCO class.

These methods appear in many forms. In addition to setting up a connection (client) to a particular hard-coded application server, forms exist that access via load balancing and can be directed at any RFC server. Forms also exist that get their data from the usual Java property files, and also methods that allow explicit decision for direct or pooled connections.

This last decision between direct or pooled connection is easy to understand. In a typical dialog application, the user will log on to the SAP system with his or her own account, transfer data, and only then, log off. This procedure makes sense because of the clear and simple authorization situation. However, one disadvantage is the additional costs that the setup and cutting of the connection involve. In a typical Web-based application, the user accounts are managed in the Web server; in the SAP system, they are usually mapped to only one or a few generic SAP users. In such cases, it is certainly more economical to use a connection from a pre-generated group (a "pool") of JCo clients to avoid paying setup and disconnection costs.

In a direct connection, the following call for generating a connection is usual:

```
mconnection =
  JCO.createClient(<connection parameters>);
```

The connection parameters can either be specified explicitly or be read in from one of the usual Java property files. The last method is more elegant in a professional environment. The generated connection can then be opened with

```
mconnection.connect();
```

and closed with

```
mconnection.disconnect();
```

after the actions are completed (e.g., using execute(), see below).

A pooled connection can either be taken from an existing pool or one that is newly created. In the second case, the pool must first be created with

```
JCO.addClientPool(key, max_connects, <connection
                          parameters>);
```

The connection parameters can take the various forms described above. The only special characteristics of this approach are that each pool contains a unique key and that the number of connections per pool must be specified. The pools of a Java Virtual Machine (JVM) are administered by a pool manager to ensure uniqueness.

If a pool is found, a connection of it can be used:

```
mconnection = JCO.getClient(key);
```

The key identifies the respective pool. The desired methods can then be executed again with the now finished connection.

After work is complete, the connection is returned to the pool with

```
JCO.releaseClient(mconnection);
```

9.2.3 Running the RFC Modules

The logical next step is to call up the RFC module on a server, based on the execute() method of the JCo.Client class.

This method appears in several overloaded forms. They all share the trait that the module call is generic. Therefore the descriptions (metadata) of the relevant import, export, or table parameters must be specified before the call is made.

The metadata specification can be performed manually (i.e., hard-coded) in the source code, or generated dynamically from information of the RFC server. Next, we'll describe a more flexible way to determine how to generate the metadata necessary for evoking RFC modules. Our goal is to be able to access the metadata during the runtime of the RFC-application and get rid of hard-coded information.

In all cases, the metadata is described in an object of the ParameterList class that is generated via the createParameterList() static method of the JCO class. A ParameterList consists of a sequence of parameters. A parameter can be a scalar (int, float, etc.), a structure, or even a whole table. Each parameter is identified by a name. With scalar parameters, each is supplemented by the specification of the JCO type (e.g., JCO.TYPE_INT, JCO.TYPE_FLOAT), the number of bytes the parameter takes up, and if necessary the number of decimal places (e.g., for JCO.TYPE_FLOAT). For compound parameters, the ID of the structure or table is added as well. A code example for the structure of such a ParameterList could look like this:

```
JCO.ParameterList mexport = JCO.createParameterList();
mexport.addInfo("EP_RESULT", JCO.TYPE_INT, 4);
```

Here an `Int` parameter of four bytes is appended to the list; it still has no value because it will be used later as an exporting parameter as the name implies. In the usual nomenclature, these are parameters that are returned by the RFC server. The `addInfo` method exists in many overloaded forms, of course, in order to deal with the various parameter types.

The tasks just described therefore are sufficient to transfer return values in case of exporting parameters. Here the server provides the values and the client provides only the space in which to store those values. To import parameters, you must specify the value of the parameter. This can be performed through a form of the `appendValue()` method:

```
JCO.ParameterList mimport = new JCO.ParameterList();
mimport.appendValue("IP_VALUE1", JCO.TYPE_INT, 4, ivalue1);
mimport.appendValue("IP_VALUE2", JCO.TYPE_INT, 4, ivalue2);
```

The call of an RFC module can then be performed explicitly via a form of the `execute()` method of the connection object, in this example, `mconnection`:

```
mconnection.execute("Z_RFC_ADD", mimport, mexport);
```

Here the RFC module, which is to be identified by its name, and the required import and export parameter lists of the method are transferred.

If the execution is successful, the `mexport` list provides the result. We'll look at how the results are used in the next section.

The most noticeable thing about the call sequence just described is that all specifications, such as the name of the RFC module and the name and form of the parameters, were specified manually and directly. As is only fitting for a good object-oriented (OO) package, the JCo package allows you to encapsulate parts or the entire specifications in objects. In a second step, an RFC module is no longer to be identified by its name, but by an object of the `JCO.Function` class:

```
JCO.Function mcall =
    new JCO.Function("Z_RFC_ADD");
```

The special thing about the `JCO.Function` object is not, of course, that it enables you to use an additional, longer way to specify the RFC module, but rather the fact that a function object contains all of the data of an RFC call. An object of this class also encapsulates the `ParameterList` objects:

```
mcall.setImportParameterList(mimport);
mcall.setExportParameterList(mexport);
```

The execution of an RFC module can now be implemented more easily:

```
mconnection.execute(mcall);
```

Note that a function object contains the values of the parameter of the current call (in our example, for instance, the integer values for the import parameter). For this reason, SAP recommends creating a new function object for each call.

The introduction of the function object has not really increased the flexibility and elegance of the code, because the parameters must still be specified manually. The third and final option is, logically, the complete generation of the metadata by querying the RFC server itself. It is common to set up a counterpart to the SAP repository in the JCo application that serves as a central storage area for the metadata of the functions on the JCo side (i.e., exchange it between the client and the R/3 System):

```
IRepository  mrepo =
    JCO.createRepository("RID", mconnection);
```

In this piece of code, a repository is generated via the static method `createRepository` and thereby linked to the RFC server—here via `mconnection`. The JCo documentation lists the exact authorizations in the SAP system that the connection used requires for access to the SAP repository data.

Alternatives to this procedure are possible, for example, generation of the repository using the equivalent constructor of the `JCO.Repository` class itself. A repository can also be set up without a connection to an RFC server. Later in the procedure however, the metadata must still be added. This can be done by building up `MetaData` using `addInfo` and then adding it to the repository via a form of the `add*InterfaceToCache` method.

We extract the metadata required to execute the RFC modules from the repository into an object of a `JCo.FunctionTemplate` class. The `JCO.FunctionTemplate` class encapsulates all necessary data on the form of the RFC module and the parameters. We don't use this class directly here, but rather the `IFunctionTemplate` interface implemented by it:

```
IFunctionTemplate mift =
    mrepo.getFunctionTemplate("Z_RFC_ADD");
```

The `mift` function template contains all relevant metadata on the Z_RFC_ADD RFC module. The query of the RFC server, here the SAP system, is performed dynamically via the repository, which also implements internal caching.

A function object can then be generated from the function template:

```
JCO.Function mcall2 = new JCO.Function(mift);
```

in which we now have to set only the current values for the import parameters:

```
JCO.ParameterList min2 = mauf2.getImportParameterList();
min2.setValue(ivalue1, "IP_VALUE1");
min2.setValue(ivalue2, "IP_VALUE2");
mconnection.execute(mcall2);
```

In the first line, the list of the input parameters—in which the parameters named "IP_VALUE1" and "IP_VALUE2" are then assigned their values—is extracted from the function object. After these preparations, the method call is also performed here.

9.2.4 Access to Data and Tables

Now our efforts will finally be repaid through data from the RFC server. In the simplest form, data from the function object is accumulated via the getExport-ParameterList method. From the ParameterList, the scalar parameters, the structures, or the relevant tables can be obtained via one of the get methods:

```
int res = mcall2.getExportParameterList().
                getInt("EP_RESULT");
```

In the same way, structures from the ExportParameterList can be obtained using getStructure. Through its fields() method, for example, a structure can deliver a FieldIterator, which works like a normal iterator and helps going through the fields in a loop. As an alternative, the fields can also be obtained via one of the get methods.

Tables are obtained from the export parameters using the getTableParameter-List() method:

```
JCO.Table mexptab =
        mcall2.getTableParameterList().getTable("ZKNA1JMS");
```

To evaluate this table, we will then run through the individual table records. The number of records is determined by the getNumRows() method. The JCo package offers various options for accessing the rows: The row with the number nr can be selected using setRow(nr), and the next row in the sequence can be selected using nextRow().

The fields of the particular row are then treated in the same way as the fields of a Structure:

```
for (int i = 0; i < mexptab.getNumRows(); i++) {
    mexptab.setRow(i);
    String mh_str = mexptab.getString("CUSTNO");
    String mh_str = mexptab.getString("NAME1");
    ...
}
```

The JCo package contains still more methods for setting the desired table row. The `firstRow()` method can be particularly useful here, to reset the focus (cursor) to the beginning of the table.

In the JCo package, tables are not only received "passively" as the result of an RFC call, but can also be actively manipulated. For these actions, the following and other methods are used: `insertRow(pos)`, which inserts a row before `pos`; `appendRow()`, which attaches a row to a table; or `deleteRow()`, which deletes the current row of a table.

In both cases, the values of the fields can then be set using `setValue(wert, name)`. Finally, rows can be deleted from the table using forms of `deleteRow`.

We cannot overemphasize that the data types of the SAP system *must* be mapped to those of the Java application when working with the JCo. The JCo performs the majority of the conversion tasks automatically; only the conversion of the time and date specifications from ABAP are worthy of special mention. ABAP programs contain different data types for time (type t) and date (type d) specifications. Java works with one data type, `Date`, which administers both pieces of information in one object. When converting ABAP variables into Java objects, developers are therefore forced to continue processing these Java variables in accordance with their ABAP source, that is, time or date. You can find the complete mapping table in the JCo documentation.

9.2.5 Complete Example Program

The commented example program (see below) shows a possible combination of the discussed actions in a JCo application. To demonstrate the use of scalar parameters, we'll resort to the simple pocket calculator model that we have used throughout this book. The `do_scalar_call()` method uses a `Function` object and two of the type `ParameterList`. A second method, `do_table_call()`, shows the more complex transfer of structures and tables and the return of table rows including their output. It uses a `FunctionTemplate` as an alternative and must also deal with the input and output structures as well as tables. Finally, the constructor of the class sets up the connection to the SAP system.

Some aspects, such as an adapted treatment of exceptional situations, were also considered. For the formation of BAPIs, note that a program guideline expects the return of a parameter named RETURN, which contains information on the result of the execution. However, the form of this parameter can differ from BAPI to BAPI.

The connection parameters are stored in the form of a Java property file in the example program. At least the following must be specified as key value pairs: jco.client.client for the target customer, jco.client.user for the login user, jco.client.passwd and jco.client.ashost for the target host (an SAP router string is possible here), and jco.client.sysnr for the instance number.

```java
import com.sap.mw.jco.*;
import java.util.*;
import java.io.*;


public class SAPIFJCo {
    private JCO.Client mconnection;
    private IRepository mrepo;

    private final String RID = "SAPIF";
    private final String connfile
                    ="connection.properties";

    public SAPIFJCo () {

        /* Get connection information */
        Properties connprops = new Properties();
        try {
            FileInputStream pf =
              new FileInputStream(connfile);
            connprops.load(pf);
            /* Display connection information
                (without password) */
            for (Enumeration en =
                        connprops.propertyNames();
                        en.hasMoreElements(); )
            {
                String pname = (String) en.nextElement();
                if (pname.indexOf("passwd") == -1) {
                    String pvalue =
                            connprops.getProperty(pname);
```

```
                System.out.println("Name: " + pname +
                                    "= " + pvalue);
            }
        }
    } catch (Exception ex) {
        ex.printStackTrace();
        return;
    }

    try {
        /* Establish connection */
        mconnection = JCO.createClient(connprops);
        mrepo = JCO.createRepository(RID,
                                    mconnection);
        mconnection.connect();
      } catch (Exception exc) {
        exc.printStackTrace();
    }
}

private int do_scalar_call(String sadd1,
                            String sadd2) {
    JCO.Function mcall = null;
    JCO.ParameterList mimport = null;
    JCO.ParameterList mexport = null;

    try {
        /* Get parameter from command line */
        int ivalue1 =
            Integer.valueOf(sadd1).intValue();
        int ivalue2 =
            Integer.valueOf(sadd2).intValue();

        /* Create function object */
        mcall = new JCO.Function("Z_RFC_ADD");

        /* Import parameter */
        mimport = new JCO.ParameterList();
        mimport.appendValue("IP_VALUE1",
                            JCO.TYPE_INT, 4, ivalue1);
```

```java
        mimport.appendValue("IP_VALUE2",
                       JCO.TYPE_INT, 4, ivalue2);

        /* Export parameter */
        mexport = JCO.createParameterList();
        mexport.addInfo("EP_RESULT",
                       JCO.TYPE_INT, 4);

        maufruf.setImportParameterList(mimport);
        maufruf.setExportParameterList(mexport);
    } catch (Exception exc) {
        exc.printStackTrace();
    }

    try {
        /* The actual synchronous call */
        mconnection.execute(mcall);

        /* Test the optional return state */
        try {
            JCO.Structure retStr =
              mcall.getExportParameterList().
              getStructure("RETURN");
            if (!(retStr.getString("TYPE").equals("")
            || retStr.getString("TYPE").equals("S")))
            {
                System.out.println("Return State = "
                        + retStr.getString("Message"));
                return(-1);
            }
        } catch (JCO.Exception jcoex) {
            System.out.println("No return state
                    available. Try to continue!");
      }

        /* Show results*/
        int res =
            mcall.getExportParameterList().
            getInt("EP_RESULT");
        System.out.println("Result of operation:"
```

```
                              + res);
        } catch (Exception exc) {
            exc.printStackTrace();
        }
        return(0);
}

    private int do_table_call(String CustLow, String CustHigh) {
        JCO.Function mcall2 = null;

        /* Customer numbers comprise ten characters */
        final int deflen = 10;
        final String defval = "0000000000";
        int i;

        try {
            /* Get function object this time via template */
            IFunctionTemplate mift =
                mrepo.getFunctionTemplate(
                  "Z_RFC_GET_MULTI_CUSTOMER");

            mcall2 = new JCO.Function(mift);

            /* Create import parameter*/
            JCO.ParameterList mimppl =
                mcall2.getTableParameterList();

            JCO.Structure mimpstr =
                mimppl.getStructure("IS_CUSTNO");
            mimpstr.setValue("I", "SIGN");
            mimpstr.setValue("BT", "OPTION");

            /* Fill until reaching ten characters */
            i = CustLow.length();
            if (i < deflen)
                CustLow = (defval + CustLow).substring(i);
            else {
                System.out.println("Error: lower customer
                                    number too long");
                return(-1);
```

```
      }
      mimpstr.setValue(CustLow, "LOW");

      i = CustHigh.length();
      if (i < deflen)
         CustHigh = (defval +
                     CustHigh).substring(i);
      else {
         System.out.println("Error: higher
                        customer number too long");
         return(-1);
      }
      mimpstr.setValue(CustHigh, "HIGH");

} catch (Exception exc) {
      exc.printStackTrace();
}

try {
      /* The call */
      mconnection.execute(mcall2);

/* Treatment of the optional return state */
      try {
         JCO.Structure retStr =
              mcall2.getExportParameterList()
              .getStructure("ET_RETURN");

         if (!(retStr.getString("TYPE").equals("")
         || retStr.getString("TYPE").equals("S")))
         {
System.out.println(retStr.getString("Message"));
            return(-1);
         }
      } catch (JCO.Exception jcoex) {
         System.out.println("No return state
                available. Try to continue!");
      }

      /* Get result table */
```

```
        JCO.Table mexptab =
          mcall2.getTableParameterList().
            getTable("ET_CUSTOMER_DATA");

        /* Create header for output */
        System.out.println("CUSTNO" + "NAME" + "COUNTRY"
                              + "CITY");

        for (i = 0; i < mexptab.getNumRows(); i++) {
            mexptab.setRow(i);
        System.out.println(mexptab.getString("CUSTNO") +
                      mexptab.getString("NAME1") +
                      mexptab.getString("COUNTRY1") +
                      mexptab.getString("CITY01"));
        }
        mconnection.disconnect();
    } catch (Exception exc) {
        exc.printStackTrace();
    }
    return(0);
  }


  public  static void main(String[] args) {

    /* Check for arguments; for debugging purposes only! */
    for (int i = 0; i <  args.length; i++)
        System.out.println(args[i]);

    SAPIFJCo sapif = new SAPIFJCo();
    sapif.do_scalar_call(args[0], args[1]);
    sapif.do_table_call(args[2], args[3]);
  }
}
```

Listing 9.1 Complete Example Program Using the JCo

9.2.6 Troubleshooting and Tracing

Any non-trivial application must eventually use procedures for handling errors and exceptional situations and for debugging. The JCo package offers several options here:

- Java exceptions are defined in the package. The basic class in the package is JCO.Exception, which is derived from java.lang.RuntimeException. The programmer must decide whether this exception and its derivatives are to be specified in code. As is well known, Java allows a choice for only this kind of exception. This is the only deviation from the general exception handling behavior in the Java language.

- The JCo provides derived exceptions, including JCO.AbapException and JCO.ConversionException. The first of these exceptions allows for reacting to exceptional situations in the RFC module. Unfortunately, RFC modules are not required to define exceptions, so this exception type must be checked in actual cases. The second exception points to internal problems in the conversion of ABAP data to Java data.

- A variant of the popular "printf" debugging is offered by the classes JCO.ParameterList, JCO.Structure, JCO.Function, and JCO.Table with the overloaded writeHTML methods. By calling up one of these methods, the current data of an object is stored as an XML file at a specified location.

- In the initial phase of JCo development, it can facilitate a better understanding to make the JCo more "talkative." An appropriate trace level analogous to that of the SAP work processes can be specified as well via a command line option of the executing JVM: java ... -Djco.trace_level=1, with parameter 1 being between 0 and 10. The trace file can also be specified via -Djco.trace_path. Tracing provides valuable monitoring information for running applications.

- Finally, ABAP debugging can also be activated from the JCo. The setAbapDebug(flag) method of the JCO.Client or JCO.Pool classes is used for this. A "True" value of the Boolean flag switches on ABAP debugging, and a "False" value switches it off. Here it must be noted that setting the underlying property, jco.client.abap_debug, using this method closes and reopens an existing connection. The setting should therefore be done before the connection is opened.

Another supplement to these options for exceptions: The JCo is not only the central point for a standalone Java application, but also for integration into a J2EE application server. According to the specification, in such a J2EE environment, no runtime exceptions may be thrown. This would make the aforementioned exceptions unusable in a J2EE environment. SAP has therefore developed a wrapper around JCO.AbapException that inherits from the general exception class and no longer from the special runtime exception. This JCO.J2EEAbapException can therefore also be used within a J2EE environment.

9.2.7 Closing Remarks

Our discussion of the JCo package has so far covered a large part of the functionality usually required in a Java client. However, this description of the JCo package is by no means comprehensive. For more information, you must consult the SAP documentation.

However, for those readers who would like to learn more about JCo, we suggest that you focus on the following four aspects of the package:

▶ In a JCO.ParameterList, individual parameters can be made inactive via one of the setActive methods. This does not actually suppress the data transfer between client and server, but it does suppress further processing by the Java layers of the JCo. In the SAP nomenclature, this additional processing is referred to as *marshalling*, a technical term that is widely used in the field of distributed systems.

▶ As of JCo Version 2.0.4, IDocs can be sent directly via the JCo by using the JCO.IDocument interface. With this, and with the tRFC, the JCo can intervene in an Application Link Enabling (ALE) environment.

▶ The RFC Library is multithreading-capable, that is, it can be used in several threads simultaneously. Java also works very intensively with threads. In future versions of the JCo, SAP will have to ensure a tighter meshing of the two concepts.

▶ For performance reasons, only a few access procedures are synchronized internally with the JCo, for example, pool and repository. For multithreading applications, ensure that you have carefully analyzed the critical paths.

To summarize, SAP provides a natural expansion of the RFC mechanism for the Java environment with the JCo package. The concepts and basic structure of an RFC client application, which have been presented in many different forms in this book, can be applied similarly to the JCo.

9.3 The Future of the SAP Java Interface

In contrast to relationships with the classical RFC environments C/C++, ActiveX, and so forth, the relationship between Java and the SAP world has not yet been finally defined. Savvy observers see the following trends:

▶ The meshing between the SAP system and Java is becoming ever tighter due to SAP's own J2EE application server and further integration into the classical ABAP application server. This makes SAP an active player on the Java stage.

▶ Another area where SAP is very much at home is being touched by the current massive marketing of Web services. This technique—for example, sending XML messages using the HTTP protocol that can then be used to call up distant methods—works very well with the efforts of SAP to be perceived as an integrator for corporate applications. With Version 1.4 of the J2EE specification, this technique will also be more intensively embedded into a Java environment. Several interesting new approaches and products can be expected from SAP in this area in particular. For example, the successful cooperation of Java and .NET Web services can offer new possibilities for SAP.

▶ As part of this tighter interplay, we can expect that the interfaces to the SAP system will be administered from a central point and can therefore be used for Web services. This central point in the current state of the art is certainly the SAP Exchange Infrastructure (XI).

In all these scenarios, the JCo will continue to play an essential role.

A   Sources and Further Reading

SAP Architecture and Administration

▶ Will, Liane: *SAP APO System Administration. Principles for effective APO System Management*. SAP PRESS 2003.

▶ Heinemann, Frédéric; Rau, Christian: *Web Programming with the SAP Web Application Server. The complete guide for ABAP and Web developers*. SAP PRESS 2003.

ABAP

▶ Keller, Horst; Jacobitz, Joachim: *ABAP Objects. The Official Reference*. SAP PRESS 2003.

▶ Keller, Horst; Krüger, Sascha: *ABAP Objects*. Addison-Wesley 2002.

▶ Matzke, Bernd: *ABAP/4. Programming the SAP R/3 System*. Second Edition, Addison-Wesley 2000.

RFC and Other Interfaces

▶ Angeli, Axel; Streit, Ulrich; Gonfalonieri, Robi: *The SAP R/3 Guide to EDI and Interfaces*. Vieweg 2000.

▶ Heinemann, Frédéric; Rau, Christian: *Web Programming with the SAP Web Application Server. The complete guide for ABAP and Web developers*. SAP PRESS 2003.

C and C++

▶ Eckel, Bruce: *Thinking in C++*. Prentice Hall 2000.

▶ Kernighan, Brian W.; Ritchie, Dennis M.: *C Programming Language*. Second Edition, Prentice Hall 1988.

▶ Stroustrup, Bjarne: *The C++ Programming Language*. Third Edition, Addison-Wesley 2000.

Object-Oriented Programming

▶ Booch, Grady: *Object-Oriented Analysis and Design with Applications*. Second Edition, Addison-Wesley 1993.

ActiveX and COM

▶ Appleman, Dan: *Developing Com/Activex Components With Visual Basic 6*. Que 1998.

- ▶ Chappell, David: *Understanding ActiveX and OLE*. Microsoft Press 1996.
- ▶ Loos, Peter: *Go To COM*. Addison-Wesley 2000.

Java

- ▶ Arnold, Ken; Gosling, James; Holmes, David: *The Java Programming Language*. Third Edition, Addison-Wesley 2000.
- ▶ Eckel, Bruce: *Thinking in Java*. Third Edition, Prentice Hall 2002.
- ▶ Sharma, Rahul; Stearns, Beth; Ng, Tony: *J2EE Connector Architecture and Enterprise Application Integration*. Addison-Wesley 2001.

Other

- ▶ Graf, Joachim: *Murphy's Computer Law*. Souvenir Press 1995.

B   About the Authors

Johannes Meiners is a graduate of business studies at the University of Applied Sciences Münster, Germany. During his studies, he focused on mathematical models for the optimization of business processes and their application in computer programs.

Currently, he works for the international SAP system reseller itelligence AG, Bielefeld, Germany, where he is responsible for the development of additional applications for R/3 and the integration of third-party components into SAP systems. In this position, he applies the different current SAP technologies such as RFC, DCOM Connector, .NET Connector, and the Java Connector (JCo).

Prof. Dr. Wilhelm Nüßer studied physics and mathematics at the Technical University (RWTH) in Aachen, Germany. After receiving his doctorate in physics in 1996, he worked for SAP for several years in training, support, and development. In the spring of 1999, he joined SAP LinuxLab—the development and porting department for SAP on Linux—where he was responsible for porting and memory management.

Since the fall of 2002, he has held the Heinz Nixdorf Chair for applied computer sciences at the University of Applied Sciences in Paderborn, Germany.

Index

Detailed guidance on all BC formats and functions

Expert instruction to call BAPIs with XML and quickly develop your own BC services

Comprehensive screenshots, flowcharts, and coding comments

66 pp., 2005, 68,00 Euro
ISBN 1-59229-052-3

Patrick Theobald

SAP° Business Connector— Applications and Development

▶ Learn about all the BC formats
▶ Call BAPIs with XML and develop your own BC services
▶ Comprehensive comments in the coding make it easy to adapt it to your specific needs

SAP° PRESS Essentials

SAP PRESS   Galileo Press

SAP Business Connector –
Applications and Development
www.sap-hefte.de

P. Theobald

SAP Business Connector – Applications and Development

SAP PRESS Essentials 3

Beginning with the initial system administration steps – connecting and monitoring one or more R/3 Systems – you'll move quickly to the development arena. Learn how to use out-of-the-box solutions (such as BAPI calls via XML) and how to implement your own custom transformations and programming services (integrated BC function packages). The examples and solutions provided are designed for immediate use, with only minor modifications. Screenshots and flow charts, along with comprehensive notes on source coding, complement the text. Plus, you'll learn about IDoc-based communication and more.

Interested in reading more?

Please visit our Web site for all
new book releases from SAP PRESS.

www.sap-press.com